The Language of the Senses
Sensory-Perceptual Dynamics in Wordsworth, Coleridge,
Thoreau, Whitman, and Dickinson

In this stimulating and original analysis of some of the most important nineteenth-century poems in English, Kerry McSweeney offers an alternative to non-referential and New Historicist critical methods.

McSweeney discusses the sensory acuity that informed Wordsworth's, Coleridge's, Thoreau's, Whitman's, and Dickinson's finest achievements and then, when blunted by illness or age, contributed to an attenuation of their creative power. He supplies a "sensory profile" or sensory history for each author and through close readings shows how this profile affected their relationship to the external world and their powers of symbolic perception.

Using perspectives gleaned from the poets themselves and an understanding of the physiological ground of perception, McSweeney establishes a compelling theoretical basis for his approach. In clear and elegant prose, he studies the physical basis of aesthetic plenitude – such as the sensory manifold of synesthesia – not only in the Romantic writers mentioned above but also in two Victorian poets, Hopkins and Tennyson.

KERRY McSWEENEY is Molson Professor of English, McGill University.

The Language of the Senses
Sensory-Perceptual Dynamics in Wordsworth, Coleridge, Thoreau, Whitman, and Dickinson

Kerry McSweeney

Liverpool University Press

© McGill-Queen's University Press 1998
ISBN 0-85323-663-1

Legal deposit second quarter 1998
Bibliothèque nationale du Québec

Printed in Canada on acid-free paper

Published simultaneously in the European
Union by Liverpool University Press

This book has been published with the help of a
grant from the Humanities and Social Sciences
Federation of Canada, using funds provided by
the Social Sciences and Humanities Research
Council of Canada.

McGill-Queen's University Press acknowledges
the support of the Canada Council for the Arts
for its publishing program.

**British Library
Cataloguing-in-Publication Data**

A British Library CIP record is available.

This book was typeset by Typo Litho
Composition Inc. in 10/12 Palatino.

For Luke and John

Contents

Preface

The premise of this book is that if Coleridge and Emerson, the principal theoreticians of English and American Romanticism respectively, were correct in identifying sensory-perceptual acuity as an essential attribute of a poet, it follows that the sensory profiles and the distinctive patterns in the interplay of the senses of individual Romantic poets are important subjects for critical investigation. In the far background of my inquiry is my undergraduate mentor at the University of Toronto, the late Marshall McLuhan, whom I first encountered in 1960 in a Renaissance poetry course from which I learned rather more about such subjects as the Inuit sensorium than about the course's ostensible subject matter. Two summers later, I was among the initiates who gathered in the St. Michael's College library to help verify the myriad quotations in the proofs of *The Gutenberg Galaxy*. It was only several years later, when as a graduate student I took McLuhan's renowned Monday night seminar on Media and Society, that I realized how sceptical I had become of the value of cultural-studies theorizing to the study of literature.

I did, however, retain an interest in what McLuhan called sensory typology. In time, this led me to the work of anthropologists interested in the sensory profiles of societies. From David Howes's *Varieties of Sensory Experience* (1991) I learned of a "crisis of representation" in his discipline caused by the dominance of the interpretative model of Clifford Geertz (8) – a "crisis" that I recognized as another instance of the interpretative "turn" taken by a number of disciplines in recent decades. In literary studies, for example, there has been a *virage* caused by the "hermeneutic universalism" of some interpretative theories and the "hermeneutic contextualism" of others (see Hiley 7). As an alternative to interpretative models, Howes offered an anthropology of the senses that would move "beyond textualism and hermeneutics" (300).

My study offers a comparable alternative – a twofold one that relates to both the status of sensory-perceptual experience in Romantic studies and readings of literary texts.

In a critique of the dominance of what he calls "ocularcentrism," Martin Jay observes that "we have increasingly come in the twentieth century to distrust perception in general and vision in particular as the ground of knowledge, often turning instead to language in all its various guises as an alternative." This has led to an overemphasis on interpretation and an "increasingly iconoclastic discursive climate" ("Rise" 318–19). Jacques Derrida, for example, does not "believe that anything like perception exists. Perception is precisely a concept ... interdependent with the concept of origin and of center and consequently whatever strikes at [this] metaphysics ... strikes also at the very concept of perception" (272).

Like my subjects, I "believe" in perception and the referential capacities of language. In this study, sensory-perceptual experience is shown to be a source or enabling condition of imaginative power in five Romantic writers (and, more briefly, in two Victorian poets). A common pattern is traced in the creative careers of five of them: sensory-perceptual acuity informs the finest achievements of Wordsworth, Coleridge, Thoreau, Whitman, and Hopkins; when this is blunted by illness or age, their creative powers attenuate markedly. And in all of my subjects, sensory ratios are shown to be an essential constituent of both symbolic perception and expansion of consciousness experiences, descriptions or representations of which are a central feature of their work. In Wordsworth's *Prelude*, for example, the dynamic interplay of eye and ear is a fundamental constituent of the "spots of time" and related experiences and thus has an important bearing on one of the most contentious areas in Wordsworth criticism: the mind/nature dialectic.

The timeliness of this contextualization could be illustrated by a review of the work done on any of my subjects over the last two decades. To take only one example, most of the attention Emily Dickinson's poetry has received during this period has been of two kinds. One is the language-talking-to-language, unrestricted-play-of-signifiers discourse that denies the referentiality of texts. In *Dickinson: The Modern Idiom*, for example, David Porter argues that Dickinson's art was "autogenetic": "almost everything in her poems is allegorized, removed from sensation into words of a privately coded intent." He speaks of Dickinson's "physical withdrawal from the referential world": the poetry "does not regard the actual world so much as words that stand for that world. Similitude no longer being the dominant form of knowledge in the poems, they become nonrepresentational and allegorical" (117, 123, 119–20).

The other kind of criticism is New Historicist, particularly feminist. While feminist critics have altered and greatly enriched our sense of Dickinson's art and achievement, it was inevitable that trade-offs would be involved. In her excellent *Undiscovered Continent: Emily Dickinson and the Space of the Mind*, for example, Suzanne Juhasz reads "Presentiment – is that long Shadow – on the Lawn" (#764) as "a tidy aphorism, a statement of general truth" (32), a calculated analogy between an abstraction and a concrete image. This emphasis follows from the book's central premise: "the mind [is] the setting for Dickinson's most significant experience"; the poet chose "to live in her mind rather than in the external world, in order to achieve certain goals and to circumvent or overcome certain forces in her environment and experience that were in opposition to those goals – particularly, the expectations and norms that a patriarchal society creates for women" (1, 4–5). My reading of the poem (in chapter 2) in perceptual terms, which I believe makes it a livelier and more interesting performance, follows from a premise opposed to those of both Porter and Juhasz: that much of Dickinson's most significant experience is referential and is found in her sensory-perceptual relationship to the natural world.

Another feminist critic has claimed that Dickinson "concentrat[es] on the sense of touch," offering as her sole evidence Luce Irigaray's statement that "a woman finds pleasure more in touch than in sight" (Dickie 31). The truth is that the dominant senses in Dickinson's poetry are sight and hearing, especially the former. Indeed, one could argue that exotropia, the serious eye disorder with which she was afflicted, was as important a factor in Dickinson's creative life as was the factor of gender.

Such an argument, however, would inevitably become reductive, and I have no intention of making it. It is one thing to go from the work of art to its conditions; but quite another to go from the conditions to the work of art. Whitman's robust good health and extraordinary haptic sensitivity, for example, are presuppositions of *Song of Myself*. But *Song of Myself*, the achieved poem, is not fully or adequately explained by his good health and haptic sensitivity. As Wordsworth insists in the preface to *Lyrical Ballads*, poems "to which any value can be attached were never produced … but by a man who, being possessed of more than usual organic sensibility, had also thought long and deeply" (*PW* ii 387–8). Similarly, while Dickinson's exotropia was a condition of her poetic practice, it would be as absurd to claim that this condition explains her creative genius as it would be to argue that *Paradise Lost* is explained by Milton's blindness. Such claims would be as patently reductive in connection with any of the subjects of this study as are critical discourses that deny

the referentiality of texts, that proceed as if poems were fully comprehensible in terms of their cultural and ideological context, and that
fail to take into account, in Wordsworth's hyperbole, the "majestic
sway" that at times he, Coleridge, Thoreau, Whitman, and Dickinson
all experienced "As natural beings in the strength of Nature" (*Prelude*
iii 193–4).

Each of my subjects has received an enormous amount of scholarly,
critical and theoretical attention. As my list of works cited indicates, I
am greatly in the debt of numerous scholars and critics. I am more
particularly grateful in various ways to Kim Blank of the University
of Victoria; Mark Jones of Queen's University; Tilottama Rajan of the
University of Western Ontario; Peter Sabor of Université Laval; Boris
Castel, editor of *Queen's Quarterly*, in which a version of part of my
chapter on Thoreau first appeared; Philip Cercone and the late Peter
Blaney of McGill-Queen's Press; my research assistant Bruce Gil-
christ, from whose training in neuroscience I benefited; Rebecca
Katzin and the members of my 1994–95 seminar on the Romantic
symbol; and, *encore une fois*, Susanne McSweeney of Collège Jean de
Brébeuf.

Note on Texts and Citations

COLERIDGE   In quoting from Coleridge, I have used wherever possible the editions in the *Collected Works*, general editor Kathleen Coburn. The text for quotations from the poems is Ernest Hartley Coleridge's edition of the *Complete Poetical Works*.

DICKINSON   The texts for all quotations from Emily Dickinson's poems and her letters are the three-volume editions edited by Thomas H. Johnson. Poems and letters are identified by the number assigned them by Johnson. In quoting from the poems, I have silently incorporated a few of the presentational emendations Johnson made for his one-volume edition *The Complete Poems of Emily Dickinson* (e.g., *its* for *it's*, *ecstasy* for *extasy*).

EMERSON   Unless otherwise noted, the text for quotations from Emerson is the Library of America edition of *Essays and Lectures*, edited by Joel Porte.

HOPKINS   The text for all quotations from Hopkins' poems is the Clarendon edition of *Poetical Works*, edited by Norman H. MacKenzie.

TENNYSON   The text for all quotations from Tennyson's poems is the second edition of *The Poems of Tennyson*, edited in three volumes by Christopher Ricks. Volume and page numbers are supplied for quotations only when their absence would make a passage difficult to find.

THOREAU   Wherever possible, the texts for quotations from Thoreau's works are those in the Princeton University Press edition of his works. For later entries from the *Journal* I have used the fourteen-volume Torrey and Allen edition of 1906.

WHITMAN   Unless otherwise indicated, the text of all quotations from Whitman's poetry and prose is the Library of America edition of the *Complete Poetry and Collected Prose*, edited by Justin Kaplan. This edition includes the text of the 1855 edition of *Leaves of Grass*, which is cited for the poems that first appeared in it (e.g., *Song of Myself* and "There Was a Child Went Forth"). But quotations from *Song of Myself* are identified by the section divisions Whitman later added to the poem.

WORDSWORTH   Unless otherwise noted, the text for all quotations from Wordsworth's poetry (except the *Prelude*) and prose is the *Poetical Works*, edited by E. de Selincourt and Helen Darbishire. For the *Prelude* I have used *The Prelude 1799, 1805, 1850*, edited by Jonathan Wordsworth, M.H. Abrams, and Stephen Gill. Unless otherwise indicated, the 1805 version is the text cited. Line numbers are parenthetically supplied for quotations from the *Prelude*. Similar information is supplied for other poems only when its absence would make a passage difficult to find.

In addition to shortened forms of titles, the following abbreviations are used in citations:

PW   Wordsworth's *Poetical Works*
  J   Thoreau's *Journal* (Torrey and Allen edition)
 *J   Thoreau's *Journal* (Princeton edition)
SM   Coleridge's *Statesman's Manual*

The Language of the Senses

ONE

Organic Sensibility

In "My First Acquaintance with Poets," William Hazlitt recalls meeting Wordsworth at Coleridge's cottage in Nether Stowey. At one point, the poet looked out of a latticed window and observed: "How beautifully the sun sets on that yellow bank!" Hazlitt remembered thinking to himself, "'With what eyes these poets see nature!' and ever after, when I saw the sun-set stream upon the objects facing it, conceived I had made a discovery, or thanked Mr. Wordsworth for having made one for me" (xvii 118). There is nothing unusual in Hazlitt's associating poetic gifts with sensory acuity. A "great Poet," Coleridge insists, must have "the *ear* of a wild Arab listening in the silent Desert, the eye of a North American Indian tracing the footsteps of an Enemy upon the Leaves that strew the Forest –; the *Touch* of a Blind Man feeling the face of a darling Child" (*Letters* ii 810). And keenness of sensation is the basis of Emerson's theory of imaginative creation. "What else is it to be a poet?" he asks; "What are his garland and singing-robes? What but a sensibility so keen that the scent of an elder-blow, or the timber-yard and corporation-works of a nest of pismires [ants] is event enough for him, – all emblems and personal appeals to him" ("Poetry" 36). This last phrase intimates what in other places Emerson and Coleridge make abundantly clear. Perception and apperception are equally necessary for the poet. Without them a natural object could never become a figure or make a personal appeal.

One way in which Coleridge emphasized the importance of organic sensibility was to describe the poet as a person who has retained into adult life the sensory-perceptual acuity of the child:

To carry on the feelings of childhood into the powers of manhood, to combine the child's sense of wonder and novelty with the appearances which every day for perhaps forty years had rendered familiar ... this is the character and privilege of genius, and one of the marks which distinguish genius from talents. And so to represent familiar objects as to awaken the minds of others to a like freshness of sensation concerning them ... this is the prime merit of genius, and its most unequivocal mode of manifestation. (*Friend* i 109–10)

To understand the connection that Coleridge makes between the childhood sensorium and poetic genius, it is necessary to become familiar with his observations on the sensory development of children.

Through studying his infant son, Coleridge was led to conclude that touch and taste are the first channels of knowledge of the outer world: "Contact – the womb – the amnion liquor – warmth + touch/ – air cold + touch + sensation & action of breathing – contact of the mother's knees + all those contacts of the Breast + taste & wet & sense of swallowing –"; "Babies touch *by taste* at first – then about 5 months old they go from the Palate to the hand – & are fond of feeling what they have taste[d] – / Association of the Hand with the Taste – till the latter by itself recalls the former – & of course, with volition" (*Notebooks* i #1414, #924).

Coleridge was correct. The senses develop in a definite sequence: tactile, auditory, visual. As the child grows, the order of precedence becomes reversed. But in the early phases of development it is "much more important to experience tactile and auditory stimulations ... than it is to experience visual ones" (Montagu 236). Eventually, vision becomes by far the most important sense, one reason being that the optic nerve has "some eighteen times more nerve endings than the cochlear nerve of the ear, its nearest competitior." And with its 800,000 fibers the eye "can transfer an astonishing amount of information to the brain, and at a rate of assimilation far greater than that of any other sense organ" (Jay *Eyes* 6). But this information only becomes meaningful on the basis of what has been previously felt and heard. As Coleridge puts it: "The first education which we receive, that from our mothers, is given to us by touch; the whole of its process is nothing more than, to express myself boldly, an extended touch by promise. The sense itself, the sense of vision itself, is only acquired by a continued recollection of touch" (*Philosophical Lectures* 115).

"In the infancy and childhood of individuals," Coleridge notes, "the first knowledges are acquired promiscuously." This was "the happy delirium, the healthful fever of the physical, moral and intellectual being, – nature's kind and providential gift to childhood. In the best good sense of the words, it is the light-headedness and light-heartedness of human life!" Nature supplies "a gay and motley chaos of facts, and forms, and thousand-fold experiences, the origin of which lies beyond the memory, traceless as life itself" (Snyder 105). This period of healthy promiscuity is the subject of Whitman's marvelous poem, "There Was a Child Went Forth," which is both a representation of a child's sensory-perceptual development and, like the first two books of Wordsworth's *Prelude*, its author's pre-history as a Romantic poet.

Whitman's poem begins in springtime as the child for the first time crosses the threshold of the early home environment into a predominantly visual post-infancy world. Outside the home, touch, taste and smell are recessive. There are some sounds, but predominantly there are sights. The child becomes part of what he sees, not what he touches, and his experiences are pristine and chaste. Touch in its role as the principal channel of sexual feeling – the sense that overwhelms the mature man in *Song of Myself* – has yet to be awakened:

> The early lilacs became part of this child,
> And grass, and white and red morningglories, and white and red clover,
>   and the song of the phoebe-bird,
> And the March-born lambs, and the sow's pink-faint litter, and the
>   mare's foal, and the cow's calf, and the noisy brood of the barnyard or
>   by the mire of the pond-side..and the fish suspending themselves so
>   curiously below there..and the beautiful curious liquid..and the
>   water-plants with their graceful flat heads..all became part of him.

The adjective "curious" refers to both subjective and objective states – it means both "eager to learn" and "exciting attention" or "awakening surprise." The fish seemingly suspended in the water of the pond are curious to the boy because in his previous experience of water inside his home anything that did not float on top sank to the bottom. The water-plants are odd in another way; "they have flat heads, unlike the other plants he knows, but they strike him as admirable nonetheless" and he thus juxtaposes what to an adult would seem two contradictory characteristics: "their graceful flat heads" (Vendler "Placing" 22).

In the next lines, the circles of sensory-perceptual awareness expand to include the sprouts in the garden, the blossoms on the apple-trees, the weeds by the road, and the humans that use the road: "the old drunkard staggering home," the schoolmistress, "the friendly boys that passed..and the quarrelsome boys" (a crucial distinction for a child), "the tidy and freshcheeked girls," and the "negro boy and girl" who are not freshcheeked but whose bare feet are notable. In the temporally elided middle of the poem, more complex and destabilizing experiences are noted as the circles of curiousness expand: the mother's wholesome odor, recalling the sensory security of infancy, contrasts with the father's minatory attributes; there is socialization ("family usages," "company"); there are powerful feelings seeking an outlet ("the yearning and swelling heart").

And, as for Wordsworth as a child, there is a tendency towards idealism: "The sense of what is real....the thought if after all it should prove unreal,/The doubts of daytime and the doubts of night-time...the curious whether and how,/Whether that which appears so is so....Or is it all flashes and specks?" Wordsworth reported that during childhood he often had to recall himself from the "abyss of idealism" through the sense of touch – by grasping at a wall or tree (*PW* iv 463). In Whitman's poem, this tendency is subsumed by the expanding circles of visual awareness that culminate in an exquisitely rendered sunset scene:

> Shadows .. aureola and mist .. light falling on roofs and gables of white
>   or brown, three miles off,
> The schooner near by sleepily dropping down the tide .. the little boat
>   slacktowed astern,
> The hurrying tumbling waves and quickbroken crests and slapping;
> The strata of colored clouds....the long bar of maroontint away solitary
>   by itself....the spread of purity it lies motionless in,
> The horizon's edge, the flying seacrow, the fragrance of saltmarsh and
>   shoremud;
> These became part of that child who went forth every day, and who now
>   goes and will always go forth every day.

This scene is a perceptual continuum stretching from the odors of the proximate shoreline, through the visual and auditory agitation of the tumbling and slapping waves and the visual particulars of the more slowly moving schooner and flying seacrow in the middle distance, to the visual limit – the horizon's edge out there and the motionless clouds and unbounded spread of purity up there. This continuum is simultaneously, not sequentially experienced; this is emphasized by the near-far alternations in the enumeration of particulars. To borrow a phrase of Whitman's from another piece of natural description, the sunset scene offers "purity without sentiment" (826). There is no subjective projection; in Friedrich Schiller's terms, it is a naive rather than a sentimental perception of the natural world.[1]

The aggregative ripples of expanding consciousness have culminated in a totality, a holistic moment. The synchronic experience at the poem's conclusion recapitulates spatially the diachronic movement of the poem outward from the maternal environment to the external world. Inscribed in its perceptual particulars is the dependence of aesthetic perception on the childhood perception that preceded it. The little boat slacktowed astern faintly recalls the lambs, the foal, the calf, and the sow's litter; the delicate color discrimination ("maroontint") recalls the pink-faint litter and the white and red morning-glories and clover seen by the child; the mud of the shore recalls the mire of the pondside; and the shoreline fragrance recalls the other olfactory image and the other *terminus a quo* in the poem – the maternal aroma.

What of the assertion that the child will "always go forth every day"? It may be taken both metaphorically (duration as the vehicle, present intensity as the tenor) and psychologically (the child/youth lives in a timeless "now," not yet having a felt awareness of his mortality). The "always" may also be considered in relation to the later-deleted last line of the poem: "And these become part of him or her that peruses them now." Here the "always" suggests indefinite temporal extension. The child/youth has grown up to become the poet who writes "There Was a Child Went Forth" and who will always go forth in the sense that his sensory-perceptual progression is re-enacted each time a reader experiences the poem.

What cannot be done is to take the "always" literally. Like Coleridge and Emerson, Whitman came in time to experience the negative effect on poetic genius of the diminution of sensory-perceptual acuity that is an inevitable part of the life cycle. Since age-related sensory changes occur gradually over a long period, beginning in adolescence or early adulthood, most persons adapt to them without difficulty. But for Romantic writers, the change could seem catastrophic. We can have "health and reason," as Emerson puts it in "Experience," and yet "have no superfluity of spirit for new creation … We are like millers on the lower levels of a stream, when the factories above them have exhausted the water" (471). This heavy change is the subject of Coleridge's Dejection Ode and Wordsworth's Intimations Ode, the latter of which was Thoreau's master-text for comprehending and articulating the devastating decline in his own sensory-perceptual powers. As for the author of "There Was a Child Went Forth": the antiphonal voice of that poem is heard in the "Sands at Seventy" section of the final edition of *Leaves of Grass*, particularly in the poem that figures the Romantic poet in old age as "The Dismantled Ship":

In some unused lagoon, some nameless bay,
On sluggish, lonesome waters, anchor'd near the shore,
An old, dismasted, gray and batter'd ship, disabled, done,
After free voyages to all the seas of earth, haul'd up at last and
    hawser'd tight,
Lies rusting, mouldering.

Coleridge's observations of the sensory development of children were part of his interest in the classification of the senses and their interaction and interdependence. Clustering his notations on these subjects (and amplifying them with other references) will introduce those aspects of sensory-perceptual experience that have a particular importance in his own work and in that of Wordsworth, Thoreau, Whitman, and Dickinson.

Coleridge was opposed to the traditional hierarchical division of the senses into higher (sight and hearing) and lower (smell, taste and touch) and to the valorization of sight as the supreme sense that had occurred in the late seventeenth century following the impact of Newton's *Opticks* and the empirically-based psychology of Locke. He was also opposed to aesthetic thinkers who equated imagination with sight and regarded the eye as the essential sensory organ upon which imagination was based.[2] The privileging of sight, Coleridge feared, could lead to a separation of subject and object. Sight and hearing present objects to the mind distinct from our perceptions of them, un-like the mixed or imperfect senses that "combine with the perception of the outward Object a distinct sense of our own Life" (*Lectures* i 36). In modern scientific terminology, touch, taste, and smell have an autocentric rather than allocentric mode of operation. It is mainly through these senses that the sixth or proprioceptive sense, the body's sense of itself, is activated. In touch, for example, both poles of the sensory experience – subjective and objective, active and passive – are present. In touching an object, I at the same time feel myself touching it: it is "as if the same stimulating event had two possible poles of experience, one objective and the other subjective" (Gibson 99). Cole-ridge believed that if unaccompanied by touch (and taste and smell), visual and auditory perceptions were "liable to cause false represen-tations of the self" (Modiano "Views" 34). For example, he came to conclude of his wife Sara that eye and ear were her "great organs" (*Letters* ii 882) to such a degree that the imbalance had resulted in

coldness perhaps & paralysis in all *tangible* ideas & sensations – all that forms *real Self* – hence she creates her own self in a field of Vision and Hearing ... & hence becomes the willing Slave of the Ears & Eyes of others. – Nothing affects her with pain or pleasure as it is but only as other people will *say it is* – nay by an habitual absence of *reality* in her affections I have had a hundred instances that the being beloved, or the not being beloved, is a thing indifferent; but the *notion* of not being beloved – that wounds her pride deeply.   (*Notebooks* i #979)

The crucial element in the constitution of *real Self* was tangible or tactual sensation, which was "not a mere moment of sensation" but a pathic merge, "the blending & unifying of the sensations that inhere in the manifold goings on of the Life of the whole man" (*Notebooks* i #979). In one of his attempts to represent this, Coleridge used a circular model, an adaptation of the medieval sense wheel, distributing the senses of hearing, sight, smell, and taste at equidistant points on a circumference and placing in the center both feeling and its direct manifestation, touch. He explained that "Feeling organized in addition to and in co-existence with the other senses is Touch"; while "Feeling organized by the absorption or subsumption of the other senses is that mysterious Sense of vital Warmth" (*Letters* iv 774). There was to be sure an essential difference between touch and feeling; the latter was "an act of consciousness having itself for its only Object, and not a Symbol or representative of any thing else. Thus I have a *sensation* of Heat, a *Feeling* of Life" (*Notebooks* iii #3605). But because they both occupied the same central place in the sensorium they were bound to dissolve into each other.

How can the visual perception of a distant object be accompanied by feeling/touch? Like Aristotle, Coleridge considered touch the originating sense; the other senses, including vision, were only acquired by a continual recollection of touch. For example, the sense of magnitude (as opposed to mere spaciousness) was dependent on the idea of substance which was in turn dependent on touch. "[A]ll our feelings & ideas of magnitude, magnitudinal sublimity, &c" are evolved "from a scale of our own bodies"; if there "were pure vision, as a perceptive sense abstracted from *feeling* in the organ of vision, why do I seek for mountains when in the flattest countries the Clouds present so many so much more romantic & *spacious* forms, & the coal-fire so many so much more varied & lovely forms?" (*Notebooks* ii #2402). Without feeling/touch, all kinds of visual tricks and specious frissons were possible, such as those described in Coleridge's own "Apologia pro Vita Sua" (1800), a poem that I shall cite in chapter 5 in discussing the deterioration of his imaginative power:

> The poet in his lone yet genial hour
> Gives to his eyes a magnifying power:

> Or rather he emancipates his eyes
> From the blank shapeless accidents of size –
> In unctuous cones of kindling coal,
> Or smoke upwreathing from the pipe's trim bole,
>   His gifted ken can see
>   Phantoms of sublimity.

In associating smell with taste and touch, Coleridge disagreed with Aristotle, who considered this sense the pivotal point between the two outer senses (sight and hearing) and the two inner senses (taste and touch). Coleridge may be judged more correct in that sight and sound are air-wave disturbances while smell is chemical and molecular, and as such closer to taste and touch. But Aristotle also had a point: smell does have unique sensory characteristics. As Poe correctly observed: "odors have an altogether idiosyncratic force, in affecting us through association; a force differing *essentially* from that of objects addressing the touch, the taste, the sight, or the hearing" (1333). The reason that the perception of odors is idiosyncratic becomes evident when the anatomy of smell is considered. The brain's processing of smells occurs through two distinct pathways. After the initial transduction from chemical to neuronal messages that occurs in the olfactory bulbs, some messages are relayed into the limbic system, an evolutionarily old and intensely emotional part of the brain. Olfaction is thus "more involved in visceral and emotional activities than in sensory information transmission" and may well cause a feeling before eliciting a concern with its meaning (Engen 4). The range of the human olfactory spectrum is wide, extending from sexual arousal to images of eternity (as in Dante's *Paradiso* and Whitman's "Crossing Brooklyn Ferry"). But the physiological dynamics of human smell are such that a person can easily be deprived of the distinctive properties of this sensory avenue and its important role in intensifying other sensory experiences – as is known to anyone who has ever eaten a gourmet dinner while suffering from a head cold.

Concerning the outer senses of sight and sound, Coleridge made an interesting comparative observation during the winter of 1798–99, when he was living in Germany:

About a month ago, before the thaw came on, there was a storm of wind; during the whole night, such were the thunders and howlings of the breaking ice [of the Lake of Ratzeburg], that they have left a conviction on my mind, that there are sounds more sublime than any sight *can* be, more absolutely suspending the power of comparison, and more utterly absorbing the mind's self-consciousness in its total attention to the object working upon it. (*Friend* i 367)

He was once again on the mark. In contrast to sight, hearing is more proximate, pervasive and penetrating. In Hans Jonas' account, sound, "itself a dynamic fact, intrudes upon a passive subject":

For the sensation of hearing to come about the percipient is entirely dependent on something happening outside his control, and ... is exposed to its happening. All he can contribute to the situation is a state of attentive readiness ... He cannot let his ears wander, as his eyes do, over a field of possible percepts ... he has no choice in the matter. In hearing, the percipient is at the mercy of environmental action, which intrudes upon his sensibility without his asking. (139)

These generalizations, however, are partial in that they refer to near or proximate sounds. When sounds are heard from a distance, the effect can be not an intrusion but an inducement to reflection and rapture. Here, for example, is a passage from the journal of Thoreau, a connoisseur of the effects of distant sounds:

Heard at a distance the sound of the bell acquires a certain vibratory hum, as it were from the air through which it passes – like a harp ... It is not the mere sound of the bell but the humming in the air that enchants me – just [as the] azure tint which much air or distance imparts delights the eye. It is not so much the object as the object clothed with an azure veil. All sound heard at a great distance thus tends to produce the same music – vibrating the strings of the universal lyre. There comes to me a melody which the air has strained. – which has conversed with every leaf and needle of the woods. It is by no means the sound of the bell as heard near at hand, and which at this distance I can plainly distinguish – but its vibrating echoes that portion of the sound which the elements take up and modulate. A sound which is very much much modified sifted and refined before it reaches my ear. (*J iv 142–3)

At a proximate distance, sight organizes a perceptual field of co-temporaneous particulars, imposing a hierarchy and figure/ground distinctions, and privileging a central object. One is able to observe dispassionately, to abstract, and to compare (see Jonas 148–9). The dynamics of distant sight are different, as an entry from Walter Scott's journal suggests: "Ah, that Distance! What a magician for conjuring up scenes of joy or sorrow, smoothing all asperities, reconciling all incongruities, veiling all absurdness, softening every coarseness, doubling every effect by the influence of the imagination" (i 172).

But the effects of distance can be more than simply charming or enchanting. Other advantages are instanced in Wordsworth's *Prelude*. In the eighth book, for example, the subject of which is "Love of Nature Leading to Love of Mankind," the poet describes standing on

Helvellyn (a peak in the Lake District) looking down on a village fair. The distance allows both the detailed observation of the human scene and a shift in focus so that it is seen against the background of the immense "circumambient world": "How little they, they and their doings, seem," Wordsworth reflects, "and yet how great,/For all things serve them" – the morning light, the silent rocks, the brooks, the peak, and the blue sky (47–61). And later in the book he recalls as a boy seeing in the distance a shepherd against the sky looking "like an aërial cross" positioned for worship (408). Also important to Wordsworth was "the way in which distance can bring about oxymoron in perception" (Ogden 254). Alpine examples are found in the *Prelude's* sixth book: the "dumb cataracts and streams of ice – /A motionless array of mighty waves" (458–9); and "the stationary blasts of waterfalls" (558) which, as we shall see, were one of the ingredients in Wordsworth's sublime experience in the Gondo Gorge.

Another characteristic of distanced sight is the "indefinite 'and so on' with which the visual perception is imbued [which] is the birthplace of the idea of *infinity*" (Jonas 150). As Ortega y Gasset has noted, as distance increases "we no longer see one thing clearly and the rest confusedly … the duality of proximate vision is succeeded by a perfect unity of the whole visual field." Distant objects become "mere chromatic entities" and can acquire illusory or apparitional qualities (824–5). In Emerson's hyperbole, it is "especially in the distant line of the horizon [that] man beholds somewhat as beautiful as his own nature" (10).

When Whitman speaks of "those beautiful wonders, the perceptions or senses" (*Notebooks* 124), the "or" seems to imply that there is little difference between the two. Coleridge is helpful both in distinguishing between these faculties and in explaining why it is practically impossible to consider them separately. A sensation is a particular kind of feeling, "a Feeling referring to some *Thing*, and not yet *organized* into a definite *Object* nor separated from the sentient Being":

The sensitive faculty is the power of being affected and modified by *Things*, so as to receive impressions from them. The Quality of these Impressions is determined partly by the nature of the sensitive faculty itself and its organs, and partly by the nature of the Things. These impressions are in the first instant *immediate Sensations*: as soon as the *attention* is directed to them, and they are taken up into the *Consciousness*, they become *Perceptions*.

A perception is "sensations organized into an Object, and thus projected out of the sentient Being." With reference to the objects of
present or past perception, "the presentations or representations of
Things," it is not possible

> to distinguish by determinate boundaries, what part proceeds from the
> sensitive faculty itself, and what from the outward Causes or the Things
> acting on the faculty ... The cause of this impossibility is that we become
> conscious both of the one and of the other in one & the same way; namely,
> as modifications of our own Being. What precedes the modification as its
> cause, we can never know; because our consciousness originates in the
> modification.   (*Notebooks* iii #3605)

This originative and constitutive power of perception is the basis of
Coleridge's conception of the creative activity of the mind, including
symbolic perception. This is the subject of the next chapter, in which
Coleridge is once again the *point d'appui*.

· TWO ·

Symbolic Perception

In the seventh chapter of *Biographia Literaria*, Coleridge develops an extended analogy for "the mind's self-experience in the act of thinking":

Most of my readers will have observed a small water-insect on the surface of rivulets, which throws a cinque-spotted shadow fringed with prismatic colours on the sunny bottom of the brook; and will have noticed, how the little animal *wins* its way up against the stream, by alternate pulses of active and passive motion, now resisting the current, and now yielding to it in order to gather strength and a momentary *fulcrum* for a further propulsion.

There are two powers at work, "which relatively to each other are active and passive"; but their operation is not possible "without an intermediate faculty, which is at once both active and passive." In "philosophical language," Coleridge explains, this intermediate faculty "in all its degrees and determinations" is called imagination, while "in common language, and especially on the subject of poetry, we appropriate the name to a superior degree of the faculty, joined to a superior voluntary controul over it" (i 124–5).

Coleridge makes the same distinction six chapters later. The primary imagination is "the living Power and prime Agent of all human Perception ... a repetition in the finite mind of the eternal act of creation in the infinite *I am*." As we have seen, for Coleridge perception (primary imagination) is "the *context* for a distinction between perceiver and perceived, not the product of that duality"; " 'reality' is understood to reside neither in an absolute subject nor in the object, but in the experienced interaction between the two" (Wheeler "Theory" 26, 17–18). The secondary imagination is "an echo of the former, co-existing with the conscious will, yet still as identical with the primary in the *kind* of its agency, and differing only in *degree*, and in the *mode* of its operation. It dissolves, diffuses, dissipates, in order to re-create." It is "essentially *vital*, even as all objects (*as* objects) are essentially fixed and dead" (i 304).

Coleridge's water-insect analogy is not the appropriate emblem for the creative activity of mind of all the subjects of this study. It is excellent for the author of "This Lime-Tree Bower My Prison" and "Frost at Midnight"; but something much faster-moving is required for Emily Dickinson – for example, her evanescent hummingbird, reeling oriole, or delirious bee. As for Whitman, his noiseless patient spider constantly unreeling filaments out of itself is perhaps the emblem one wants, though something more dynamic and erotic would be preferable for the poet of *Song of Myself* – perhaps the stallion in section 32 of that poem, who is "fresh and responsive" to the caresses of its rider: "His nostrils dilate ... his well built limbs tremble with pleasure."

But what these writers, and Wordsworth and Thoreau, all have in common is that perception or primary imagination is an essential aspect of the creative process. So is the detection of analogies. A key premise for all of them is, in Emerson's formulation, a "radical correspondence between visible things and human thoughts": "Every natural fact is a symbol of some spiritual fact. Every appearance in nature corresponds to some state of the mind, and that state of the mind can only be described by presenting that natural appearance as its picture ... man is an analogist, and studies relations in all objects ... neither can man be understood without these objects, nor these objects without man" (20–1).

When the particular "man" in question is a poet, there is nothing unusual about this declaration. Aristotle, for example, regarded the mastery of metaphorical language – the ability to perceive similarities that was an inborn gift and could not be taught – as *the* distinguishing feature of the poet (49). Emerson was in complete agreement: "As a power [poetry] is the perception of the symbolic character of things, and the treating them as representative: as a talent it is a magnetic tenaciousness of an image" ("Poetry" 27). In the particular case of natural facts and spiritual facts, the former are the vehicles of metaphorical relationships; the tenors are mental, psychological, and emotional states. In *Nature*, Emerson provides examples: "An enraged man is a lion, a cunning man is a fox, a firm man is a rock, a learned man is a torch ... flowers express to us the delicate affections" (20).

But these are conventional, even hackneyed figures. What is distinctive about the Romantic use of such tropes, what makes Emerson's assertion a key Romantic postulate, is the emphasis on the
perception of an analogy between subject and natural object. Writing
in 1829, the critic Francis Jeffrey considers it axiomatic that "the very
essence of poetry ... consists in the fine perception and vivid expression of that subtle and mysterious Analogy which exists between the
physical and the moral world – which makes outward things and
qualities the natural types and emblems of inward gifts and emotions" (474). A principal reason why in the Romantic period this analogical activity of mind came to be considered the distinguishing
feature of poetry is suggested by a passage in Coleridge's *Statesman's
Manual*. It occurs when he turns his attention from the scriptural revelation of God to "the great book of his servant Nature":

I have at this moment before me, in the flowery meadow, on which my eye is
now reposing, one of its most soothing chapters ... For never can I look and
meditate on the vegetable creation without a feeling similar to that with
which we gaze at a beautiful infant that has fed itself asleep at its mother's
bosom, and smiles in its strange dream of obscure yet happy sensations. The
same tender and genial pleasure takes possession of me, and this pleasure is
checked and drawn inward by the like aching melancholy, by the same whispered remonstrance, and made restless by a similar impulse of aspiration. It
seems as if the soul said to herself: from this state hast *thou* fallen! Such
shouldst thou still become, thy Self all permeable to a holier power! thy Self
at once hidden and glorified by its own transparency, as the accidental and
dividuous in this quiet and harmonious object is subjected to the life and
light of nature which shines in it ... (71)

The best gloss on this passage is Schiller's description of the relationship of the modern poet to the natural world in his *Naïve and
Sentimental Poetry* (1795–6): "Our feeling for nature is like the feeling
of an invalid for health." The reason natural scenes so deeply affect
their human perceivers is that we are responding to "the serene
spontaneity of their activity, existence in accordance with their own
laws, the inner necessity, the eternal unity with themselves. *They
are what we were*," says Schiller: "they are what *we should once again
become*." Natural scenes are "not only the representation of our lost
childhood, which eternally remains most dear to us, but fill us with
a certain melancholy"; they are also "representations of our highest
fulfilment in the ideal, thus evoking in us a sublime tenderness"
(105, 84–5).[1]

In the subjects of this study, the varieties of inner/outer analogical figuration range from the emblematic to the implicit, the determinate to the polysemous, and the metaphorical to the metonymic. At one end of the spectrum are examples of the charm that attends natural phenomena as, in Wordsworth's phrase, "they present to Fancy's choice/Apt illustrations of the moral world,/ Caught at a glance, or traced with curious pains" (1850 *Prelude* xiv 317–20). Both of the following are superior examples of elaborate tracing:

Truth considered in itself and in the effects natural to it, may be conceived as a gentle spring or water-source, warm from the genial earth, and breathing up into the snow drift that is piled over and around its outlet. It turns the obstacle into its own form and character, and as it makes its way increases its stream. And should it be arrested in its course by a chilling season, it suffers delay, not loss, and waits only for a change in the wind to awaken and again roll onwards.   (Coleridge *Friend* i 65)

Again I scent the white water-lily ... It is the emblem of purity, and its scent suggests it. Growing in stagnant and muddy [water], it bursts up so pure and fair to the eye and so sweet to the scent, as if to show us what purity and sweetness reside in, and can be extracted from, the slime and muck of earth ... What confirmation of our hopes is in the fragrance of the water-lily! ... The foul slime stands for the sloth and vice of man; the fragrant flower that springs from it, for the purity and courage which springs from its midst.   (Thoreau *J* vi 352–3)

The tenor of both figures is an idealized abstraction with a generalized inspirational import; but neither figure seems arbitrarily developed or mere rhetorical embellishment. Both presuppose attentive observation of natural phenomena, and in each case it appears as if observation has stimulated reflection. Both bring to mind Thoreau's generalization that it is "as language that all natural objects affect the poet ... He sees a flower or other object, and it is beautiful or affecting to him because it is a symbol of his thought, and what he indistinctly feels or perceives is matured in some other organization" (*J* v 359). Both figures, however, depend on conceptual transference rather than a single intense perceptual act or the detection of a complementarity between perceiver and perceived. Both might even be thought to answer to Coleridge's complaint:

never to see or describe any interesting appearance in nature, without connecting it by dim analogies with the moral world, proves faintness of

Impression. Nature has her proper interest; & he will know what it is, who believes & feels, that every Thing has a life of it's own, & that we are all *one Life*. A Poet's *Heart & Intellect* should be *combined, intimately* combined & *unified*, with the great appearances in Nature – & not merely held in solution & loose mixture with them, in the shape of formal Similies.[2]   (*Letters* ii 864)

Stronger impressions and more intimate combinations of inner and outer are found in the following two passages:

Does Lust call forth or occasion Love? – Just as much as the reek of the Marsh calls up the Sun. The sun calls up the vapor – attenuates, lifts it – it becomes a cloud – and now it is the Veil of the Divinity – the Divinity transpiercing it at once hides & declares his presence – We *see*, we are conscious of, *Light* alone; but it is Light embodied in the earthly nature, which that Light itself awoke & sublimated.   (Coleridge *Letters* iii 305)

> As Frost is best conceived
> By force of its Result –
> Affliction is inferred
> By subsequent effect –
>
> If when the sun reveal,
> The Garden keep the Gash –
> If as the Days resume
> The wilted countenance
>
> Cannot correct the crease
> Or counteract the stain –
> Presumption is Vitality
> Was somewhere put in twain.   (Dickinson #951)

Unlike the first two examples, the tenors of these figures are not idealized abstractions but processive emotional states, and the detailing of similarity between natural and spiritual processes yields psychological insight. Moreover, the appositeness of the analogy (the intimacy of the combination) is not exhausted in the tracing. For example, in addition to its explicit tenor, the second example also suggests that affliction brings a blighting, numbing deadness to the affective and perceptual life. But while these two examples are different from the first two in degree of impression and of complementarity of subject and object, they are similar in that they also involve conceptual transference and thus make one reluctant to cite either passage as an exemplification of subject and object sharing in the common life of all.

The next two passages contain still more intimate combinations of inner and outer:

> Presentiment – is that long Shadow – on the Lawn –
> Indicative that Suns go down –
>
> The Notice to the startled Grass
> That Darkness – is about to pass –   (Dickinson #764)

Lo! – with the rising sun it [a tree or flower] commences its outward life and enters into open communion with all the elements, at once assimilating them to itself and to each other. At the same moment it strikes its roots and unfolds its leaves, absorbs and respires, streams forth its cooling vapour and finer fragrance, and breathes a repairing spirit, at once the food and tone of the atmosphere, into the atmosphere that feeds *it*. Lo! – at the touch of light how it returns an air akin to light, and yet with the same pulse effectuates its own secret growth, still contracting to fix what expanding it had refined. Lo! – how upholding the ceaseless plastic motion of the parts in the profoundest rest of the whole it becomes the visible organismus of the whole *silent* or *elementary* life of nature and, therefore, in incorporating the one extreme becomes the symbol of the other; the natural symbol of that higher life of reason, in which the whole series (known to us in our present state of being) is perfected, in which, therefore, all the subordinate gradations recur, and are re-ordained *"in more abundant honor."*   (Coleridge *SM* 72)

The subject of Dickinson's poem is not an idealized abstraction or generalized emotional state but rather a mood or sudden feeling. The analogy is connotative rather than denotative, suggestive rather than determinate. It depends not on conceptual transference or associative tracing but on a perceptual/emotional intuition (it is not *the* long shadow, but *that* long shadow). What is intuited or felt is the coextensiveness of inner and outer that is figured by the transferred epithet "startled." There is no suggestion of conceptual transference; intense perception of the natural fact is itself the trigger of the analogy, and the act of analogical perception is delicately inscribed in the poem.

The passage from the *Statesman's Manual* is a more extended example of an analogical figure that inscribes the act of perceiving the analogy. It is the climax of Coleridge's meditation on the flowery meadow outside his window, the beginning of which was cited above. In that poignant reflection, Coleridge had discovered or been reminded of a counterpart in himself to the light of the sun – the "light of conscience" or, rather, the potential of that internal power to compose what is "accidental and dividuous" in his nature into an harmonious unity (*SM* 71). But, as Margery Sabin has pointed out, in that analogical perception the burden of "correspondence between nature and spirit falls on the metaphor of light, and there seems no reason other than religious and literary tradition to call conscience a light. The 'light of conscience' is a figure of speech, perhaps only an arbitrary verbal convention" (205). As soon as he had composed the passage, Coleridge seems to have had the same realization:

But ... I seem to myself to behold in the quiet objects, on which I am gazing, more than an arbitrary illustration, more than a mere *simile*, the work of my own Fancy! I feel an awe, as if there were before my eyes the same Power, as that of the Reason – the same power in a lower dignity, and therefore a symbol established in the truth of things. I feel it alike, whether I contemplate a single tree or flower, or meditate on vegetation throughout the world, as one of the great organs of the life of nature.   (72)

A single plant is now perceived as a symbol of the processes of the life of the natural world, which is itself a "natural symbol" of the inner life of reason with which it is felt to be coextensive. That is to say, a metonymical or synecdochal relationship, rather than simply a metaphorical one, is the basis of the analogy.

For Coleridge, this contiguous relationship is the distinguishing feature of the natural fact as symbol. It is "not a metaphor or allegory or any other figure of speech or form of fancy, but an actual and essential part of that, the whole of which it represents" (*SM* 79). While the gentle spring in the passage quoted above is an allegorical emblem of truth, the plant in the flowery meadow is a symbol of the one life within and abroad. An allegory is simply "a translation of abstract notions into a picture-language which is itself nothing but an abstraction from objects of the senses"; a symbol is "characterized by a translucence of the Special in the Individual or of the General in the Especial or of the Universal in the General. Above all by the translucence of the Eternal through and in the Temporal" (*SM* 30).

"Above all by the translucence of the Eternal through and in the Temporal." Coleridge was as much or more interested in natural facts as figures and symbols of the transcendent as he was in them as figures or symbols of inner states. So was Emerson, who in *Nature* is at pains to point out that the correspondence of outer nature to inner nature is only one of the two ways in which nature is symbolic: "Have mountains, and waves, and skies, no significance but what we consciously give them, when we employ them as emblems of our thoughts?" The answer (quoting Swedenborg) is that "'The visible world and the relation of its parts, is the dial-plate of the invisible'." For Emerson, there is no doubt as to which of the two kinds of "spiritual facts" is superior: "the noblest ministry of nature is to stand as the apparition of God. It is the organ through which the universal spirit speaks to the individual, and strives to lead back the individual to it" (24, 40).

This lower/higher mode of Romantic symbolic perception of natural facts is no more new than the inner/outer mode. As Coleridge observes: "it has been the music of gentle and pious minds in all ages, it is the *poetry* of all human nature, to read [the natural world] in a figurative sense, and to find therein correspondences and symbols of the spiritual world" (*SM* 70). Had not Paul written in his Epistle to the Romans (1:20) that "the invisible things of Him from the creation of the world are clearly seen, being understood by the things that are made"? This mode also has the same qualitative range as the inner/outer mode. At one end, there are conventional or arbitrary figures involving conceptual transference, like those in a poem written by Wordsworth at the beginning of the post-Romantic decades of his career:

> Yes, it was the mountain Echo,
> Solitary, clear, profound,
> Answering to the shouting Cuckoo,
> Giving to her sound for sound!
>
> Unsolicited reply
> To a babbling wanderer sent;
> Like her ordinary cry,
> Like – but oh, how different!
>
> Hears not also mortal Life?
> Hear not we, unthinking Creatures!
> Slaves of folly, love, or strife –
> Voices of two different natures?
>
> Have not *we* too? – yes, we have
> Answers, and we know not whence;
> Echoes from beyond the grave,
> Recognised intelligence!

> Such rebounds our inward ear
> Catches sometimes from afar –
> Listen, ponder, hold them dear;
> For of God, – of God they are.   (ii 265–6)

The poem's first two stanzas present a two-part natural fact: the sounds of the cuckoo and the enhanced echoes of these sounds. The remainder of the poem is devoted to the spiritual truth for which the natural fact is made to stand. Human beings, if not babbling wanderers, are unthinkingly in the grip of lower passions. But "we" have the ability to distinguish sounds of "two different natures": terrestrial sounds and higher sounds from beyond that do not simply echo, are not merely what cuckoos can hear, but that come from another realm of being, that are "of God" and "beyond the grave."

Wordsworth's crude emblem or allegory is not rooted in a perceptually intense experience and requires no special sensitivity to the natural world. Indeed, the poem turns on the assumption of a discontinuity between man and nature owing to the former's privileged access to intimations from a supernatural world. In Romantic symbolic perception, on the other hand, the emphasis is as much on the perceiver as on the perceived; their relationship is dynamic rather than static, and depends on the disposition of the perceiver. "In the transmission of the heavenly waters," as Emerson extravagantly said, "every hose fits every hydrant ... Every thing must be taken genially, and we must be at the top of our condition, to understand any thing rightly" (676).

But the more attention is drawn to the importance in symbolic perception of the subjective state of the perceiver, the more equivocal the fit between subject and object can come to seem. This problem is the subject of a number of Emily Dickinson's poems on the phenomenology of perception. "Of Bronze – and Blaze" (#290), for example, is an epistemological satire warning of the dangers at the idealistic extreme of symbolic perception. The poem describes the comical results of too ardent an identification with an extraordinary natural fact, the northern lights or aurora borealis. Their majestic self-sufficiency and sovereign unconcern "infects" the "simple spirit" of the poem's speaker "With Taints of Majesty," prompting her to enter into ludicrous, self-destructive competition with "their competeless Show":

> I take vaster attitudes –
> And strut upon my stem –
> Disdaining Men, and Oxygen,
> For Arrogance of them.

In another poem (#668), the speaker asserts that " 'Nature' is what we see –/The Hill – the Afternoon –/Squirrel – Eclipse – the Bumble bee" and that it is also "what we hear –/The bobolink – the Sea –/ Thunder – the Cricket." But these empirical definitions are qualified by counterstatements – "Nay – Nature is Heaven ... Nay – Nature is Harmony" – suggesting that the natural world is not the aggregate of the various particulars presented to the senses but a perceptually integrated whole that is more than the sum of its parts and that can sometimes seem an ideal essence. In this poem, the conclusion is that "Nature is what we know" even if we "have no art to say" what precisely we know about it.

In other poems, however, Dickinson is less confident – for example #1071:

> Perception of an object costs
> Precise the Object's loss –
> Perception in itself a Gain
> Replying to its Price –
> The Object Absolute – is nought –
> Perception sets it fair
> And then upbraids a Perfectness
> That situates so – far –

The "Object Absolute," the *Ding-an-sich*, cannot be known and is thus without value, a nought. What can be known is one's perception of the object, the value or "Gain" of which is dependent on the intensity of the perception (the "Price" paid for it). But a dearly purchased object may have an enticing beauty or ideal quality that paradoxically places it at a distance from us ("so Heavenly far" in a variant reading) or that it can only retain when it is at a distance. We thus perceive a fairness or perfectness that we cannot possess. "The sea is lovely," as the later Emerson observed, "but when we bathe in it, the beauty forsakes all the near water. For the imagination and senses cannot be gratified at the same time. Wordsworth rightly speaks of 'a light that never was on sea or land,' meaning, that it was supplied by the observer" (1110).

Emerson's animadversions anticipate the mid-century British critique of symbolic perception. In *The Finer Optic: The Aesthetic of Particularity in Victorian Poetry*, Carol Christ shows that in contrast to the Romantics, perceptual particulars in the poetry of Tennyson, Browning, Hopkins, and D.G. Rossetti are not "representative of a moment of imaginative experience that becomes in some way universal ... but merely descriptive of a single moment of consciousness." The difference, Christ suggests, is symptomatic of the Victorians' gradual loss of "the Romantic assurance that there existed universal correspondences ... between the imagination and the sensible world" (12–14).

A negative critique of the Romantic belief in the correspondence between states of mind and natural facts is also a conspicuous feature of Victorian aesthetic thinking. In the third volume of *Modern Painters*, for example, John Ruskin offers an extended analysis of what he terms the "pathetic fallacy" – the projection on to natural objects of the emotions and feelings of the perceiver. Poets of the first order like Homer, Dante, and Shakespeare were able to see and describe natural objects without subjective distortion. The pathetic fallacy was commonly the practice, not of bad poets, but of poets of the second order like Wordsworth, Keats, and Tennyson. Such poets were imaginative, not fanciful; and the employment of the pathetic fallacy allowed them to express and communicate the emotional and psychological truth of their subjective state. But it did so at the cost of producing "a falseness in all our impressions of external things" (v 205). To avoid this falseness was of enormous importance: "the greatest thing a human soul ever does in this world is to *see* something, and tell what it *saw* in a plain way ... To see clearly is poetry, prophecy, and religion, – all in one ... The true Seer always feels as intensely as anyone else; but he does not much describe his feelings" (v 333–4).[3]

There was criticism from the other side of the Atlantic as well. In *Pierre or, the Ambiguities* (1852), for example, Herman Melville has his narrator caustically observe: "Say what some poets will, Nature is not so much her own ever-sweet interpreter, as the mere supplier of that cunning alphabet, whereby selecting and combining as he pleases, each man reads his own peculiar lesson according to his own peculiar mind and mood" (402). So severe are aspects of Melville's critique of Romantic symbolic perception that they anticipate the deconstructive critique of the past thirty years.[4] Melville did to the optimistic postulates of Emerson's *Nature* what deconstructive commentators like Hillis Miller and Paul de Man did to the constructive readings of Romantic literature by M.H. Abrams and others. Abrams' summa, *Natural Supernaturalism* (1971), celebrates the success of "the central enterprise" of the Romantic period: "to join together the 'subject' and 'object' that modern intellection had put asunder, and thus to revivify a dead nature, restore its concreteness, significance, and human values, and re-domiciliate man in a world which had become alien to him" (*Breeze* 96). But even before this work was published, its premises had begun to be attacked.

One of the most influential assaults was de Man's analysis of the Romantic symbol in "The Rhetoric of Temporality" (1969). In the early nineteenth century, so his argument runs, there was a longing for "a transcendental source" or ground of being (192). The temptation "for the self to borrow ... the temporal stability that it lacks from nature" could not be resisted; the result was "the spiritualization of the symbol" (197, 192). For de Man, a non-spiritualized symbol is an allegory, "a sign that refers to one specific meaning and thus exhausts its suggestive potentialities once it has been deciphered" (188). Allegory "designates primarily a distance in relation to its own origin, and, renouncing the nostalgia and the desire to coincide, it establishes its language in the void of this temporal difference" (207). Symbol on the other hand offers an illusory identification with the not-self: its "main attraction" is its "appeal to the infinity of a totality" – a "supersensory totality" (188–9). In their flight from temporality and an "authentically human destiny," Romantic poets became "trapped in the contradiction of a pseudo dialectic between subject and object" (206, 198). Romantic symbolic perception was thus a "defensive strategy" or mystification that attempted to suppress self-knowledge of an "authentically temporal predicament" (208).

De Man's analysis was in turn equally strongly attacked. Thomas McFarland, for example, complained that the Coleridgean symbol was wrongly identified by de Man with metaphorical diction. In contrast to allegory, a symbol remains intimately bound up with the world of organic nature. It partakes of "the highest cognitive efforts of the mind" and its structure is "one of cognitive synecdoche, not rhetorical mystification." Far from being a mystification, symbol is "a direct accounting of human perception" (52). There were also historical distortions: the dialectic of subject and object, for example, is "intrinsic to human awareness and therefore cannot be restricted to Romantic thought" (46). On this last point, McFarland might well have cited a passage from Coleridge that reads like a pre-emptive refutation of de Man:

In a self-conscious and thence reflecting being, no instinct can exist, without engendering the belief of an object corresponding to it, either present or future, real or capable of being realized: much less the instinct, in which humanity itself is grounded: that by which, in every act of conscious perception, we at once identify our being with that of the world without us, and yet place ourselves in contra-distinction to that world. Least of all can this mysterious pre-disposition exist without evolving a belief that the productive power, which is in nature as nature, is essentially one (i.e. of one kind) with the intelligence, which is in the human mind above nature ... So universally has this conviction leavened the very substance of all discourse, that there is no language on earth in which a man can abjure it as a prejudice, without employing terms and conjunctions that suppose its reality, with a feeling very different from that which accompanies a figurative or metaphorical use of words.   (*Friend* i 497–8)

De Man's essay is now more than a quarter century old. From this perspective, it is clear that while Abrams and other commentators were unquestionably too constructive and totalizing in their reading of the Romantics, often mistaking "the poem, an intentional object, for a natural object" (Chandler 467), de Man made the error of conflating these commentators with the subjects of their discourse. He is more telling as a critic of totalizing organicist commentators than as a critic of Romantic poetry. In my view, what most weakens de Man's argument is the apparent paucity of his literary-historical knowledge of the rich body of nineteenth-century British and American Romantic literature. This material, in which the dialectic of subject and object is a given, contains a variety of engagements of the imagination and the natural world and a corresponding diversity in the kinds and modalities of symbolic perception.

But de Man does not distinguish between inner/outer and lower/ higher symbolic perception; he does not allow for the variety of engagements among poets – Keats's "camelion Poet," for example, as opposed to poets of the "wordsworthian or egotistical sublime" (*Letters* i 387). Nor does his agenda allow him to recognize the variety that is the result of the changing ratios and intensities of sensory and perceptual engagement within writers. In this regard, de Man's misuse of the Fenwick note on the Intimations Ode is as telling as his apparent ignorance of Coleridge's thinking about symbol in the years preceding the definition in *Statesman's Manual* (which de Man cites from a secondary source).

As an antidote to de Manian deconstruction, I offer Whitman's expansive celebration of symbolic perception in section 6 of *Song of Myself*:

A child said, What is the grass? fetching it to me with full hands; How could I answer the child? ... I do not know what it is any more than he.

I guess it must be the flag of my disposition, out of hopeful green stuff woven.

Or I guess it is the handkerchief of the Lord,
A scented gift and remembrancer designedly dropped,
Bearing the owner's name someway in the corners, that we may see
   and remark, and say Whose?

Or I guess the grass is itself a child ... the produced babe of the
   vegetation.

Or I guess it is a uniform hieroglyphic;
And it means, Sprouting alike in broad zones and narrow zones,
Growing among black folks as among white,
Kanuck, Tuckahoe, Congressman, Cuff, I give them the same, I receive
   them the same.

And now it seems to me the beautiful uncut hair of graves.

Later in this section, Whitman remarks of his cornucopic generation
of tropes: "O I perceive after all so many uttering tongues!" But the
tongues are not contradictory or mutually exclusive. The grass is a
polysemous symbol, but it is not split up into a multiplicity of arbitrary signifieds (like the doubloon in *Moby-Dick*) because there is a
single perceiver with a radiating intensity of affirmative apprehension. *The flag of my disposition*: in this trope, the grass, a natural fact, is
the vehicle of a metaphor, the tenor of which is the inner being of the
perceiver. *The handkerchief of the Lord*: a fresh instance of the Pauline
lower/higher correspondence by which invisible things are understood by the things that are visible. In this delightful trope, the *Deus
absconditus* is figured as a coquette, who flirtatiously leaves a token of
herself to be found. *The grass is itself a child*: this is "a tautological
answer to the questioner, the 'produced babe of the vegetation' mirroring the 'child'" (Blasing 123). It is also a metaphorical figuring of
the one life within and abroad. Unlike the passage's first trope, however, the vehicle here is human (a child), the tenor natural (the vegetation). *A uniform hieroglyphic*: the grass as an emblem ("symbolic object
represent[ing] a set of values" [Dupriez 443]) of democratic equality.
The beautiful uncut hair of graves: a metaleptic grace-note. Here the
grass is a synecdochal symbol of the participation of humans in the
nitrogen cycle – an instance of the "procreant urge of the world" (#3)
and its "perpetual transfers and promotions" (#49).
   As the section continues, it becomes apparent that this recognition
of the symbiotic life of man and nature is a step towards the assertion
that the dead "are alive and well somewhere;/The smallest sprout

shows there is really no death." The natural fact of the sprouting grass becomes a trope for spiritual immortality. In Thoreau's similar figure, "human life ... dies down to the surface, but puts forth a green blade to eternity" (*J i 470). Behind Whitman's radiant apprehension of immortality, however, is the spectre of an authentically temporal destiny, of which there are numerous intimations in *Song of Myself* and the other poems in the first edition of *Leaves of Grass*: maggots and rats; beetles rolling balls of dung; the turbid pool in the autumn forest and the black stems that decay in its muck; gashed bodies on battlefields; the massacre of the Alamo's defenders; a deathbed scene with its smell of camphor, useless medicines, helpless physician, and grieving family. It is true that there are numerous assertions of the opposite – that "there is nothing but immortality" ("To Think of Time"). But the very frequency of these asseverations is itself evidence of Whitman's recessive recognition of his mortality.

What happened to Whitman and his poetry when his powers of symbolic perception waned and he no longer felt deathless is part of the subject matter of a later chapter. The subject of the next chapter is the representation of expansion of consciousness experiences in which mortal limitations seem transcended.

THREE

Sublime or Mock Sublime?

Emerson's *Nature* contains a well-known description of an expansion of consciousness experience: "Standing on the bare ground, – my head bathed by the blithe air, and uplifted into infinite space, – all mean egotism vanishes. I become a transparent eye-ball; I am nothing; I see all; the currents of the Universal Being circulate through me; I am part or particle of God" (10). Descriptions and representations of such experiences are a central feature of Romantic literature. In "Tintern Abbey," Wordsworth speaks of a "blessed mood" during which "we are laid asleep/In body, and become a living soul" able to "see into the life of things." Shelley describes a "state called reverie" in which those subject to it feel "as if their nature were dissolved into the surrounding universe, or as if the surrounding universe were absorbed into their being. They are conscious of no distinction" (*Prose* 174). Emily Dickinson calls these states "Heavenly Moments ... A Grant of the Divine" (#393); Melville's term is the "'all' feeling" (*Letters* 131). Whitman's disciple, Richard Maurice Bucke, uses the term "cosmic consciousness"; while Robert Jay Lifton employs "experiential transcendence" to describe the mode of "symbolic immortality" involving "extraordinary psychological unity, intensity of sensual awareness, and inexpressible illumination and insight" (82–3). Yet another term is "natural mystical experience," which R.C. Zaehner uses to denominate the merging of consciousness and nature – the ecstatic state in which the boundaries of space and time seem transcended, everyday reality seems pathetically unreal, and death becomes unthinkable (*Mysticism* 41).

It is far from easy to distinguish these experiences from three other types of experience: religious mystical experiences; neurological episodes or other psychically generated phenomena; and substance-induced transformations of consciousness. Concerning the first, for example, Zaehner takes a strict line, insisting that natural mystical experiences, which are often undergone by those who are not otherwise known as mystics, have nothing in common with traditional religious mysticism. They are unlike both Hindu mysticism, which is characterized by complete absorption of the individual soul into the Absolute, and "the normal type of Christian mystical experience in which the soul feels itself to be united with God by love." For Zaehner, only these two kinds of experience, both of which have as a *sine qua non* "the exclusion of all that we normally call Nature," may be properly described as religious (*Mysticism* 29, 33). On the other hand, in his *Varieties of Religious Experience*, William James is inclusive rather than exclusive in proposing "four marks" – ineffability, noetic quality, transiency, and passivity – which, "when an experience has them, may justify us in calling it mystical" (380–1).

Concerning the second kind of experience, it is interesting to consider the "ecstatic aura" sometimes experienced by epileptics just before the onset of a seizure. A detailed description of such an experience occurs in Dostoevsky's *The Idiot*: in a moment of "extraordinary illumination," Prince Myshkin's brain "seemed to flare up momentarily and all his vital forces tense themselves at once in an extraordinary surge." His consciousness was filled with "pure, harmonious gladness and hope, and filled too with the consciousness of the ultimate cause of all things." During "these gleams and lightning-flashes of heightened self-awareness, and hence also of 'higher existence'," there is a "profound experience of infinite happiness" and an understanding of the hitherto strange biblical phrase, "there should be time no longer" (237–8).

This sounds very much like the ecstatic experiences found in the subjects of this study, and like Zaehner's description of natural mystical experiences. Indeed, Joseph Frank, Dostoevsky's biographer, uses Zaehner's terminology in his discussion of what the Russian novelist experienced at the beginning of his epileptic attacks (194–8). To the question of whether such neurologically triggered episodes are identical with experiences of expanded consciousness found in nineteenth-century Romantic literature, some might well answer as Prince Myshkin does: if the experiences are equally transporting, what does it matter? The gleams and lightning flashes that preceded his attacks, he reflects, "were no weird figments brought on by hashish, opium, or wine, degrading the intellect and distorting the soul"; and even if his illness were the cause, "what does it matter ... if the end-result, the instant of apprehension, recalled and analysed during recovery, turns out to be the highest pitch of harmony and beauty, conferring a sense of some hitherto-unknown and unguessed completeness, proportion, reconciliation, an ecstatic, prayerful fusion with the supreme synthesis of life?" (237).

The same argument has been made concerning expansions of consciousness triggered by intoxicants, anaesthetics, and other substances. Dostoevsky's prince insists on a distinction between them and the ecstatic aura experience. So does Emerson, who warned of the "dangerous attraction for men" of opium and alcohol, which were "the semblance and counterfeit of [the] oracular genius" (414). But Aldous Huxley in *The Doors of Perception and Heaven and Hell* and R.A. Durr in *Poetic Vision and the Psychedelic Experience* both argue that there is no qualitative difference between substance-induced and other forms of expansion of consciousness experiences.

Huxley celebrated the life-enhancing properties of mescalin, which when correctly administered "changes the quality of consciousness more profoundly and yet is less toxic than any other substance in the pharmacologist's repertory" (5). Huxley explained that the drug inhibits the production of enzymes regulating the supply of glucose to the brain cells, thus lowering the brain's biological efficiency and permitting "the entry into consciousness of certain classes of mental events, which are normally excluded" by the regulating mechanism of the brain and the nervous system (76). When Huxley took mescalin, habitual perceptions were superseded by a "sacramental vision of reality" (15). Perception itself was "enormously improved"; visual impressions, for example, were greatly intensified as the eye recovered "some of the perceptual innocence of childhood, when the sensum was not immediately and automatically subordinated to the concept" (18). Other effects detailed by Huxley are also similar to those found in natural mystical experiences, such as the merging of inner and outer, and the suspension of spatial and temporal categories. Durr compares Huxley's "open-eyed psychedelic vision" to literary texts "celebrating the everyday world," arguing that "the similarities between the world of psychedelic vision and the world of imaginative vision are numerous, striking, and of the essence"; that they share "a fundamentally identical power of apprehension, or mode of being" (vii-xii).

Are Durr and Huxley correct, or can one make category distinctions and qualitative discriminations between fortuitous experiences and those chemically induced? Is there, for example, a difference between Whitman's visionary experience of the universe held together by love, as represented in the fifth section of *Song of Myself*, and the distinctly droll proclamations of a fifty-year-old widow who was given LSD in a clinical setting and whose utterances while under the drug's influence were recorded:

I am Love. Love. Love. Love. Love. ... Negroes and little fishes, lampshades and vinegar. These I love. Coats and hats and three-ring pretzels. Radios and Russians, bobolinks and tree sap, medicine chests and Freud and the green line down the center of the street on St Patrick's Day, these I love. These I cherish. ... Hair spray and Buddha and Krishna Menon. My love overfloweth to all. My nephew – and mushrooms. Red cars, red caps, porters, Martin Luther King, Armenians, Jews, Incas, and John O'Hara. Love. Love. Love. Love. Big yellow Chrysanthemums and the sun and pancakes and Disneyland and Vermont and cinnamon and Alexander the Great. The UN and aluminium foil and apple cider and cigars. Clark Gable, Tony Curtis and salamanders, crochet, the aurora borealis and dimples, mustard plasters and even Mayor Wagner. I am just bursting with joy, with love.   (qtd in Zaehner *Drugs* 95)

There is also the considerable problem of making qualitative distinctions between fortuitous and self-induced (rather than chemically induced) experiences. An example of the latter is the degree of sublimity attained by Tennyson through repeating his name over and over. Replying to Benjamin Paul Blood, the American author of *The Anaesthetic Revelation and the Gist of Philosophy*, Tennyson told this precursor of Huxley that while he had "never had any revelations through anaesthetics":

A kind of waking trance I have frequently had, quite up from boyhood, when I have been all alone. This has generally come upon me thro' repeating my own name two or three times to myself silently, till all at once, as it were out of the intensity of the consciousness of individuality, the individuality itself seemed to dissolve and fade away into boundless being, [a state] where death was an almost laughable impossibility, the loss of personality (if so it were) seeming no extinction but only true life.   (Collins 153–4; *Memoir* i 320)

Zaehner regards this experience as a bona fide form of natural mystical experience; but Philip Collins suggests that "such a self-regarding technique may strike us as a form of spiritual masturbation" (154). Collins does not say, however, how he would qualitatively distinguish this from something more penetrative and less onanist – from, for example, the visionary experience represented in the climactic ninety-fifth poem of Tennyson's *In Memoriam*, a precondition of which, as the preceding poem makes clear, is Tennyson's having ceased actively to desire the experience.

A instructive example of this difficulty is found in the opening section of Coleridge's "Hymn before Sun-rise, in the Vale of Chamouni" (1802):

> Hast thou a charm to stay the morning-star
> In his steep course? So long he seems to pause
> On thy bald awful head, O sovran *Blanc*,
> The Arve and Arveiron at thy base
> Rave ceaselessly; but thou, most awful Form!
> Risest from forth thy silent sea of pines,
> How silently! Around thee and above
> Deep is the air and dark, substantial, black,
> An ebon mass: methinks thou piercest it,
> As with a wedge! But when I look again,
> It is thine own calm home, thy crystal shrine,
> Thy habitation from eternity!
> O dread and silent Mount! I gazed upon thee,
> Till thou, still present to the bodily sense,
> Didst vanish from my thought: entranced in prayer
> I worshipped the Invisible alone.
>
> Yet, like some sweet beguiling melody,
> So sweet, we know not we are listening to it,
> Thou, the meanwhile, wast blending with my Thought,
> Yea, with my Life and Life's own secret joy:
> Till the dilating Soul, enrapt, transfused,
> Into the mighty vision passing – there
> As in her natural form, swelled vast to Heaven!

In a letter of 1819, Coleridge glosses this passage by stating that he had long "been accustomed to *abstract* and as it were unrealize whatever of more than common interest my eyes dwelt on; and then by a sort of transfusion or transmission of my consciousness to identify myself with the Object." He also reports that Wordsworth had "censured the passage as strained and unnatural, and condemned the Hymn in toto ... as a specimen of the Mock Sublime" (*Letters* iv 974–5). The basis of Wordsworth's condemnation is suggested by comments made to Henry Crabb Robinson in 1812 criticizing in Coleridge "a sort of dreaminess which would not let him see things as they were": Coleridge preferred using his "extraordinary powers [to summon] up an image or series of images in his own mind" to "the influence of external objects" (qtd in Parrish 41).

How does one judge this matter? Is the experience Coleridge describes bona fide or bogus, sublime or mock sublime? For that matter, how can a literary critic ever be certain of a correspondence between the after-the-fact verbal representation of an experience of expanded consciousness and the experience itself, or even be certain that there ever was an experience? In my view, there are three methodological keys to a successful consideration of these questions.

(*a*) The first is to place the text under consideration in its biographical and literary context. In the case of Coleridge's "Hymn before Sun-rise," the crucial context (described in my fifth chapter) is the precipitate decline of the poet's health during the early 1800s and consequently of his sensory acuity – particularly his sense of feeling/ touch, the weakening of which is instanced in the so-called emancipation described in "Apologia pro Vita Sua." There is also a letter contemporaneous with the composition of the "Hymn" in which Coleridge explains that the experience he placed in an Alpine vale had actually occurred on Scafell in the Lake District. There he says he had "involuntarily poured forth a Hymn in the manner of the *Psalms*, tho' afterwards I thought the Ideas &c disproportionate to our humble mountains – & accidently lighting on a short Note in some swiss Poems, concerning the Vale of Chamouny, & it's Mountain, I transferred myself thither, in the Spirit, & adapted my former feelings to these grander external objects" (*Letters* ii 864–5). But other letters and a long journal entry concerning his experiences on Scafell suggest that no sublime effusion of the kind described in the poem had occurred there. This suggestion is strengthened by the evidence first brought to light by De Quincey in 1834: that Coleridge's poem has an "unacknowledged obligation" to Friederike Brun's poem "Chamouny beym Sonnenaufgange."[1] Thus, although one cannot ever be absolutely certain that Coleridge had never had an experience tallying with the one represented in his "Hymn," convincing evidence suggests that Wordsworth was correct in condemning the poem as a specimen of the mock sublime.

(*b*) The second methodological key is to pay particular attention to the perceptual basis (or otherwise) of the experience. It is obvious that in low forms of the sublime the perceptual basis is crucial: the experience is triggered when a given sense is freed from its customary groove. But the perceptual basis can be equally important in less crude experiences. Consider, for example, a distinctive feature of a number of Tennyson's poems, to which several commentators have called attention: a glimmering shape or light, usually white, seen against a dark background evokes powerful feelings of reassurance and comfort. Examples are the tablet glimmering in the dark church in poem lxvii of *In Memoriam*; the white kine in poem xcv of the same work; and the "stream that flashest white" in "In the Valley of Cauteretz."

How can this association be explained? F.E.L. Priestley uses a gambit common in literary-critical discourse – pseudo-explanation by means of learned allusion: "A dim whiteness gleaming in a dark background is always for [Tennyson] a symbol of reassurance, a faint but adequate glimmer of light in the darkness, analogous to the 'candle of the Lord' of the Cambridge Platonists" (161). But this explains nothing.

Is there, one might well ask, a perceptual reason why this visual image resonates with such positive intensity for the severely myopic Tennyson? When a bright object is seen against a dark background, there is an increase in the "temporal integrating time" needed in order for the eye to take in the object. It is "as when a photographer uses a longer exposure in dim light" (Gregory 83).[2] This presupposes intense attention on the part of the perceiver. The result is a deeper, more last-ing visual impression. At the same time, the slowness plus the con-centration of attention has a tranquillizing effect.

The best example is found at the close of "Audley Court," where the color of the illumination seen against a dark background is green: [3]

> ere the night we rose
> And sauntered home beneath a moon, that, just
> In crescent, dimly rained about the leaf
> Twilights of airy silver, till we reached
> The limit of the hills; and as we sank
> From rock to rock upon the glooming quay,
> The town was hushed beneath us: lower down
> The bay was oily calm; the harbour-buoy,
> Sole star of phosphorescence in the calm,
> With one green sparkle ever and anon
> Dipt by itself, and we were glad at heart.

The flashing buoy and its effect on the speaker have elicited critical commentary of the pseudo-explanation-by-allusion sort (e.g., Nichols 137–9), but the passage can be much more satisfactorily discussed in terms of the dynamics of perception. It comes at the close of an account of a peaceful, quietly joyful day that two old friends have spent together. As they saunter back to the quay, their spirits are at peace with all. One perceptual aspect of the scene that intensifies the peacefulness is spatial breadth. Coleridge distinguished between vertical distant views and horizontal ones: while the former induce excitement and intense emotion, the latter are calming (*Notebooks* ii #2357). The other important aspect is the intensity of visual impres-sion made possible by the longer integrating time. This is intimated stylistically by the one-sentence description prolonged over many

lines, and was further enhanced, twenty-five years after the poem
was first published, by the addition of the antepenultimate line – the
time it takes to say the line, prolonged by the abundance of long
vowels, mimes the slow integrating time during the descent.

But what about ecstatic expansions of consciousness? After all, in
some visionary experiences the senses and the objects of perception do
not figure. Blake, for example, insisted that "Natural Objects always
did & now do Weaken deaden & obliterate Imagination in Me"; "I
question not my Corporeal or Vegetative Eye any more than I would
Question a window concerning a Sight I look thro it & not with it" (655,
555). With other writers, it is a different matter. Wordsworth, whose
dependence on natural objects infuriated Blake, is a good example. The
well-known accounts of visionary experience in "Tintern Abbey" are
generalized reformulations of past experiences, which are summarized
but not represented. But in Wordsworth's representations of sublime
experiences, the vital role played by perception is usually clear. One
example is "A Night-Piece," which I must quote in toto.

> —The sky is overcast
> With a continuous cloud of texture close,
> Heavy and wan, all whitened by the Moon,
> Which through that veil is indistinctly seen,
> A dull, contracted circle, yielding light
> So feebly spread that not a shadow falls,
> Chequering the ground – from rock, plant, tree, or tower.
> At length a pleasant instantaneous gleam
> Startles the pensive traveller as he treads
> His lonesome path, with unobserving eye
> Bent earthwards; he looks up – the clouds are split
> Asunder, – and above his head he sees
> The clear Moon, and the glory of the heavens.
> There, in a black-blue vault she sails along,
> Followed by multitudes of stars, that, small
> And sharp, and bright, along the dark abyss
> Drive as she drives: how fast they wheel away,
> Yet vanish not! – the wind is in the tree,
> But they are silent; – still they roll along
> Immeasurably distant; and the vault,
> Built round by those white clouds, enormous clouds,
> Still deepens its unfathomable depth.
> At length the Vision closes; and the mind,
> Not undisturbed by the delight it feels,
> Which slowly settles into peaceful calm,
> Is left to muse upon the solemn scene.   (*PW* ii 208–9)

Unlike Blake, Wordsworth's observer is looking with the eye and not through it. The essential given of the poem is that visual perception of distant objects offers an experiential basis for the idea of infinity: "the unfolding of space before the eye, under the magic of light bears in itself the germ of infinity – as a perceptual aspect" (Jonas 151). As the celestial quiet is emphasized by its contrast with the sound of the wind in the nearby tree, so the depth of the vault is emphasized by its contrast with the clouds. As Kenneth R. Johnston points out: "that the cloud-veil changes from visual obstruction to visual aid implies that limitations upon vision are helpful ... By its contrasting of ground and background of vision, 'A Night-Piece' ... suggests that the eternal dimension would not be recognized without the natural scene. Literally, it would lack focus" (22). But Johnston does not note the principal cause of this striking effect, which is, so to speak, a perceptual trick: "they wheel away/Yet vanish not." The moon and stars seem to wheel away, but in fact they are stationary. What has happened, to use Coleridge's phrasing in the Dejection Ode, is that the clouds "give away their motion to the stars." Thus, perceptual experience is a *sine qua non* of this striking instance of the distinctively Wordsworthian sense of the permanent in the transitory ("still they roll along") that Tennyson found in the "something" of "Tintern Abbey" whose "dwelling is the light of setting suns" (Page 176).

In the opening lines of Coleridge's "Hymn before Sun-rise," the most conspicuous use of figurative language is the simile comparing the speaker's visual apprehension of the mountain to "some sweet beguiling melody,/So sweet, we know not we are listening to it." The intensification and interpenetration of the senses is often found in representations of expansion of consciousness experiences. Could this synesthetic image therefore be taken as evidence that the account has some kind of perceptual grounding? The question raises important methodological considerations that must be addressed at some length.

Synesthesia, the not uncommon experience of one modality of sense experienced in terms of another, might be considered a bodily trope or metaphor in which one sense is the tenor and another the vehicle. An example is "sonogenic synesthesia, in which music provokes intense visual experiences or cutaneous paraesthesias" (Stein and Meredith 9). The most common occurrence of the former is *audition colorée* – sounds received as colors – which is often found in children and in accounts of chemically altered states of consciousness, such as those induced by mescalin and hashish.

But synesthesia has two meanings: it is *both* a quality or kind of perception and a figurative use of language. The former is called clinical or psychological synesthesia; the latter literary synesthesia. In his

Unity of the Senses: Interrelations among the Modalities, Lawrence E. Marks provides a good deal of interesting information about synesthesia from the scientific point of view. His eighth chapter is concerned with "synesthetic metaphor in poetry," which is considered from a strictly psychological aspect. For Marks, synesthesia in poetry reflects the convergence of the senses – their analogical properties and the correspondences between different senses. As authorities, he cites Aristotle and Coleridge, the latter of whom wrote that "the poet must … understand and command what Bacon calls the *vestigia communia* of the senses, the latency of all in each, [especially] the excitement of vision by sound and the exponents of sound" (*Biographia* ii 128). Marks might have also cited Edmund Burke's observations concerning "a chain in all our sensations," a "general agreement of the senses": they "bear witness to each other … bear an analogy to, and illustrate one another" (110, 113, 126).

Unfortunately, Burke did not consider how the interpenetration of the senses might contribute to the emotional intensities of his subject – the sublime. And Marks' discussion does not address aspects of his subject relating to intensity and expansion. He does say that a "universal synesthetic capacity" can be aroused "by powerful sensory-esthetic experiences," and he does recognize intensity as a classic example of a "suprasensory attribute" or quality – that is, a dimension of sensory experience not limited to a single sense modality (8, 5). But he does not consider that an essential characteristic of synesthetic metaphors is that they indicate or express intensity. Nor does he consider that the unity of the senses in synesthetic perception corresponds to, is coextensive with, the apprehension of the unity of the external world (and of the perceiver and the world).

He also fails to take into account the question of whether the representation of a given synesthetic experience is neurological or literary. How far, for example, are synesthetic comparisons in a poem the result of the poet's intention to produce certain artistic effects as opposed to their being representations of his/her perceptual experiences? In many instances, it is the former. As Glenn O'Malley has explained: "it is precisely an inescapable oddness and mystery about intersense harmony (its supersensuousness, so to speak) which imaginative adaptations of synesthetic expression often hope to exploit." In order to convey "sensuous intimations of spiritual perception, rather than to achieve psychological verisimilitude, intersense metaphors and synesthetic concepts may be designed to represent a transcendence of ordinary experience" (398). Dante's *Divine Comedy*, for example, is "one of the best illustrations of a philosophic or spiritual use of intersense metaphor and of synesthetic conceptions." There is a synesthetic registration of the movement upward from the *Inferno* in which intersense analogies are rare and negative ("the sun is silent"; "every light [is] mute") through to the *Paradiso*, in which the distinctions among the senses largely dissolve (409–10).

The conclusion seems to me clear: for the literary critic, no distinction can be made between the poet's experience and his representation of it in words. Consequently, all synesthesia should be considered literary synesthesia. When we talk about the poet's experience we are in fact talking about his/her representation in words and figures of a putative experience. But these representations can be compared and contrasted, and distinctions made among them. This includes qualitative discriminations between superior representations and inferior ones like Byron's derivative synesthetic images, Swinburne's metronomic ones, or the bombast of Dylan Thomas' "Poem on his Birthday" ("I hear the bouncing hills/Grow larked and greener ... and the dew larks sing/Taller ...").[4]

(*c*) The third methodological key, then, is to pay close attention to the language and style of the representation. "Veracity," declares Emerson, "is that which we require in poets ... The poet writes from a real experience, the amateur feigns one. ... Style betrays you ... We detect at once by it whether the writer has a firm grasp on his fact or thought, – exists at that moment for that alone" ("Poetry" 29, 31, 33). Let us return to the opening lines of Coleridge's "Hymn before Sun-rise." Surely F.R. Leavis' point is well taken: "Coleridge makes a dutiful show of the sublime, but it amounts to little more than the explicit 'awful,' 'rave' ... and 'dread'" (234). For another critic, the forced language makes it seem "as if Coleridge were trying to make something happen rather than expressing what had happened" (Haven 76). What both these critics are suggesting is that Coleridge was insincere.

Sincerity as a critical term has fallen into disrepute in the twentieth century. In a recent attempt to re-establish its usefulness in the criticism of lyric poetry, Malcolm Budd has persuasively argued that "defects in sincerity, or forms of insincerity, can properly be attributed on the basis of the manner in which a person expresses his feeling or the style of his self-communion." Lack of sincerity or "imaginative integrity" on the part of the implied author "can be revealed by such features as the use of inflated language, vague emotional clichés, the lack of precision and the manner of the poem's indebtedness to other poetry" (142–3). In Ezra Pound's blunter formulation: "Technique is the test of sincerity" (Hall 25).

The qualitative difference between Whitman's representation of the visionary experience of love in the fifth section of *Song of Myself* and that of the psychedelic widow quoted above would become patent in a literary-critical analysis that paid close attention to technique and style. Neither I nor anyone else can presume to know with certainty whether Whitman is recounting an actual experience, as Richard Maurice Bucke and William James believed; whether he is offering a "dramatic representation … conceived in the imagination," as James E. Miller thinks (6–7); or whether he is making an intertextual maneuver – "a considered re-vision" of the transparent eye-ball experience in Emerson's *Nature* (Gatta 176). But I am sure that the fifth section of *Song of Myself* is sincere in Budd and Pound's use of the term. The passage is discussed in my sixth chapter; like all the close readings in this study, it is informed by attention to biographical and literary context, sensory-perceptual dynamics, and language and style.

FOUR

Wordsworth's Mighty World
of Eye and Ear

No poet has been more concerned with the sources of his creative power than Wordsworth. Much of his finest poetry is not only the effluence of what in the prospectus to *The Recluse* he calls the "dread Power!/Whose gracious favour is the primal source/Of all illumination"; it is also about the genesis and nature of this power. Sometimes Wordsworth speaks of it as a gift:

> to me I feel
> That an internal brightness is vouchsafed
> That must not die, that must not pass away.
> Why does this inward lustre fondly seek,
> And gladly blend with outward fellowship?
> Why do *they* shine around me whom I love?
> Why do they teach me whom I thus revere?   (*PW* v 335–6)

These questions are not rhetorical. Wordsworth really did not understand the nature and operation of this gift any more than in section 50 of *Song of Myself* Whitman understood the similar force at work in him. Like Wordsworth, the American poet did "not know what it is…. but I know it is in me"; it seemed connected with a larger force outside the self ("Something it swings on more than the earth I swing on"), and it was not "chaos or death" but "form and union and plan," "happiness," and even "eternal life."

The imagery of blending and mutual giving in Wordsworth's lines suggests that the internal brightness is in a symbiotic relationship with the outside world. When consciousness and the goodly universe are fused, the result is an experience of transport, an expansion

of consciousness, a sense sublime. At other times, however, Wordsworth seems to describe creative power as something whose source
is loss. Among the qualities attributed to a poet in the preface to
Lyrical Ballads, for example, is "a disposition to be affected more than
other men by absent things as if they were present" (*PW* ii 393). And
while the speaker of "The Solitary Reaper" does not know the language in which the Highland maiden (a figure of the poet) is singing,
he is in no doubt that the emotion her "melancholy strain" powerfully and memorably communicates is loss.

Whitman's poetry also contains an alternative, loss-based account of
the sources of his creative power. The explanation for his opposing
accounts – gain versus loss, gift versus deprivation – is that Whitman
was not the same man in 1860 that he had been in 1855, and the change
had resulted in a radical reassessment of the nature and genesis of his
creative power. In Wordsworth, the distinction between gift and deprivation is less clear-cut. The key point is that while he seems to offer
differing accounts of the sources of his power, he never doubted that
its origin was in his childhood and adolescence and was intimately
connected with his felt recollections of earlier experiences and states of
being. "The days gone by," including those from "the dawn almost/
Of life," are "the hiding-places of [his] power" (xi 333–5).

In the first book of the *Prelude*, Wordsworth turns from the creative
vexations of the present to his earliest memories in the hope "that I
might fetch/Invigorating thoughts from former years" (648–9). He
reviews his early life in order to reassure himself that his childhood
among the rivers, lakes, mountains, and shepherds of Cumberland
had uniquely equipped him to be a great poet. The subject of the
Prelude thus becomes the sources of Wordsworth's creative power. But
even this thorough examination of his development does not yield a
clear explanation. In what was recollected from "the days gone by"
one again finds the contrasts of gift versus deprivation, internal brightness versus internal darkness. As Wordsworth says, he "grew up/
Fostered alike by beauty and by fear" (i 305–6).

Freud begins *Civilization and its Discontents* with a discussion of what
he calls the "oceanic" feeling. A friend had written saying that in his
previous work, *The Future of an Illusion*, Freud failed to appreciate
"the true source of religious sentiments," which were found in "a
peculiar feeling" present in himself and in many others, "a sensation
of 'eternity', a feeling as of something limitless, unbounded – as it
were 'oceanic'." These views caused Freud "no small difficulty. I can-

not discover this 'oceanic' feeling in myself." There being no physio-logical signs to describe, one had to fall back on the "ideational content" with which the feeling was first associated. This seemed to be "a feeling of an indissoluble bond, of being one with the external world as a whole." Its source was apparently in early childhood: "An infant at the breast does not as yet distinguish his ego from the exter-nal world as the source of the sensations flowing in upon him." Gradually, however, the developing ego learns to make distinctions between inner and outer and to detach itself from the external world; eventually the "reality principle" comes to dominate development. "Our present ego-feeling is, therefore," says Freud, "only a shrunken residue of a much more inclusive – indeed, an all-embracing – feeling which corresponded to a more intimate bond between the ego and the world without it" (1–5).

In book ii of the *Prelude* (237–87), Wordsworth makes his own analysis of the oceanic feeling. The similarities with Freud's thinking are up to a point remarkable, but the differences are equally striking. "Blessed the infant babe," Wordsworth begins, "For with my best conjectures would I trace/The progress of our being." From his mother's breast and eye, feelings pass into the life of the infant "like an awakening breeze," quickening his mind and perceptual faculties. In the sensations derived from the "beloved presence" of the mother,

> there exists
> A virtue which irradiates and exalts
> All objects through all intercourse of sense.
> No outcast he, bewildered and depressed;
> Along his infant veins are interfused
> The gravitation and the filial bond
> Of Nature that connect him with the world.
> Emphatically such a being lives,
> An inmate of this active universe.

"Such, verily," says Wordsworth, "is the first/Poetic spirit of our human life." But he immediately goes on to speak of the growing dominance of what Freud calls the reality principle. The first poetic spirit, the great birthright of our being, is "By uniform controul of after years/In most abated and suppressed." An obvious question arises: why does the gift survive in some while it is extinguished in most? Why, for example, did it survive in Wordsworth? Part of the answer is given in the first two books of the *Prelude*, which describe how dur-ing childhood Wordsworth's infant sensibility was "augmented and sustained" (ii 287) through intense perceptual experiences. The other part of the answer is the affective memory, which sustained the poet's gift in post-childhood years and enabled him to tap the distinctive power of those intense early experiences.

Understanding why they were powerful, however, was a different matter. It was difficult to separate the "naked recollection" of past events from "what may rather have been called to life/By after-meditation" (iii 646–8). And there was the recurrent problem of the perceptual and affective overlay of past and present. This difficulty is imaged in the fourth book's comparison of the autobiographical poet "Incumbent o'er the surface of past time" to looking over the side of a slow-moving boat on still water. One sees many "beauteous sights" on the bottom, but "fancies more"; often "perplexed" by surface reflections, one "cannot part/The shadow from the substance" (252–63). There was also the considerable problem of present beliefs or preoccupations affecting the representation and evaluation of past experiences. In the manuscripts that record the growth of the *Prelude* from the two-book version of 1799, through the 1805 to the 1850 version, there are numerous instances of Wordsworth's reinterpreting early experiences and assigning different meanings to them.[1]

Wordsworth calls the most important of his earlier experiences "spots of time." The passage in book xi of the 1805 *Prelude* in which these crucial moments are described contains a notable example of dubious reinterpretation prompted by after-meditation:

> There are in our existence spots of time,
> Which with distinct preeminence retain
> A renovating virtue, whence, depressed
> By false opinion and contentious thought,
> Or aught of heavier or more deadly weight
> In trivial occupations and the round
> Of ordinary intercourse, our minds
> Are nourished and invisibly repaired –
> A virtue, by which pleasure is enhanced,
> That penetrates, enables us to mount
> When high, more high, and lifts us up when fallen.
> This efficacious spirit chiefly lurks
> Among those passages of life in which
> We have had deepest feeling that the mind
> Is lord and master, and that outward sense
> Is but the obedient servant of her will.
> Such moments, worthy of all gratitude,
> Are scattered everywhere, taking their date
> From our first childhood – in our childhood even
> Perhaps are most conspicuous. (257–78)

A puzzling feature of this passage is the emphasis both on experiences of "our first childhood" and on experiences that show the mind to be "lord and master" and "outward sense ... but the obedient servant of her will." As we shall see, the two childhood experiences that Wordsworth proceeds to describe in book xi hardly show the mind to be lord and master of anything. Of course, one understands that in each case what the child Wordsworth experienced depended on his emotional state. In the first, for example, an "ordinary sight" became invested with "visionary dreariness" (xi 308, 310) because of the internal disposition of the perceiver, a child not six years old who had just undergone a subjectively terrifying experience. But neither episode shows the child's mind as in any way autonomous, self-sufficient, or possessing lordly prerogatives.

Of what can Wordsworth have been thinking? The lord-and-master lines were not in the original 1799 version of the spots of time passage and, as Sybil Eakin has shown, such notions played no role in his initial description and evaluation of the two episodes. Moreover, in other places in the 1805 *Prelude* Wordsworth had been much concerned with the question of the relative contribution made by each of the two participants in the mind-nature relationship. In book ii, for example, he poses the question of why in his seventeenth year he saw "blessings spread around me like a sea." Was it "the power of truth/ Coming in revelation"? Or was it the result of his own transference of enjoyment on to "unorganic natures," thus "Coercing all things into sympathy" (405–14)? A number of passages suggested that the answer was found not in the master-servant model but in a symbiotic model –

> A balance, an ennobling interchange
> Of action from within and from without:
> The excellence, pure spirit, and best power,
> Both in the object seen, and eye that sees.   (xii 375–8)

The passage in book xi can thus be explained as a later interpolation by the post-1804 Wordsworth, as he reassesses his early experiences in the light of his growing concern with the mind's capacity to move beyond nature and access the transcendent.

While many commentators have regarded ennobling interchange as the essence of the Wordsworthian mind-nature dialectic, another line of Wordsworth criticism has been more sceptical. In the 1960s this reading came under pressure from three influential commentators, each of whom attached great importance to three crucial passages in the *Prelude* that seemed to privilege mind/imagination over nature: the interpolation in book xi; the crossing the Alps episode in book vi; and the ascent of Snowdon episode in book xiii. Paul de Man observed that in the second of these Wordsworth "goes so far as to designate the earth by the astonishing periphrase of 'Blank abyss,'" and to insist that the imagination can only come into full play when "the light of sense goes out" and its activity becomes "its own perfection and reward" ("Intentional" 77). Harold Bloom insisted on a "hidden conflict between Poetry and Nature in Wordsworth" that reminded him of the Russian proverb "two bears in one den" (145). And Geoffrey Hartman emphasized the apocalyptic tendency of Wordsworth's imagination: "By apocalyptic I mean that there is an inner necessity to cast out nature" (49).[2]

These antithetical readings were in turn strongly opposed by critics like Jonathan Wordsworth and Thomas McFarland. The latter, for example, insisted that Bloom's and Hartman's views could not be maintained "except by disregarding overwhelming evidence to the contrary." Nature was not in opposition to Wordsworth's imagination; his "poetic genius and his poetic achievement were inseparable from an enormous imaginative intensity about nature and natural objects" (30, 36). I believe that the case made by Coleridgean commentators can be strengthened if attention is concentrated on the perceptual particulars of Wordsworth's representations of the spots of time and related experiences rather than on his after-the-fact explanations that, in Hartman's own phrase,"usually overlay rather than deepen insight"(xvii). There can of course be no question of recovering what the child Wordsworth actually experienced. Naked recollections do not exist in the text, for they are necessarily mediated by the words of the adult poet, whose verbal representations of early experiences will inevitably differ from the experiences themselves. On the other hand, one is interested in the sources of Wordsworth's creativity primarily because of the quality of the poetry that is its effluence; and these are found in his representations of childhood experiences, not in his generalizations about them. In Thomas Hardy's terms, the reader of the *Prelude* should be primarily concerned with Wordsworth's powerfully articulated "impressions" rather than his shifting "convictions" (408).

In his recollections of the poet, Thomas De Quincey recalls an incident that occurred one midnight when he and Wordsworth had walked out from Grasmere to wait for the carrier bringing the London newspapers. At intervals, Wordsworth would lie flat on the road and place his ear to the ground to see if he could catch any sound of distant wheels. Once, as he was rising from the ground, his eye caught a bright star "that was glittering between the brow of Seat Sandal and of the mighty Helvellyn." Wordsworth gazed at the star "for a minute or so" and then made the following observation:

I have remarked, from my earliest days, that, if under any circumstances, the attention is energetically braced up to an act of steady observation, or of steady expectation, then, if this intense condition of vigilance should suddenly relax, at that moment any beautiful, any impressive visual object, or collection of objects, falling upon the eye, is carried to the heart with a power not known under other circumstances. Just now ... when I raised my head from the ground, in final abandonment of hope for this night, at the very instant when the organs of attention were all at once relaxing from their tension, the bright star hanging in the air above those outlines of massy blackness fell suddenly upon my eye, and penetrated my capacity of apprehension with a pathos and a sense of the infinite, that would not have arrested me under other circumstances.   (160)

Wordsworth illustrated "the same psychological principle" with reference to his poem about the mountain boy blowing mimic hootings to the owls. This poem was first published in the 1800 edition of *Lyrical Ballads* under the title "There was a Boy" and subsequently placed among "Poems of the Imagination" in later arrangements of his works. But it was also included in the 1805 *Prelude*, and earlier versions, written partially in the first person, are found among the drafts of the 1799 *Prelude*. There is therefore good reason for considering "There was a Boy" as a spot of time experience that is deployed in the third person in book v of the *Prelude* to suit the structural and thematic plan of that extended work, just as the two episodes explicitly called spots of time were moved to book xi from their proper chronological position in books i and ii. Here is the 1805 text:

> There was a boy – ye knew him well, ye cliffs
> And islands of Winander – many a time
> At evening, when the stars had just begun
> To move along the edges of the hills,
> Rising or setting, would he stand alone
> Beneath the trees or by the glimmering lake,
> And there, with fingers interwoven, both hands
> Pressed closely palm to palm, and to his mouth
> Uplifted, he as through an instrument
> Blew mimic hootings to the silent owls
> That they might answer him. And they would shout

Across the wat'ry vale, and shout again,
Responsive to his call, with quivering peals
And long halloos, and screams, and echoes loud,
Redoubled and redoubled – concourse wild
Of mirth and jocund din. And when it chanced
That pauses of deep silence mocked his skill,
Then sometimes in that silence, while he hung
Listening, a gentle shock of mild surprise
Has carried far into his heart the voice
Of mountain torrents; or the visible scene
Would enter unawares into his mind
With all its solemn imagery, its rocks,
Its woods, and that uncertain heaven, received
Into the bosom of the steady lake.   (389–413)

Attention is initially directed to the evening horizon, the place
"Where earth and heaven do make one imagery" (*PW* i 247). Low-
hanging stars seem to be moving along the edges of the hills, thus
imparting a sense of animation to the natural world. Against this cre-
puscular background occur two of the most unruffled experiences of
expanded consciousness represented in Wordsworth's poetry. As the
boy strains to hear the owls' replies, which have been coaxed into
being by his own mimetic skill (which presupposes an intimate and
patiently acquired knowledge of natural phenomena), the pauses of
deep silence seem to mock his efforts. They also raise the intensity
of his perceptual expectation to such a pitch that when, to quote De
Quincey, "his attention [begins] to relax – that is, in other words,
under the giving way of one exclusive direction of his senses, [begins]
suddenly to allow an admission to other objects" (161), the result is
an extraordinary perceptual experience. The visible scene enters into
the boy's mind "unawares" because it, unlike the owls' hootings, has
been unsought. The scene includes the image of the darkening ("uncertain") sky, reflected on ("received into") the surface ("bosom") of
the steady lake. The memorable sweetness of this perception and
its powerful effect are unobtrusively intimated – the aptness of the
expression matching that of the experience described – by the way
in which the quiet fusion of sky and water, metaphorically described
in human terms, intimates the fusion of the natural setting and the
inner being of the boy – a fusion that had already been suggested at
the beginning of the passage by the mingling of terrestrial and celestial on the horizon.

But this is not the passage's principal felicity. As Walter Pater
observes: "Clear and delicate at once, as he is in the outlining of visible
imagery, [Wordsworth] is more clear and delicate still, and finely

scrupulous, in the noting of sounds" (43). As he strains to hear the now silent owls, the boy hears something else, something from beyond quotidian perceptual limits that gives "a gentle shock of mild surprize" and carries "far into his heart the voice/Of mountain torrents." The perceptual dynamics of this quietly transporting experience are suggested by Thoreau's observation that "All sound heard at the greatest possible distance produces one and the same effect, a vibration of the universal lyre, just as the intervening atmosphere makes a distant ridge of earth interesting to our eyes by the azure tint it imparts to it" (*Walden* 123). In his description, Wordsworth uses two metaphors to suggest the effect on the boy of hearing such vibrations. One is the humanizing metaphor – the sound of the mountain torrents described as their "voice" – which is comparable in effect to the similar metaphors already noted in the closing lines of the passage. The other metaphor also intimates the interpenetration of human perceiver and natural setting, though in this case a natural term is used to describe a human quality. Its suggestiveness was finely caught by De Quincey: "This very expression, 'far', by which space and its infinities are attributed to the human heart, and to its capacities of re-echoing the sublimities of nature, has always struck me as with a flash of sublime revelation" (161).

"There was a Boy" has two further points of interest. One is Wordsworth's later comment on the poem: "Guided by one of my own primary consciousnesses, I have represented a commutation and transfer of internal feelings, co-operating with external accidents, to plant, for immortality, images of sound and sight, in the celestial soil of the Imagination" (*PW* ii 440n). Prima facie, it is hard to see how such idealizing commentary can be justified. A "heaven" is mentioned, but in reference only to the evening sky, which is "uncertain" because it is being reflected in the shifting waters of the lake, and also for the same reason that the lake is glimmering rather than shining: because of the waning of the light. The entire thrust of the poem concerns the interpenetration of man and nature, not of human and suprahuman. On the other hand, it is from the limits of the perceptible, the threshold of the transcendent, that the voice of mountain torrents comes; the terrestrial and celestial mingle on the horizon; and when a vibration of the universal lyre is felt, there is a sense of contact with something beyond, for the description of which a supernatural vocabulary ("immortality," "celestial") would seem unavoidable.

The final point is a related one. In his essay, "Why Distant Objects Please," Hazlitt notes that "Distance of time has much the same effect as distance of place" (viii 256). If one thinks about "There was a Boy" in the context of the informing concerns of the *Prelude*, one soon becomes aware of the force of this analogy. Just as the distant, barely perceptible voice of mountain waters is carried far into the boy's heart (whereas the very same sound heard from a closer distance would be unremarkable and unmemorable), so the childhood spots of time gain part of their power from the very fact that they are distant in time, and that from a temporal rather than a spatial perspective they are on the border between the perceptible and imperceptible, the immanent and what is beyond, and are therefore potentially capable of striking vibrations on the universal lyre. Thus, implicit within this spot of time is a spatial model of the temporal relationship between early experience and adult consciousness that helps to account for the lasting power of the remembered moments.

In De Quincey's anecdote and in "There was a Boy" the perceptual displacement is from the aural to the visual. When the flow of heightened sensitivity moves in the opposite direction, the resultant impact on the consciousness of the Wordsworthian perceiver can be less sweetly penetrating than roughly unsettling. One example is the second of the two spots of time described in book xi. But before turning to these two crucial episodes, we first need to consider Wordsworth's sensorium and the eye-ear relationship in his poetry, and to examine some of the moments of intense perceptual experience described the books i and ii of the *Prelude*.

In the preface to *Lyrical Ballads*, Wordsworth declares that a poet must be a man "possessed of more than usual organic sensibility" (*PW* ii 387–8), by which phrase is meant the capacity to receive impressions through the senses. In the case of Wordsworth himself, the capacities of his lower senses were less, not more, than usual. Robert Southey reported that his friend "had no sense of smell," a deprivation also noted by James Payn, who observed that Wordsworth could not distinguish the scent of a beanfield in bloom (Smith 1, 11–12). As with odors, few gustatory impressions are found in Wordsworth's poetry. Nor is there evidence of a strong haptic capacity.[3] Hearing and especially sight are the dominant senses in Wordsworth's poetry.

Wordsworth describes his younger self as having an eye that "evermore" was looking for "the shades of difference / As they lie hid in all exterior forms / Near or remote, minute or vast." His sight "Could find no surface where its power might sleep" (iii 157–9, 164). The "manifold distinctions ... Perceived in things where to the common eye / No difference is" produced "gentle agitations of the mind" that contributed to the expansive sense of seeing "blessings spread around me like a sea" (ii 317–20, 414). This unceasing activity of discrimination makes vision the dominant perceptual organ in Wordsworth's poetry. In the preface to *Lyrical Ballads*, the poet is referring to metre, and consequently to the ear, when he speaks of "the pleasure which the mind derives from the perception of similitude in dissimilitude" as the "principle [which] is the great spring of the activity of our minds, and their chief feeder" (*PW* ii 400). But in quotidian perceptual experience this spring is fed primarily through the eye and not the ear. So dominant is the role of sight that it is "in every stage of life/The most despotic of our senses" (xi 172–3). At one point Wordsworth feared that the hegemony of the eye would reduce him to being a mere connoisseur of visual sensations. He was also concerned with the tyranny that sight (together with the analytic powers of the mind) could exercise in post-adolescent life over the creative faculties. In book xi the spots of time experiences are introduced to explain why in the despondent period after the failure of his hopes for the French Revolution he did not long remain under the tyranny of an eye that brought him "vivid but not profound" delights. It is the very reason one would expect: because he "had felt/Too forcibly, too early in my life,/ Visitings of imaginative power" for this condition to last (188, 250–2).

One of the ways of overcoming the power of the eye was through internalizing the object of visual perception: the bodily eye was superseded by "the inward eye" and "the mind's eye." In "Resolution and Independence," for example, the speaker's dejection gives way to a more resolute state of mind as a result of the self-reparative activity of his imagination, which internalizes the figure of the aged leech-gatherer and re-creates him as a type of human endurance. Three visual images describe the aged figure: a huge stone; a sea beast crawled forth to sun itself; a motionless cloud. But the transforming power of the imagination becomes intense only when the dominance of the visual begins to abate:

> The old Man still stood talking by my side;
> But now his voice to me was like a stream
> Scarce heard; nor word from word could I divide;
> And the whole body of the Man did seem
> Like one whom I had met with in a dream;
> Or like a man from some far region sent,
> To give me human strength, by apt admonishment.

This adult creative experience, so the imagery suggests, recapitulates an intense perceptual experience of the Wordsworthian child. The "body of the Man" is carried from the external world far into the consciousness of the poet, just as the sound of distant mountain torrents is carried far into the heart of the boy.

A second way of overcoming the eye's dominance was by "replacing sight with sound, or in less definite cases, by shifting the emphasis from sight to sound" (Miyagawa 32). In "Resolution and

Independence," the visual images are superseded by an auditory image (the old man's voice as a stream scarce heard) as the process of internalization occurs. A more fully articulated example is found at the beginning of the discharged-soldier episode in book iv of the *Prelude* (363–99). Wordsworth is describing what happened to him one night while indulging "a favourite pleasure" – walking alone along the public road on a summer night. As he mounts a steep ascent, the road before him, glittering in the moonlight, seems like a river (a "wat'ry surface") flowing along to join "the brook/That murmured in the valley" – murmured rather than, say, babbled because its sound is heard from a distance. As he walks, "in my own despite" (i.e., passively) the young man receives "amusement" from such near visual objects as intrude on his "listless sense,/Quiescent and disposed to sympathy." But as he enters more deeply into the stillness of the "silent road" he begins to have a deeper experience. His body is described as "drinking in/A restoration," and, as this sweet state of being intensifies, the dominance of the ear is again noted: "I looked not round, nor did the solitude/Speak to my eye, but it was heard and felt."

A manuscript fragment from the late 1790s contains the following notation:

> The clouds are standing still in the mid heavens;
> A perfect quietness is in the air;
> The ear hears not; and yet, I know not how,
> More than the other senses does it hold
> A manifest communion with my heart.   (v 343)

In thinking about why hearing is so privileged rather than sight it is helpful to recall Coleridge's observation that sounds can be "more sublime than any sight *can* be" because they can more fully suspend "the power of comparison" (in Wordsworth's phrase, the ability to perceive "manifold distinctions") and more completely absorb "the mind's self-consciousness in its total attention to the object working upon it" (*Friend* i 367). It is also helpful to reflect on an observation made by Hazlitt in "Why Distant Objects Please": "Sounds, smells, and sometimes tastes, are remembered longer than visible objects, and serve, perhaps, better for links in the chain of association," because "they are in their nature intermittent, and comparatively rare; whereas objects of sight are always before us, and, by their continuous succession, drive one another out. The eye is always open," while the ear "is oftener courted by silence than noise; and the sounds that break that silence sink deeper and more durably into the mind. I have for this reason," Hazlitt says, "a more present and lively recollection of certain scents, tastes, and sounds than I have of mere visible images, because they are more original, and less worn by frequent repetition" (viii 258).

When Hazlitt gives particular examples from his own past (the taste of barberries, the smell of a brick kiln, certain musical sounds), it is hard not to think of the non-visual touchstones of vision in Proust's *À la recherche du temps perdu* in which through involuntary memory the past is recovered: the taste of a *madeleine* cake soaked in tea; hearing an exquisite passage in a musical composition; stepping on an uneven paving stone; the touch of a starched napkin. As has long been recognized, there are similarities between Wordsworth and Proust concerning the importance of affective memory and the tremendous power of special moments from the past to irradiate the present. But there are important differences as well.

Near the beginning of *À la recherche du temps perdu*, the adult narrator, weary and dispirited, soaks a *madeleine* in a cup of tea and takes up a spoonful of the mixture. When it touches his lips, a transformation occurs:

at once the vicissitudes of life had become indifferent to me ... I had ceased now to feel mediocre, contingent, mortal. Whence could it have come to me, this all-powerful joy? I sensed that it was connected with the taste of the tea and the cake, but that it infinitely transcended those savours, could not, indeed, be of the same nature. Whence did it come? What did it mean? How could I seize and apprehend it?   (i 48)

The answer was that the tea-soaked *madeleine* had evoked the memory of long-ago Sunday mornings of his childhood when he would visit Aunt Léonie in her room. The all-powerful joy was not found in the childhood experience itself, but in the fusion of two temporal moments, one belonging to the adult present, the other to the childhood past, that had been triggered by the involuntary memory of a sense impression. Near the end of the novel, the narrator reflects that the reality of his life is found in just such fortuitous moments of connection "between these immediate sensations and the memories which envelop us simultaneously with them" (iii 924). For him, truths based on sense impressions are more profound than truths directly apprehended by the intellect. The former were material in that they derived from and were triggered by sensory experience, but they were also transcendent. While the moments of rapture lasted he could not have said whether he was in the one temporal medium or the other; what was experienced was "in some way ... extra-temporal" (iii 904).

In Wordsworth, the involuntary operation of memory has not the same emphasis, although it is hardly the case that he had other than fortuitous access to the past experiences that were the hiding places of present power. Furthermore, in Proust the particular perceptual memory is simply the trigger of recollection; it is not the pivotal point of the recollected experience or in itself a cause of the intensity of impression that makes the experience memorable. This is why the vivid childhood experiences evoked in the *Prelude* do not affect the present in the same way that those in Proust do. An essential aspect of the difference is that in Wordsworth's spots of time and related experiences the dominant senses are invariably sight and hearing – the two least physically involving of the senses. Unlike smell, taste and touch, these senses can be deeply engaged by what is at a distance from the perceiver. In the *Prelude*, the sights and sounds that strike most deeply are often those at the perceptual limit and thus able of themselves to evoke feelings of sublimity and transcendence. The importance in later life of these childhood experiences is not that they can be recovered intact. It is rather that these early experiences of sublimity are the source of future experiences of expanded consciousness.

In book ii, Wordsworth describes being out alone at night during childhood

> listening to sounds that are
> The ghostly language of the ancient earth,
> Or make their dim abode in distant winds.
> Thence did I drink the visionary power.

These fleeting moods of exultation, during which he had "felt whate'er there is of power in sound/To breathe an elevated mood, by form/Or image unprofaned" (that is, undiluted by visual perceptions) were valuable not because they suggested that the mind is its own lord and master, but because they permanently sensitized his consciousness:

> the soul –
> Remembering how she felt, but what she felt
> Remembering not – retains an obscure sense
> Of possible sublimity, to which
> With growing faculties she doth aspire.   (326–38)

Most of the memorably intense experiences recounted in the first two books of the *Prelude* are more particularly and concretely described and as a result show more clearly the central role of perception. Take, for example, the ice-skating passage (i 452–89). Words-worth describes how he would sometimes leave his playmates and skate off alone "To cut across the image of a star/That gleamed upon the ice." When he attempted to do so, the reflection moved away from him as he approached. Because of the remoteness of the re-flected object, the skater would never have been able to cross the star's reflection on the ice, which achievement would remain, no matter how long the attempt, what in book vi is called a "something evermore about to be." In the next lines, Wordsworth recalls that when, after skating hard, he suddenly stopped short "yet still the solitary cliffs/Wheeled by me." It seemed as if the visible world had a perceptible life and motion of its own – seemed, that is, a showing forth of the force of the something that rolls through all things.

In the fullest representation of a glacial frisson, the effects are primarily aural:

> So through the darkness and the cold we flew,
> And not a voice was idle. With the din,
> Meanwhile, the precipices rang aloud;
> The leafless trees and every icy crag
> Tinkled like iron; while the distant hills
> Into the tumult sent an alien sound
> Of melancholy, not unnoticed; while the stars,
> Eastward, were sparkling clear, and in the west
> The orange sky of evening died away.

As in "There was a Boy," the coming on of night amplifies the audi-tory aspect of the scene, allowing a non-visual apprehension of the reciprocity of human and natural. The noise of the children's activity is given back as an alien sound by the distant hills, as a reverberating ringing by the nearer precipices, and as a tinkle by the icy crags and leafless trees. Coleridge, the first commentator on this passage, explained the last acoustic effect, which is not an echo: "When very many are scating together, the sounds and noises give an impulse to the icy trees, and the woods all round the lake *tinkle*" (*Friend* i 368). The visual equivalent of a tinkle is a twinkle or a sparkle, and in the climax of the passage the eye is raised to the evening horizon, where the setting sun has left a swathe of orange and made perceptible the sparkle of the stars – just as it has the tinkling of the trees.

Other intense childhood experiences were more destabilizing. One of them describes how in springtime the young Wordsworth would climb to the high places of lonely peaks to plunder ravens' nests. He describes himself hanging precariously upside down above a nest while "the loud dry wind" blew "with what strange utterance" through his ears and, to turn to the scene's visual aspect, "the sky seemed not a sky/Of earth, and with what motion moved the clouds" (i 347–50). The perceptual foundation of this description needs no underlining. As Emerson observes, if one bends over and looks at a landscape through one's legs, the "pleasure mixed with awe" that is experienced would be "a low degree of the sublime" (34). In the case of the child above the raven's eggs, this low form of visually induced ecstasy is intensified by the strangeness of the wind's sound.

Another experience – the famous boat-stealing episode (i 372–426) – was more deeply disorienting. One evening Wordsworth chanced upon a shepherd's boat "by the shores of Patterdale, a vale/Wherein I was a stranger," and impulsively took the boat and rowed out into the lake. There he has an experience similar in kind to, but more psychologically complex in origin and different in degree of intensity from, what he experienced on another evening on another lake when he suddenly stopped short on his skates and sensed the solitary hills wheeling around him. In this episode, "huge and mighty" natural forces seem to stride after the boy while he is on the lake. For many days after his mind "Worked with a dim and undetermined sense/Of unknown modes of being," as these forms moved slowly through his mind by day and troubled his dreams at night.

What is the cause of this powerfully destabilizing experience? One factor is the boy's state of mind as he rows the stolen boat out into the lake. He already feels a degree of guilt about what he is doing: "It was an act of stealth/And troubled pleasure." The oxymoronic last phrase is particularly suggestive. At one level, the boy's pleasure is qualified by an inner uneasiness because of his transgression. But it is also intimated that at a deeper level of consciousness a part of the boy's pleasure is owing to the very fact of its being "troubled," that is, of its being felt to be illicit. That this act has darkly intensified the boy's experience is further suggested by the aggressive energy with which he rows. Even hints of a sexual element in his energy enter as he "lustily" dips his oars into the lake and rises "upon the stroke" with the boat.

The turning point in the episode is a startling perceptual experience. As the boy rows outward into the lake he is looking backward at the receding shore and "a rocky steep" rising above it. But he reaches a point on the lake's surface where, because his angle of vision has changed, this steep ceases to be the bound of the horizon. Suddenly from behind that unexceptional elevation, "a huge cliff,/As if with voluntary power instinct,/ Upreared its head." What has happened is that to the unusually stimulated and apprehensively intense consciousness of the boy the second cliff, the sudden appearance of which has surprised him, seems a hugely minatory apparition. As he begins frantically to row, the changing angle of his vision reveals more of the cliff, which "growing still in stature … like a living thing/ Strode after me." It is clear that the boy has projected onto the cliff both his own emotional state and the "measured motion" of his vigorous rowing. Thus, the episode is fully explicable in perceptual terms. The boy is scared out of his wits by the fortuitous conjunction of heightened sensitivity caused by the "troubled pleasure" of his internal condition and a particularly striking example of a not uncommon perceptual experience.

The experience is of course memorable. But what the account of the boat-stealing episode, and the other accounts of specific early experiences in the first two books of the *Prelude*, do not directly address is how these experiences relate to adult creative power and visionary capability. It is in connection with the two childhood experiences described in book xi – the spots of time explicitly so called – that Wordsworth does address this difficult subject. It is clear that Wordsworth himself did not fully understand the peculiar continuing power of the two episodes – he was in no doubt that he had experienced something vitally important; but what he had experienced and why it remained incandescent were more complicated matters.

In the first spot of time (xi 278–315) a very early experience is recalled – "I was then not six years old." Though scarcely able to hold a bridle, the child is taken for a horseback ride. He begins the outing with "proud hopes"; but this little rise in the five-year-old ego is soon deflated when through "some mischance" he is separated from his guardian. Doubtless feeling increasingly apprehensive, the boy dismounts and, leading his horse down "the rough and stony moor … and stumbling on," comes to the valley bottom "where in former times/A murderer had been hung in iron chains" and where, owing to local superstition, the murderer's name had been carved in monumental writing on the turf by the mouldered gibbet-mast. After the boy's eye takes in the scene, he "forthwith" leaves the spot and reascends to the bare common. What he sees there – or rather how he sees – shows that he has undergone a subjectively terrifying experience. He sees

> A naked pool that lay beneath the hills,
> The beacon on the summit, and more near,
> A girl who bore a pitcher on her head
> And seemed with difficult steps to force her way
> Against the blowing wind. It was, in truth,

An ordinary sight, but I should need
Colours and words that are unknown to man
To paint the visionary dreariness
Which, while I looked all round for my lost guide,
Did at that time invest the naked pool,
The beacon on the lonely eminence,
The woman, and her garments vexed and tossed
By the strong wind.

This passage powerfully conveys the visionary state of the boy's consciousness through understatement and repetition, which are appropriate rhetorical registers both for the description of an ordinary sight
and for the communication of the sheer desperate lostness of the five-
year-old boy. No feelings of guilt or of troubled pleasure are projected
onto extraordinary natural sights as night comes on. There is rather
primal terror in the broad daylight and a consequent expansion of
consciousness – a "visionary dreariness" in which a naked pool, a
lonely beacon, and a woman struggling against the wind are powerfully registered on the boy's sensitized consciousness and come to
stand as elemental emblems of his subjective sense of desolation.

In the 1799 two-part *Prelude* Wordsworth ended his account of the
first spot of time with the lines quoted above. By 1805, he had supplied a thirteen-line coda that attempted to account for the continuing
power that the memory held for him. Before examining this coda, one
might first ask if there is anything in the description itself that can
help explain its continued power. A notable aspect of the representation is that no specific perceptual occurrence serves as the trigger of
expanded consciousness. (It should be noted, however, that the boy
moves abruptly from an enclosed space to an open one, and from a
sheltered and presumably silent location to one where a strong wind
is blowing.) On the other hand, in the 1799 text, an extremely interesting metaphor is employed at the beginning of the episode. In emphasizing the fact that the experience was a very early one, Wordsworth
remarks that it is "of an early season that I speak,/The twilight
of rememberable life" (i 297–8). He does not say the *dawn* of rememberable life. Had he done so, one would have had a conventional
figure in which the cycle of an individual's life is compared to the
diurnal cycle, early childhood being equated with dawn, and so on.
But Wordsworth specifies the twilight, a more complex figure that becomes suggestive as soon as the terms of the comparison are understood. Something far removed in time, at the very limit of what is
recoverable by memory, is compared to something at the spatial limit
of visual perception.

One can therefore suggest that part of the reason the first spot of time is so memorable is simply that it was such an early experience. But in the 1805 coda (xi 315–27), Wordsworth does not suggest anything so direct. A "blessèd season" in later life is described, when the poet, his sister Dorothy, and his future wife strolled in daily presence of the "ordinary sight." It is weakly asserted by means of a limp rhetorical question that, when they did so, the radiance of their mutual love was enhanced for the poet – was made "more divine" – by his remembrances of "the power/They left behind." What is being claimed here – the transformation of dreariness into radiance – is in essence an adaptation of the Christian *felix culpa* paradox: destabilizing early experiences – "obstinate questionings" and "blank misgivings" are two of the names they are given in the Intimations Ode – later come to have a positive value. The principal difficulty with this part of the coda is not, so to speak, with the doctrine, but with the implicit restriction of the after-effect to the setting in which it first occurred. As is clear from other episodes in the *Prelude*, physical proximity is by no means a precondition for the continued efficacy of early experiences. The metaphorical phrase "spots of time" does not refer to the fixing of temporal events in space but rather to the emancipation of temporal experiences from the spatial order.

The last three lines of the coda, however, break away entirely from temporal and spatial determinants (the time of early love and the particular setting) to state with convincing directness the essential point of contact between intense childhood experiences and intense later experiences: "So feeling comes in aid/Of feeling, and diversity of strength/Attends us, if but once we have been strong." In the first spot of time, the boy was hardly strong in the sense of being lord and master of his situation. But what he experienced was strongly experienced, and this early activation of intense feelings creates the capacity and hence the possibility of his experiencing other feelings of comparable intensity in later life. *What* the child felt is less important than *how* he felt; through the memory of the latter an "obscure sense/Of possible sublimity" is retained.

The second spot of time (xiii 344–88), which dates from Wordsworth's fourteenth year, is more complicated than the first, if not more complex. As one would expect, a principal reason is the subjective consciousness of the older perceiver. The major difficulty concerns the interrelationship between two temporally close past events. The first is Wordsworth's experience while he waited impatiently for the sight of the horses that would take him and his brothers home from school for the Christmas holidays. The second event is his reaction to the unexpected death of his father less than ten days later. A summary of this second event is interpolated into the middle of the description of the first.

If this interpolation is set aside for the moment and the earlier experience examined on its own terms, it can be seen that the experience turns on the dynamics of sensory perception, more particularly on the displacement of one sense by another. "Feverish, and tired, and restless," and "impatient for the sight" of the horses, Wordworth climbed to a craggy summit that gave a view of "at least a long half-mile" of two roads, by one of which the horses would be arriving. The day was stormy, rough and wild and the visibility poor. The boy sat down on grass "half sheltered by a naked wall," with a single sheep on one side of him and a "whistling hawthorn" on the other. There he waited and watched, "Straining my eyes intensely as the mist/Gave intermitting prospect of the wood/And plain beneath."

What happened next is not immediately reported, for at this point a summary of the later event (the father's death and the boy's reaction to it) is interpolated. Then there is a return to the original experience of waiting for the horses. Afterwards (that is, after the death of the father), this experience became vividly memorable:

> the wind and sleety rain,
> And all the business of the elements,
> The single sheep, and the one blasted tree,
> And the bleak music of that old stone wall,
> The noise of wood and water, and the mist
> Which on the line of each of those two roads
> Advanced in such indisputable shapes –
> All these were spectacles and sounds to which
> I often would repair, and thence would drink
> As at a fountain.

Given the texts we have been examining, it can hardly be doubted that what happened to make this experience so memorable, and so pregnant with restorative power, was not simply a subsequent event but a perceptual experience similar to that described in the De Quincey anecdote and in "There was a Boy" – save that the perceptual displacement was from sight to hearing and the experience was not sweetly transporting. "Though it may appear strange," Edmund Burke notes in his treatise on the sublime, "that such a [perceptual] change as produces a relaxation, should immediately produce a sudden convulsion; it is yet most certainly so" (134). The boy's attention had been energetically braced up to an act of intense visual observation. But the predominantly aural particulars of his immediate surroundings ("all the business of the elements") had suddenly penetrated his "capacity of apprehension" in a roughly unsettling way that left a lasting resonance in memory. In Wordsworth's figure, the experience became a fountain from which he continued to "drink." The same verb is used in the passage in book ii in which Wordsworth describes his boyhood self "drink[ing] the visionary power" that flowed from the night-time sounds of the natural world. And at the root of both images is the primal imbibing of the child at the mother's breast.

It is thus possible to explain part of the lasting power of the first experience described in the second spot of time without reference to the interpolated later experience. The latter takes up the space in the account of the earlier experience where the notation of the sudden relaxation of the organs of visual perception straining to catch sight of something far off would have come. In the interpolation, Wordsworth sketches a different explanation of the power of the remembered "business of the elements": in the time immediately after his father's death the boy came to associate this desolating event with what he had experienced on the summit. It had "appeared/A chastisement" for his having waited in "such anxiety of hope," and it had caused him to bow low to God, who, the boy believed, "thus corrected my desires."

Whether it is at all reasonable for the boy to have felt this way is not in question. The reported information, which does not *ipso facto* strain credulity, is simply that he did come to associate the two events in this way. The moot point is the inference of the adult poet searching for the hiding places of his power: that the second event caused the first experience to become impregnated with significance so that "afterwards" it remained incandescent in his memory. One need not disagree entirely with the after-recollection. The problem is with the implication of causality. Through association, the second event may well have added enormously to the power of the memory of the first. But this does not mean that the power of the first experience is dependent on the power of the second. After all, the first experience must have been memorably intense and destabilizing in its own right for the boy to have imagined that it warranted such a powerful divine rebuke. Like the enhanced radiance of young love in the first spot of time, the sense of divine rebuke exemplifies the power of the experience rather than explaining it; and it is implicitly misleading in suggesting that the affective power of the experience is dependent upon proximity (spatial in one case, temporal in the other). A *sine qua non* of the power of the second spot of time, implicit in the representation of the experience at the craggy summit, is the dynamics of perception.

Attention to perceptual dynamics also throws light on two of the most important episodes in the *Prelude* – the ascent of Mount Snowdon and the crossing of the Alps. The former (xiii 1–119) describes the night-time ascent of the Welsh mountain that Wordsworth made when he was twenty-one. He and a companion were climbing at night because they wished to see the sunrise from the mountain top. The poet walked in silence, his head bent earthward, his "eager pace" match-ing his "no less eager thoughts," which are not specified but obvi-ously centered on the anticipation of seeing a spectacular sunrise. The night was close and warm; "a dripping mist/Low-hung and thick" covered all of the sky. "Hemmed round on every side by fog and damp," the climbers could see little until they reached the summit, which on this particular night was on an exact level with the top of the heavy-hanging, mist-laden clouds. As a result, upon reaching the summit Wordsworth experienced a sudden perceptual displacement:

> For instantly a light upon the turf
> Fell like a flash. I looked about, and lo,
> The moon stood naked in the heavens at height
> Immense above my head, and at the shore
> I found myself of a huge sea of mist,
> Which meek and silent rested at my feet.
> A hundred hills their dusky backs upheaved
> All over this still ocean, and beyond,
> Far, far beyond, the vapours shot themselves
> In headlands, tongues, and promontory shapes,
> Into the sea, the real sea, that seemed
> To dwindle and give up its majesty,
> Usurped upon as far as sight could reach.

The visual scene, with its mixture of land and land-like clouds, is spectacular in its own right; but as the representation of the Snowdon experience reaches its climax a third displacement occurs. This time it is not from anticipated sunrise to full moon, or from darkness to light and closeness to expansive vision, but the unsettling shift from seeing to hearing. At a mediate distance from the summit/shore of the cloud/ocean is

> a blue chasm, a fracture in the vapour,
> A deep and gloomy breathing-place, through which
> Mounted the roar of waters, torrents, streams
> Innumerable, roaring with one voice.

Once this extraordinary spectacle has "passed away," it is followed by an equally spectacular meditation that "rose in me that night/ Upon the lonely mountain." In retrospect, the scene becomes figural: "The perfect image of a mighty mind,/Of one that feeds upon infinity." The power that Nature had thrust forth "upon the senses" now comes to stand for

> the express
> Resemblance – in the fullness of its strength
> Made visible – a genuine counterpart
> And brother of the glorious faculty
> Which higher minds bear with them as their own.

Thus, through the conceptual transference made possible by hindsight, what was perceived from the top of Snowdon becomes an emblem or allegory of the autonomy of higher minds whose imaginations have no need of a reciprocal relationship with the natural world because they have the power to dominate "all the objects of the universe."

Nonetheless, if one attends to the description of what Wordsworth saw and heard that night rather than to the after-meditation, to the impression rather than the retrospective convictions, striking similarities between the Snowdon episode and the poet's childhood experiences become apparent. The first point, already intimated, is the importance of the perceptual dynamics. Take, for example, Wordsworth's sudden apprehension of the tsunami of sound roaring up from the blue chasm. As Hartman explains, this apprehension "cannot be sudden except psychologically": if Wordsworth "does not hear the stream of sound, which must have been there all along, it is because his senses were fixed by [a] visual image." The usurpation of sight is so strong that "it masks the continuous sound, and the re-entry of the latter into consciousness appears like a breakthrough. Though the vision … is about nature, it is also about the poet's perception of nature" (185).

Furthermore, a degree of interdependence between the experience itself and the transcendent after-claims becomes apparent if one recalls the experience of the boy who blew mimic hootings to the owls but came to hear instead the "voice of mountain torrents" that was carried far into his heart – by which metaphor, as De Quincey noted, space and its infinities were attributed to the human heart. In the Snowdon after-meditation, Wordsworth uses the same spatial metaphor (though on a scale that registers the difference between a moving sea of clouds and a steady lake, and between the roar of waters and the barely heard sound of distant streams): a mighty mind is "exalted by an under-presence,/The sense of God, or what-soe'er is dim/Or vast in its own being." And when the mighty mind is described as one that "feeds" upon infinity, it is impossible not to recall the child Wordsworth drinking visionary power from the sounds of the night winds and, earlier still, the oceanic feelings of the infant feeding at the mother's breast.

Of the crossing the Alps episode in book vi, David Ellis has observed that "If one could momentarily put on one side the inter-polated tribute to Imagination … then it would be more obvious that Wordsworth's apocalyptic vision of the Alps … can be read as dependent on the relaxation of will [I would say, with De Quincey, on the relaxation of an intense condition of perceptual vigilance] which ensues when he learns he has already crossed them" (65). But there is no reason why this interpolation cannot be momentarily set aside, just as the interpolation in the waiting-for-horses episode was. Wordsworth presents his crossing of the Alps as an example of a powerful emotion, "a deep and genuine sadness" (492) that over-came him during his continental peregrinations in the summer of 1790 when he was twenty. He and his companion had looked for-ward to savoring the actual moment when they would cross the Alps. But they had mistaken their route, become disoriented and, when finally set right by a peasant, discovered that they had in fact already made the crossing. Wordsworth says that the "dull and heavy slackening" in attention that ensued when they realized their mistake was "soon dislodged" (549–51). Certainly there is nothing dull about the famous description of the Gondo Gorge (556–72) which they then entered and through which they journeyed down-ward for several hours:

> The immeasurable height
> Of woods decaying, never to be decayed,
> The stationary blasts of waterfalls,
> And everywhere along the hollow rent
> Winds thwarting winds, bewildered and forlorn,
> The torrents shooting from the clear blue sky,
> The rocks that muttered close upon our ears –

Black drizzling crags that spake by the wayside
As if a voice were in them – the sick sight
And giddy prospect of the raving stream,
The unfettered clouds and region of the heavens,
Tumult and peace, the darkness and the light,
Were all like workings of one mind, the features
Of the same face, blossoms upon one tree,
Characters of the great apocalypse,
The types and symbols of eternity,
Of first, and last, and midst, and without end.

Despite the statement that his disappointment was soon dislodged, it is obvious that Wordsworth had in fact experienced a severe inner displacement, as he had done years before when he had come upon the mouldered gibbet-mast, and that he entered the gorge in a heightened perceptual state similar to that of the boy when he had fled the valley bottom and reascended the bare common. In the gorge, Wordsworth's frustrated intensity of expectation reaches a vertiginous pitch. It is the perceiver rather than the winds who is "bewildered and forlorn." The "*sick* sight/And *giddy* prospect of the raving stream" (my italics) refer principally to a human rather than a natural condition. The giddy effect is also conveyed by the fact that the description is a composite of Wordsworth's sequential perceptual experiences as he descended the gorge. As Elizabeth Helsinger has noted, there is "no sense of the perceiver's location in the passage; almost every visual element is plural, and the spectator is somewhere in the midst of woods, waterfalls, winds, torrents, rocks, crags, clouds" (99). To his intensified perceptions, the rocks and drizzling crags seem to speak with a human voice, while his visual distance from other aspects of the scene makes for a perceptual oxymoron (Ogden 254) – "the stationary blasts of waterfalls" – that compounds the effect of the natural-cycle oxymoron of "woods decaying, never to be decayed." These perceptual particulars, together with the more general fused contrasts of tumult and peace, darkness and light, mirror the interpenetration of consciousness and landscape and exemplify the "paradox of immanence and transcendence" that Merleau-Ponty identified as an essential characteristic of all perception: "immanence, because the perceived object cannot be foreign to him who perceives; transcendence, because it always contains something more than what is actually given" (16).

In the last lines of the passage, however, a new element enters into the representation of Wordsworth's experience in the gorge.

"Characters," "types," and "symbols": these allegorizing terms suggest the supersession of intense perceptual activity by an idealizing after-meditation in which, as in the Snowdon episode, transcendent notes are sounded. This is a different kind of imaginative activity from that occurring earlier in the passage. The objects of perception are here translated into "characters"; the inner/outer, subject/object dynamic is replaced by a lower/higher schema; vertiginous intensity is controlled by conceptual transference. The last five lines of the passage, that is to say, seem just as much a later interpolation (or interpretation) by Wordsworth as does the address to imagination that had been temporarily put to one side but must now be examined.

Commentators agree that this interpolation records a sudden realization of the significance of his 1790 experience that came to Wordsworth in 1804 while recreating the experience in verse. It is the recognition that beyond the natural or material sublime there is a higher sublime where "greatness make[s] abode." This is experienced in "visitings/Of awful promise, when the light of sense/Goes out in flashes that have shewn to us/The invisible world" (532–6). "Blest in thoughts/That are their own perfection and reward" (545–6), the mind, as Stephen Gill puts it, "outsoars the material sublime with glimpses of infinitude." But while Gill acknowledges the transcendent thrust of this passage, he nonetheless insists on the primacy of the imagination-nature linkage. Wordsworth "is not Blake," and while his imagination may transcend both memory and natural objects and give glimpses of the invisible world, "its ground" is nonetheless in this world (71).

What does not seem to have been noticed by Gill and other Coleridgean commentators is that the interpolation itself can be used to make this point. The flash of insight that Wordsworth experienced in 1804 was into the cause of his profound dejection on learning that he had crossed the Alps without realizing it. The sadness he then felt, Wordsworth subsequently realized, revealed an "under-thirst/Of vigour" (489–90) in him that he ultimately identified as a longing for the transcendent. "Our destiny," the exultant poet proclaims,

> Our destiny, our nature, and our home,
> Is with infinitude – and only there;
> With hope it is, hope that can never die,
> Effort, and expectation, and desire,
> And something evermore about to be.   (538–42)

These lines appear to refer to something in the transcendent future beyond what can be attained by the union of the mind and the visible universe, and thus to anticipate the Snowdon after-meditation and its claims for an autonomous imagination or "mighty mind" with unmediated access to an invisible world. But this is not entirely the case. For one thing, as William Empson points out, there is ambiguity in Wordsworth's saying that "the light of sense/Goes out in flashes that have shewn to us/The invisible world": "goes out" can mean both "proceeds from" and "fails" (or "is extinguished"). This verbal ambiguity "drives home the paradox" that (in terms cognate with those used by Empson) the showing forth of the invisible world both transcends and is dependent upon perceptual experience (294–5). One should also recognize that, as in the second spot of time, the recollected experience unquestionably has a perceptual basis to which the interpolated material may well make a synergistic addition, but which does not of itself cause the experience to occur or to be memorable. And of course, as we have seen, in book ii of the *Prelude* the "sense of something evermore about to be" – there called "an obscure sense/Of possible sublimity" (336–7) – is shown to be rooted not in the invisible world but in intense perceptual experiences of childhood.

To speak of the relationship between childhood experiences and transcendent intimations is inevitably to bring into the discussion "Ode: Intimations of Immortality from Recollections of Early Childhood." In later life Wordsworth remarked that "to the attentive and competent reader the whole sufficiently explains itself." But he had earlier told a correspondent that the poem rested "entirely upon two recollections of childhood, one that of a splendour in the objects of sense which is passed away, and the other an indisposition to bend to the law of death as applying to our particular case. A Reader who has not a vivid recollection of those feelings having existed in his mind cannot understand the poem" (*PW* iv 463–4). For a reader lacking these prerequisites, the next best thing is a knowledge of the spots of time and related experiences that we have been considering.

The fourth stanza of the ode ends with two urgent questions: "Whither is fled the visionary gleam?/Where is it now, the glory and the dream?" The remainder of the Intimations Ode attempts to find an answer to these insistent interrogatives as well as to the unstated question concerning what can sustain the person who has ceased to be a child and is daily travelling ever further from the dawn of his life and its visionary intensities and ever closer to "the darkness of the grave."

The positive part of the answer begins in the ninth section with an abrupt exclamation:

> O joy! that in our embers
> Is something that doth live,
> That nature yet remembers
> What was so fugitive!

In the ashy darkness of our adult existence there remains in memory a glowing remnant of the visionary intensity of childhood. The gleam and the glory have vanished from out there, but an afterglow remains within. So does the memory of two other kinds of early experiences, with which we have become familiar. The first is

> those obstinate questionings
> Of sense and outward things,
> Fallings from us, vanishings;
> Blank misgivings of a Creature
> Moving about in worlds not realised,
> High instincts before which our mortal Nature
> Did tremble like a guilty Thing surprised.

In his turn-of-the-century essay on Wordsworth, A.C. Bradley observes that "the best commentary on a poem is generally to be found in the poet's other works" and that the closing lines of the boat-stealing episode in the second book of the *Prelude* furnish the best commentary on these difficult but unquestionably central lines (133). Equally apposite "commentary" is provided by a number of the other destabilizing early experiences recounted in the *Prelude*, especially the two explicitly denominated spots of time.

The other kind of early experience that remains incandescent in the adult memory are

> those first affections,
> Those shadowy recollections,
> Which, be they what they may,
> Are yet the fountain light of all our day,
> Are yet a master light of all our seeing.

Here the synesthetic image of "fountain light" fuses the drinking-in quality of the oceanic feeling that has its origin in the child at the maternal breast with the celestial visual imagery employed earlier in the ode. The stanza concludes with the assertion that, by enabling us to make contact with the childhood time when we felt part of a larger unbounded continuum, the felt memory of these two kinds of early experience can supply a sustaining sense of continuity in time.

The complex image at the stanza's close becomes comprehensible as soon as it is seen against the correct background:

> Hence in a season of calm weather
> Though inland far we be,
> Our Souls have sight of that immortal sea
> Which brought us hither,
> Can in a moment travel thither,
> And see the Children sport upon the shore,
> And hear the mighty waters rolling evermore.

In this image, spatial distance (from the seashore to far inland) is used as a metaphor of temporal distance (between childhood and adult life). In certain moments of good weather someone far inland can catch sight of the sea. It is described as "immortal" because in Wordsworth's figure tenor and vehicle are allowed to blur together: like the inland traveller looking back at the sea on a clear day, "our souls" through memory can regain contact with the oceanic ("immortal") feelings of childhood. As we have seen, the intensity of such feelings, whether sweet or unsettling, was often characterized by perceptual displacement, as one is reminded by the final lines of the passage in which the inland traveller's visual image of children sporting on the shore is superseded by a more powerful auditory image of the permanent in the transitory: the sound of "mighty waters rolling evermore."

Writing in 1886, Gerard Manley Hopkins identified the Intimations Ode as the poem in which Wordsworth's "insight was at its very deepest ... when he wrote that ode human nature got [a "shock"], and the tremble from it is spreading" (*Correspondence* 148). Coleridge and Thoreau, the subjects of the next two chapters, both felt the tremble. For them, Wordsworth's poem was an essential point of reference in reflecting on and coming to terms with the dulling of their organic sensibilities and the decay of their rare powers of symbolic perception.

FIVE

Coleridge's Blessed Interval

In the first chapter of *Biographica Literaria*, Coleridge speaks of "a long and blessed interval" in his earlier life, "during which my natural faculties were allowed to expand, and my original tendencies to develope themselves: my fancy, and the love of nature, and the sense of beauty in forms and sounds" (i 17). The time was 1795–8, when Coleridge was in his mid-twenties. It began with his engagement to Sara Fricker, whom he married in September 1795. However unpromising the circumstances of their coming together and unhappy the eventful outcome of their marriage, Coleridge initially found that "Domestic Happiness is the greatest of all things sublunary" (*Letters* i 158). During this period, he also became a father and found a patron and friend in Thomas Poole; his long-standing friendship with Charles Lamb deepened; William and Dorothy Wordsworth became close friends; and the former became one half of an extraordinary creative association.

Coleridge also came into sustained, intimate contact with the natural world for the first time: initially at Clevedon for three months in late 1795; then from the beginning of 1797 to September 1798 at Nether Stowey, also in Somerset, where he lived in a cottage within walking distance of a variety of scenic places and prospects. "I love fields & woods & mounta[ins] with almost a visionary fondness," Coleridge writes in a letter of March 1798, "and because I have found benevolence & quietness growing within me as that fondness [has] increased, therefore I should wish to be the means of implanting it in others." He then quotes Wordsworth on man's "shadowy Sympathies with things that hold/An inarticulate Language." Once taught to love natural objects, "The Joy of that pure principle of Love" would necessarily lead a person to "seek for objects of a kindred Love/In fellow-natures, & a kindred Joy" (*Letters* i 397–8). The inter-amplifying love of natural objects and fellow natures is one of a number of minglings, mirrorings and doublings that characterize this period of Coleridge's life – the time when Memory and Hope "sang the same note" and blended "with each sweet *now* of/My felicity,"

> Like Milk that coming comes & in its
> easy stream Flows ever in, upon the
> mingling milk, in the Babe's murmuring
> Mouth/or mirrors each reflecting each.
> (*Notebooks* ii #3107)

The difference that personal happiness and closeness to nature made in Coleridge's life are registered in his poetic development. He later recalled that

> In the great City rear'd, my fancy rude
> By natural Forms unnurs'd & unsubdued
> An Alien from the Rivers & the Fields
> And all the Charms, that Hill or Woodland yield[s],
> It was the pride & passion of my Youth
> T' impersonate & color moral Truth
> Rare Allegories in those Days I spun,
> That oft had mystic senses oft'ner none.
> Of all Resemblances however faint,
> So dear a Lover was I, that with quaint
> Figures fantastically grouped I made
> Of commonest Thoughts a moving Masquerade.
> (Whalley 17–18)

An example is "Sonnet: To the Autumnal Moon," written in 1788. Its octet describes the moon as seen at different times; the sestet, beginning "Ah such is Hope!", finds parallels between the lunar tableaux and the virtue that is "as changeful and as fair." The parallels are emblematic figurations of the pre-Romantic type: resemblances traced with curious pains that necessitate conceptual transference. The result is a rhetorical proclamation of an overdetermined message addressed to anyone within shouting distance. The sonnet also illustrates other features of his early verse that by the later 1790s Coleridge had come to recognize as defects: "the swell and glitter both of thought and diction," the "profusion of double-epithets, and a general turgidness" (*Poems* ii 1145).

Another characteristic of the early poetry is the absence of vivid sensory notations and images. In the sonnet, the "I" is only nominally present and his eye is as "weak" and "dimly peering" in the literal sense as the moon (in one of its appearances) is in the figurative. In contrast, the poetry Coleridge wrote in the later 1790s is full of acute visual notations. Here, for example, is the description from "Reflections on Having Left a Place of Retirement" of what Coleridge saw from the top of a "Mount sublime" that commanded a view of the Bristol Channel:

> Oh! what a goodly scene! *Here* the bleak mount,
> The bare bleak mountain speckled thin with sheep;
> Grey clouds, that shadowing spot the sunny fields;
> And river, now with bushy rocks o'er-brow'd,
> Now winding bright and full, with naked banks;
> And seats and lawns, the Abbey and the wood,
> And cots, and hamlets, and faint city-spire;
> The Channel *there*, the Islands and white sails,
> Dim Coasts, and cloud-like hills, and shoreless Ocean –
> It seem'd like Omnipresence! God, methought,
> Had built him there a Temple: the whole World
> Seem'd *imag'd* in its vast circumference:
> No *wish* profan'd my overwhelmèd heart.
> Blest hour! It was a luxury, – to be!

In contrast to the autumnal-moon sonnet, this descriptive passage is dramatic rather than didactic: "The speaker is not merely an observer and commentator standing apart from what he describes ... [He] is now involved in an experience which is intrinsically significant. [The images] reveal the movement of the speaker's mind from one mode of apprehension (the perception of things) to another (the apprehension of wholeness)" (Haven 54–5). The perceptual discrimination is sharp; the monochrome pattern of black speckled with white on the near mountain is reversed in the dark on bright patterns in the middle distance – both the fields in strong sunlight with spots of shadow and the "bright" river dotted with rocks. The eye is then led beyond the human habitations to wider vistas – first the channel spotted with islands and sails and then the vast unpatterned expanse of ocean and sky. The mirroring of one part of the natural scene by another is more than simply refreshing; it is awe-inspiring. The expansion of consciousness, coextensive with the expansion of the poet's intense visual apprehension, culminates in a sense of something big and indivisible. This sense is intensified by perceptual dynamics unremarked (or unrecorded) at the time but noted in the analysis of such vistas that Coleridge made eight years later in his *Notebooks* (i #1675): "The View of an extensive Plain, all cultivated, from a high mountain, would be merely an amusing object – a curiosity … were it not for the imposingness of the situation from which we view it – the feelings, possibly worked on by the air &c. Hence, the advantage of Sea, & Lake in these Views – they take off the *littleness* & picturishness – the Camera obscura effect."

Personal happiness, a sense of community, closeness to nature, sensory acuity and the physical health it presupposes – all simultaneously experienced in the sweet *now*: this is the biographical basis of Coleridge's later description of the genius of youth: "all genius exists in a participation of a common spirit. In joy individuality is lost." To have "genius is to live in the universal, to know no self but that which is reflected not only from the faces of all around us, our fellow creatures, but reflected from the flowers, the trees, the beasts … A man of genius finds a reflex to himself, were it only in the mystery of being" (*Philosophical Lectures* 179). Coleridge wrote most of his finest poetry during this blessed interval, including "Kubla Khan" and "The Rime of the Ancient Mariner." My interest is in the four principal conversation poems, each addressed to a different member of his intimate circle: "The Eolian Harp" to Sara Fricker in the time just before their marriage; "This Lime-Tree Bower my Prison" to Charles Lamb; "Frost at Midnight" to his infant son; and "The Nightingale" to William and Dorothy Wordsworth. In these poems, a wealth of delicately inscribed sensory notations and blendings of thought and feeling are the poetic distillation of the time when "every sense, each thought, & each sensation/Lived in my eye, transfigured, not supprest" (*Notebooks* ii #3107). Mirrorings and blendings of inner and outer, lower and higher, micro and macro, are the signs of Coleridge's felt sense that "every Thing has a life of it's own, & that we are all *one Life*" (*Letters* ii 864). But as we shall see, while these poems represent and enact the apprehension of the one life, they also problematize it.[1]

My pensive Sara! thy soft cheek reclined
Thus on mine arm, most soothing sweet it is

To sit beside our Cot, our Cot o'ergrown
With white-flower'd Jasmin, and the broad-leav'd Myrtle,
(Meet emblems they of Innocence and Love!)
And watch the clouds, that late were rich with light,
Slow saddening round, and mark the star of eve
Serenely brilliant (such should Wisdom be)
Shine opposite! How exquisite the scents
Snatch'd from yon bean-field! and the world *so* hush'd!
The stilly murmur of the distant Sea
Tells us of silence.

Thus begins "The Eolian Harp," the first and least aesthetically satisfying of the four poems. The lines recapitulate the evolution of
Coleridge's poetic manner: conventional, even hackneyed, figures –
the emblematic jasmin, myrtle and star – give way to a more active
and fresh perception of the natural world. Kathleen Wheeler has
tracked the "gradual progression through the imagery from a state
of relative passive observation, to a highly responsive, articulate level
of appreciation": the twilight used as a metaphor for a state of mind
poised between passive and active; the "humanizing qualification" of
"saddening" and the "progressive immediacy of [its] participial
form" – the first indications of an active, imaginative response to
the scene; and the "delightful topographical design" in which "the
'landscape' of the heavens is now mirrored by the landscape of the
earth in terms of the relations amongst the predominant elements"
(*Creative* 67, 70, 72).

The subtle transition from sluggish to more active perception
may also be traced in the lulling, murmuring flow of the lines, which
encourages the loosening of habitual responses, and in the effects of
the waning of the light. As visibility diminishes, the visual arrange-
ment of clouds and stars above is superseded by the olfactory and
aural arrangements at ground level of beanfield on one side and sea
on the other. At the climax of the passage, a delicious sensory felicity
occurs: the speaker becomes aware of silence through the one exception to it – a far-off sound that does not intrude on the silence
but seems part of it; the murmur is "stilly," that is, partaking of the
motionlessness and quiet of the scene. This oxymoronic registration
also brings the suggestion of the one life, of nature as potentially or
incipiently animate – the sea's "murmur" as of a voice.

This anticipates the more elaborate figuration in the center of the
poem of the "mute still air" as "Music slumbering on her instrument." In these lines, the atmosphere is *still* (calm and silent) but *still*

(nonetheless) pregnant or instinct with musical sound – as *air* (atmosphere) is homologous with the *air* (musical strain) that is actualized by the wind-harp. This similarity is signalled by the repetition in the second half of the antepenultimate lines of each stanza: "the world *so* hush'd"/"a world so fill'd." The movement is from the particular, scarcely heard, and microcosmic to a macrocosmic expansion of consciousness that is rooted in, and coextensive with, the sensory-perceptual particulars.

What fills the hushed world are the sounds of "that simplest Lute,/ Placed length-ways in the clasping casement." In lines 14–25, the sounds are mainly figured in delicately erotic terms. By "the desultory breeze caress'd," the lute seems

> Like some coy maid half yielding to her lover,
> It pours such sweet upbraiding, as must needs
> Tempt to repeat the wrong!

As its strings are "boldlier swept" by the breeze, the lute produces "a soft floating witchery of sound" that is likened to the sound made by elves in "Fairy-Land"

> Where Melodies round honey-dropping flowers,
> Footless and wild, like birds of Paradise,
> Nor pause, nor perch, hovering on untam'd wing!

Erotic undertones are again detectable. This passage does not describe a spiritualizing of the mind as does the "Omnipresence" passage in "Reflections on Having Left a Place of Retirement," the other conversation poem of 1795. The sound is bewitching rather than blessed; the melodies induce an oceanic ("soft floating") state of feeling/touch – a mode of the polymorphously perverse. In Whitman's phrase, from the description of a similarly induced experience in section 26 of *Song of Myself*, it is like being "steeped amid honeyed morphine." It is not an imaginative state unprofaned by wish in which the intellect is raised to an apprehension of God; it rather resembles the fulfillment of a wish expressed by Coleridge in a letter of 1797: like the Hindu god Vishnu "to float about along an infinite ocean cradled in the flower of the Lotos, & wake once in a million years for a few minutes – just to know that I was going to sleep a million years more" (*Letters* i 350).

The next lines contain no erotic or regressive undertones; this is not surprising given that they were composed and added to "The Eolian Harp" two decades after its first publication:

> O! the one Life within us and abroad,
> Which meets all motion and becomes its soul,
> A light in sound, a sound-like power in light,
> Rhythm in all thought, and joyance every where –
> Methinks, it should have been impossible
> Not to love all things in a world so fill'd;
> Where the breeze warbles, and the mute still air
> Is Music slumbering on her instrument.

This passage reflects Coleridge's later philosophical and scientific reading, as Abrams has shown (*Breeze* 158–91), but in essence it represents how Coleridge felt at times during the later 1790s. The dominant trope in the passage, synesthesia, functions as a Coleridgean symbol in absorbing sensory particulars into a perceptual totality and thus linking part to whole. Moreover, secondary qualities like light and sound are fused with primary qualities like motion (see Rajan "Displacing" 470). Joy or joyance is the name of this feeling; it presupposes the supersession of onlooker consciousness by participatory consciousness. In the former, "we think of ourselves as separated beings, and place nature in antithesis to the mind, as object to subject, thing to thought, death to life"; the latter is "that intuition of things which arises when we possess ourselves, as one with the whole" (*Friend* i 520–1).

The later-interpolated passage is followed by the description of a visually rather than aurally induced expansion of consciousness culminating in pantheistic speculation. The breeze animates the passive lute just as

>   on the midway slope
> Of yonder hill I stretch my limbs at noon,
> Whilst through my half-clos'd eye-lids I behold
> The sunbeams dance, like diamonds, on the main,
> And tranquil muse upon tranquillity;
> Full many a thought uncall'd and undetain'd,
> And many idle flitting phantasies,
> Traverse my indolent and passive brain,
> As wild and various as the random gales
> That swell and flutter on this subject Lute!
>   And what if all of animated nature
> Be but organic Harps diversely fram'd,
> That tremble into thought, as o'er them sweeps
> Plastic and vast, one intellectual breeze,
> At once the Soul of each, and God of all?

In Wheeler's tracing, these lines "are full of indications about the imaginative experience" – for example, the twilight-like mixture of active and passive ("half-clos'd eye-lids" and the ambiguous "stretch my limbs," which can mean either vigorous exercise or recumbent relaxation) leading to speculations that reach out "into the mystery of existence and the individual's relation to nature" (*Creative* 79–80). My reading notes the self-induced aspect of the poet's squinting and finds instead a return to the indolent and indulgent mode of the "witchery of sound" passage that ultimately takes one beyond sensory-perceptual experience ("intellectual" means "beyond the senses") into vertiginous neo-Platonic musings that are less integral to the poem than the one-life passage (see House 75).

These speculations bring a "mild rebuke" from pensive Sara, prompting the speaker's recantation. Her "more serious eye" bids Coleridge to "walk humbly with my God" and to abjure what he now identifies as

> shapings of the unregenerate mind;
> Bubbles that glitter as they rise and break
> On vain Philosophy's aye-babbling spring.

In the light of the poem's ending, the speaker's opening figurations – the emblemizing of the flowers and the star followed by a fresher, more active perception of the natural world, may be read as part of a strategy of address to his less imaginative and more conventionally Christian fiancée. The goal was presumably to encourage a more perceptually active response to nature and thus a more sensuous mode of being in the world. But the strategy led the speaker down the road of excess and culminated in Sara's understandable rebuke. An indolent and passive brain, after all, is not the most desirable quality in a prospective husband and parent; nor is the cultivation of "feelings all too delicate for use" or the tendency to nurse "in some delicious solitude … slothful loves and dainty sympathies."

These phrases are from the contemporaneous conversation poem, "Reflections on Having Left a Place of Retirement," in which *in propria persona* Coleridge voices the same sentiments that are put into Sara's eye. They suggest that while his recantation at the end of "The Eolian Harp" explicitly refers to the "intellectual breeze" passage, it implicitly qualifies everything that has gone before, including the one-life passage. The near pun in "aye-babbling spring" nicely focuses the poem's ambivalence about itself. The question of egotism in poetry was one on which Coleridge had equivocal views, as can be seen by juxtaposing two contemporaneous entries in his notebooks: "Poetry without egotism comparatively uninteresting"; "Poetry – excites us to artificial feelings – makes us callous to real ones" (i #62, #87).

By June of 1797, when Coleridge returned to the creative mode of the conversation poem, this dichotomy appearred to have been resolved. "This Lime-Tree Bower my Prison" is a much more aesthetically successful composition than "The Eolian Harp" – more all of a piece, with better transitions and modulations, and a greater naturalness and subtlety in the inner/outer figurations. There is no ideological tension – no dissonance between pantheistic tendencies and Christian supernaturalism. In the poem, natural objects "evident to ear and eye are veilings of the Almighty Spirit; they clothe and render that spirit sensible"; but they are not the essence of that spirit (Engell 84). Nor is there a vocational tension between "feelings all too delicate for use" and the Christian life of other-regarding activity. The poem shows the value, the good, of the creative activity of mind – even if the wholesome moral is spelled out in its least poetically interesting lines (59–67). There is also no sexual subtext in the poem: the relationship of speaker to addressee is that of close friendship. Charles Lamb, "my gentle-hearted Charles," had been Coleridge's intimate friend since their school days and they had recently drawn even closer after Lamb's "strange calamity" (in a fit of madness, his sister Mary had killed their mother).

The poem's occasion is explained in a headnote: "some long-expected friends" (Lamb, and William and Dorothy Wordsworth) had arrived for a visit, but on the morning of their arrival Coleridge had "met with an accident" (Sara had spilled a skillet of boiling milk on his foot) that kept him from walking during the whole of their stay. Thus, "This Lime-Tree Bower" opens with the speaker vexed at being immobile and confined to his bower while his friends are imagined to "Wander in gladness." He is even feeling a little sorry for himself: he has lost, he says, "Beauties and feelings" that could have added to his inventory of sweet memories. His sense of confinement and immobility is reflected in his initial conjecture that his friends have descended into a confined and uncheering place:

> that still roaring dell, of which I told;
> The roaring dell, o'erwooded, narrow, deep,
> And only speckled by the mid-day sun;
> Where its slim trunk the ash from rock to rock
> Flings arching like a bridge; – that branchless ash,

> Unsunn'd and damp, whose few poor yellow leaves
> Ne'er tremble in the gale, yet tremble still,
> Fann'd by the water-fall! and here my friends
> Behold the dark green file of long lank weeds,
> That all at once (a most fantastic sight!)
> Still nod and drip beneath the dripping edge
> Of the blue clay-stone.

The primary meaning of "still" in each of its three occurrences is "nonetheless": even in June the flow of the water is strong; although the ash leaves and the weeds are not moved by the breeze, they do tremble or nod because of the atmospheric displacement caused by the waterfall. All three instances also have a secondary suggestiveness: the oxymoronic sense of moving in place – the visual equivalent of the stilly murmur at the beginning of "The Eolian Harp."

The last notation, "the dripping edge/Of the blue clay-stone," is a diminished echo and mirroring of the roaring water of the stream and an instance of a distinctive feature of "This Lime-Tree Bower" – the numerous pairings of macro and micro, spectacular and commonplace. The suggestion is that nothing is unconnected or singular in the continuum of nature, that there is a rhythm in the external world. This in turn relates to a final aspect of the triple use of "still": as with another fantastic sight, "the stationary blast of waterfalls" in the Gondo Gorge in book vi of the *Prelude*, the perceptual oxymoron carries the suggestion of the coexistence or complementarity of the abiding in the transient.

One other notable aspect of the description of the roaring dell is that it records the poet's increasing intensity of perceptual recollection and empathetic identification with what his absent friends are experiencing – a movement of mind from a passive notion of perception as the reception and storing of pleasing data to a more dynamic notion (which is synonomous with the increasing engagement of the secondary imagination with the materials of the poem). The friends are first imagined to have "perchance" come to the dell. The next verb referring to them is "Behold"; like "Wander," it is indicative, but its positioning at the beginning of a line makes it incipiently imperative. It suggests both the friends' and the poet's intense aesthetic delight in the scene and their experience of a certain degree of awe ("a most fantastic sight") in the perceptual paradox; and it prefigures the dominance of the imperative mood in the climax of the next section.

A sensory displacement occurs in the white space between the first and second sections: from the roaring dell to the silent hill-top edge; from a close-up, particularized perception of natural objects to an expansive vista of distanced objects – from the long lank weeds to the "many-steepled tract magnificent," from the wet blue clay-stone to the kindling blue ocean. Now the poet fully achieves imaginative release from his sense of confinement in the bower and subjection to peevish feeling. This movement brings into focus another of the poem's macro-micro mirrorings: Charles Lamb had "pined/And hunger'd after Nature, many a year, in the great City pent" and had suffered a great calamity, while Coleridge is experiencing only a brief confinement as a result of a trifling domestic mishap. Just as external nature is to revive Charles, so Coleridge will be revived through his imaginative involvement in Charles' revivification.

This section represents a further transition – a movement from seeing to gazing that culminates in vision:

> Ah! slowly sink
> Behind the western ridge, thou glorious Sun!
> Shine in the slant beams of the sinking orb,
> Ye purple heath-flowers! richlier burn, ye clouds!
> Live in the yellow light, ye distant groves!
> And kindle, thou blue Ocean! So my friend
> Struck with deep joy may stand, as I have stood,
> Silent with swimming sense; yea, gazing round
> On the wide landscape, gaze till all doth seem
> Less gross than bodily; and of such hues
> As veil the Almighty Spirit, when yet he makes
> Spirits perceive his presence.

The imperative verbs register the shift from onlooker consciousness to participatory consciousness, the hallmark of which is the sense of the oneness of, and of oneness with, the external world (see Kirkham 132). Coleridge had quoted a version of the last six lines in a letter of October 1797: "frequently *all things* appear little [to me] … the universe itself – what but an immense heap of *little* things? – I can contemplate nothing but parts, & parts are all *little* … My mind feels as if it ached to behold & know something *great* – something *one & indivisible* … But in this faith *all things* counterfeit infinity" (*Letters* i 349). What is apprehended is a sense of the abiding in the transient – in Wordsworth's formulation in "Tintern Abbey," "a sense sublime/Of something far more deeply interfused,/Whose dwelling is the light of setting suns." In the phrase "less gross than bodily," *gross* has the sense of dense, thick, solid; not ethereal, transparent, or impalpable. The meaning of *bodily* is clear from the phrase that follows in manuscript versions of the passage: "a living Thing/Which acts upon the mind." Gazing takes on "the character of a spiritual communion and loses its 'grosser' meaning as an experience of the eye" (Ball 41). The "Almighty Spirit ... makes Spirits perceive": the same word is used for both divine and human. In this complex reciprocity, it is as a spirit (not as a body) that the Spirit is perceived; but this is possible only because the Spirit spiritualizes the body.

"A delight," the poet declares at the beginning of the third section, "Comes sudden on my heart, and I am glad / As I myself were there." His imaginative participation in his friends' gazing brings release and a re-perception of his own surroundings:

> Nor in this bower,
> This little lime-tree bower, have I not mark'd
> Much that has sooth'd me. Pale beneath the blaze
> Hung the transparent foliage; and I watch'd
> Some broad and sunny leaf, and lov'd to see
> The shadow of the leaf and stem above
> Dappling its sunshine! And that walnut-tree
> Was richly ting'd, and a deep radiance lay
> Full on the ancient ivy, which usurps
> Those fronting elms, and now, with blackest mass
> Makes their dark branches gleam a lighter hue
> Through the late twilight; and though now the bat
> Wheels silent by, and not a swallow twitters,
> Yet still the solitary humble-bee
> Sings in the bean-flower.

Even in this confined space, Coleridge now finds examples of "the poetry of nature" (*Biographia* ii 5): the transparent foliage, the broad and sunny leaf dappled by shadow, the rich colors of the walnut-tree, the golden light of the setting sun on the ivy, the lighter greens of the ivy against the dark mass of arborial foliage. There is the additional aesthetic charm of the mirroring of the first two stanzas in the third (to which Wheeler [*Creative* 140–1] has called attention): the dell relates to the bower, the ash to the walnut-tree, the foliage in one place to that in the other, the bark on the ocean to the bat against the sky. Finally, the solitary humble-bee sings in the bean-flower, a natural mirroring or companionable form of the poet – solitary, humble (non-egotistical), but nonetheless expressing itself musically. The bee's still audible sound echoes the big sound of the "still roaring dell" in an aurally diminished way, just as the "late twilight" is a visual diminution of the gloriously setting sun of the second stanza.

This section of the poem also has the same pattern of progression as the first two (see Benzon 1100): intense sensory and perceptual activity with gradual narrowing of focus, followed by discursive reflection ("methinks," "I shall know") and then by epiphany:

> when the last rook
> Beat its straight path along the dusky air
> Homewards, I blest it! deeming its black wing
> (Now a dim speck, now vanishing in light)
> Had cross'd the mighty Orb's dilated glory,
> While thou stood'st gazing; or, when all was still,
> Flew creeking o'er thy head, and had a charm
> For thee, my gentle-hearted Charles, to whom
> No sound is dissonant which tells of Life.

There is a double reference in "the mighty Orb's dilated glory." It refers not only to the sun, but also to an eye become "soliform" as the subjective precondition for the perception of the sun's radiance: "in order to direct the view aright," as Plotinus says (in Coleridge's translation), "it behoves that the beholder should have made himself congenerous and similar to the object beheld. Never could the eye have beheld the sun, had not its own essence been soliform" (*Biographia* i 114–5n). Thus, the end of "This Lime-Tree Bower" contains a diminished sunset version of spirits perceiving Spirit because they have been spiritualized by it. And the declension from "vanishing in light" to "creeking o'er thy head" – from the visually distant to the aurally near; from sublimity to being "sooth'd"; from ecstasy to "charm" – encapsulates the poem's key contrast between distant perceptual stimulations of sublime feelings and sustaining natural particulars nearer at hand. Since the difference is one of degree, not of kind, the controlling trope is synecdoche: no natural sight or sound is dissonant because each tells of the one life in which it participates.

The non-problematic charm of "This Lime-Tree Bower" is missing from "Frost at Midnight," which Coleridge wrote the following February. The natural setting of the poem is the cold darkness and silence of a winter midnight: there is little sensory acuity because there is little to be acute about. The loudness of the "owlet's cry" clashes with the silence – unlike the "stilly murmur of the distant sea" at the opening of "The Eolian Harp." With no sense of the one life within and abroad, Coleridge's thought has no rhythm: the dead calm "disturbs/ And vexes meditation with its strange/And extreme silentness."

There is a comparable stillness inside the cottage. Coleridge's "cradled infant slumbers peacefully"; a "thin blue flame" lies without quivering on the "low-burnt fire." The "sole unquiet thing" is a film fluttering in the grate. *Faute de mieux*, the "idling Spirit" of the poet, "every where/Echo or mirror seeking of itself," seems to find in the film "dim sympathies with me who live,/Making it a companionable form." There is nothing at all unusual in this; as Coleridge observes in *The Friend*, "In a self-conscious and thence reflecting being, no instinct can exist, without engendering the belief of an object corresponding to it, either present or future, real or capable of being realized" (i 497). But one must distinguish among the kinds of corresponding thought to be realized – that is, among the interpretations made of natural facts. Like the low-burnt fire, the fluttering film is a suggestive metaphor of the speaker's "idling spirit." But he "interprets" the film as a "companionable form" or answering other and thus as giving evidence of the one life within and abroad. As such, the film would appear to be what in the *Statesman's Manual* Coleridge calls an "arbitrary illustration … a mere *simile*, the work of my own Fancy" (72).

In the next verse paragraph, attention shifts from present to past as the speaker recalls a childhood experience in which the fluttering of a film in a grate was given another subjective meaning, this time projected not by him alone but by popular superstition. As a footnote explains: "In all parts of the kingdom these films are called *strangers* and supposed to portend the arrival of some absent friend." As a child, Coleridge had believed this superstition; often at Christ's Hospital in London, where he had been sent to school at the age of ten, after gazing at a fluttering film in the evening, the next morning in class he would watch the door in expectation of the arrival of someone from his Devon birthplace: "For still I hop'd to see the *stranger's* face,/Townsman, or aunt, or sister more beloved." The reader is not told whether the arrivals presaged by the film occurred, but it must have been the case that they did not. Popular superstition posits in the film a meaning or a human reference that it does not possess and is therefore bound to result in disillusionment. If an object is to function as "a symbol established in the truth of things" (*SM* 72), its meaning must be discovered, not imposed.

This verse paragraph also contains the representation of a memory of his birthplace that as a schoolboy Coleridge had once had: a summer fair-day during which the church bells rang all day, stirring and haunting the child with "a wild pleasure," in part because they

seemed a portent – seemed "like articulate sounds of things to come."
Even in the speaker's childhood, then, there was longing and unfulfillment. At that time it was prospective; at school in London it was
retrospective. Thus a mirroring effect: the boy at school longing backward in time to his "sweet birth-place" recovers a memory of himself
longing forward in time for "things to come." Moreover, this cameo in
the middle of "Frost at Midnight" itself mirrors the surrounding text
in which the adult speaker first remembers back in time to his childhood and then looks forward to the "things to come" for his infant son
asleep in the cradle next to him.

In the following stanza, Coleridge recalls that during his years
at Christ's Hospital he was "pent 'mid cloisters dim,/And saw
nought lovely but the sky and stars" – that is, his only experience of
the natural world was the visual observation of distant objects with
no proximate sensory contextualization. In contrast, he foresees that
during his son's crucially formative years he shall

> wander like a breeze
> By lakes and sandy shores, beneath the crags
> Of ancient mountain, and beneath the clouds,
> Which image in their bulk both lakes and shores
> And mountain crags: so shalt thou see and hear
> The lovely shapes and sounds intelligible
> Of that eternal language, which thy God
> Utters, who from eternity doth teach
> Himself in all, and all things in himself.
> Great universal Teacher! he shall mould
> Thy spirit, and by giving make it ask.

One might have expected the self-imaging to be represented by lakes
mirroring shores, crags, and clouds. But the kind of self-reflecting harmony described is different: this imaging relies on a perceiver to make
the connection, to note the similarities. Unlike the "echo or mirror seeking" of the adult speaker, however, it does not involve subjective projection onto nature. The syntax of this eternal language largely consists
of parallelism, chiasmus and repetition. The lakes, shores and mountain crags are each twice named; "lovely shapes and sounds intelli-
gible" is chiasmic, as is God's teaching "Himself in all, and all things in
Himself." These constructions are syntactic mirrorings of God's eternal
natural language which, as a Coleridgean symbol, is "always *tautegori-*
cal," always "expressing the *same* subject but with a difference ... in
contra-distinction from metaphors and similitudes, that are always *alle-*
gorical" (*SM* 30n).

But this natural language is one to which only children have access. In his poem of 1796, "The Destiny of Nations," Coleridge declares that "all that meets the bodily sense I deem / Symbolical, one mighty alphabet / For infant minds." The purpose of the alphabet is that "we may learn with young unwounded ken / The substance from the shadow." The post-childhood wound is self-consciousness, the loss of the feeling of coextensiveness with the natural world, which prompts the longing for a "companionable form" out there.

The long-term benefits of having learned the divine language are asserted at the close of "Frost at Midnight":

> Therefore all seasons shall be sweet to thee,
> Whether the summer clothe the general earth
> With greenness, or the redbreast sit and sing
> Betwixt the tufts of snow on the bare branch
> Of mossy apple-tree, while the nigh thatch
> Smokes in the sun-thaw; whether the eave-drops fall
> Heard only in the trances of the blast,
> Or if the secret ministry of frost
> Shall hang them up in silent icicles,
> Quietly shining to the quiet Moon.

For Coleridge's infant son, the poem's ending is prospectively positive: all seasons shall be sweet *to thee*.[2] In "This Lime-Tree Bower," Coleridge's other-regarding vision of Charles Lamb's vision had a positive value for himself as well as for Lamb. It is not at all clear that the same may be said for his vision of his son's future in "Frost at Midnight." The first of the two whether/or constructions may be associated with the future of the infant: sweetness in all seasons – even in winter, which is beautifully figured as a red-breasted bird singing on a branch and flanked by white snow and green moss.

The second construction refers principally to the adult. The "whether" clause describes "the eave-drops fall / Heard only in the trances of the blast." A *blast* is a blowing or strong gust of wind. The principal meaning of *trance* is a passage, a way through (from the Latin *transitus*); in the aural sense of this line, the precise meaning would be a pause or suspension. But the more usual meaning of the word is an unconscious or insensible condition, a suspension of consciousness, an intermediate state between sleeping and waking, or a state of mental abstraction from external things. All of these meanings are suggestive in relation to the perceiving consciousness of the poem. At this second level of meaning the trances are a kind of hypallage or transferred epithet (like the "swimming book" at line 38) referring to the speaker's idling or abstracted state. We have, then, another instance of the doubling or mirroring of inner and outer: the breaths of the infant inside the cottage fill up the vacancies and momentary pauses (the trances) in the speaker's thought, while outside the drip of the eave-drops is heard in the trances of the blast. Does this count as an instance of the one life? If so, it is a minimal one. And it is further problematized by the fact that the storm or blast of wind may be taken as a figure for the spirit or consciousness of the adult, vexed by its sense of separation from external reality.

The second alternative in the final whether/or construction is found in the final lines of the poem:

> Or if the secret ministry of frost
> Shall hang them up in silent icicles,
> Quietly shining to the quiet Moon.

Like the description of the lakes, shores and crags, that of the icicles makes use of repetition. The last line repeats the word "quiet" first in its abverbial, then its adjectival, form, both of which reinforce the silence in the previous line. The image is also a repetition in that the icicles are reflecting the light of the moon, which in turn is reflecting that of the sun. Thus, both the recursive rhythm of the lines and the icicles' reflective capability suggest that the image has a one-life, not subjectively imposed, symbolic suggestiveness.

But precisely what is being suggested? Are the icicles a companionable form for the speaker? They come into being as a result of the "ministry of frost" which, in a hint of the homey, hangs them up on the eaves as if hanging out the washing. The religious connotations of ministry also suggest, if not the existence of a providential order, at least that one is at home in nature and that, since the icicles' arrival is represented as the result of an intentional act, there is a force in the natural world responsive to human need. But the operation of the frost is secret; and like the secret strength of things that compels Shelley's attention in "Mont Blanc," it cannot be known whether it is benevolent, malevolent, or utterly indifferent to human need.

The secrecy of the frost, like the silence of the icicles, encapsulates a root paradox of symbolic perception: if a natural object is permitted to function symbolically, without the imposition of subjective interpretations, then its meaning will tend to be known only to itself and what it will tend to figure forth is its own compelling mysteriousness. The silent icicles may thus be considered a symbol of the silence of the natural world in response to the emotional interrogation by the poet searching for a companionable form. It would seem that, for the adult who has lost the child's sense of wonder, there can be no companionable form, though there may be simulacra. "Never can love make consciousness and ascription equal in force," as Emerson sadly observes in "Experience": "There will be the same gulf between every me and thee, as between the original and the picture" (488).

"The Nightingale," composed in April 1798, two months after "Frost at Midnight," has numerous intertextual connections with the conversation poems that preceded it. The echoes and repeated motifs and images indicate Coleridge's concern to work through pressing questions concerning symbolic perception and the one-life apprehension – concerns presumably made more urgent by the problematic ending of "Frost at Midnight." Indeed, "The Nightingale" is an anatomy of these subjects, containing examples of no fewer than eight different subject-object relationships.

From the point of view of the one life, the poem's opening is distinctly unpromising:

> No cloud, no relique of the sunken day
> Distinguishes the West, no long thin slip
> Of sullen light, no obscure trembling hues.

What is not there in the west is a sunset – not a spectacular sunset as in "This Lime-Tree Bower" or even a "slow saddening round" as at the beginning of "The Eolian Harp." What is not there is an attenuated, obscure sunset – a "sullen" sunset. The adjective, a transferred epithet, suggests not only a sluggish perceptual or imaginative state, but also a gloomy, unsociable temperament with a predisposition to melancholy projection – like that found in the poets who made sunsets an opening cliché of eighteenth-century melancholy poetry (see R.H. Hopkins 438). Their representative in "The Nightingale" is the figure posited in lines 16–21:

> some night-wandering man whose heart was pierced
> With the remembrance of a grievous wrong,
> Or slow distemper, or neglected love,
> (And so, poor wretch! filled all things with himself,
> And made all gentle sounds tell back the tale
> Of his own sorrow).

This profile recalls a number of poems Coleridge himself had written in his early twenties and described in two prefaces of 1796, which expound and defend the kind of poem "in which some lonely feeling is developed." The finest examples were those compositions "in which moral Sentiments, Affections, or Feelings, are deduced from, and associated with, the scenery of Nature," thereby creating "a sweet and indissoluble union between the intellectual and the material world" (*Poems* ii 1139).

But this is not the only figure of the poet in the opening section of "The Nightingale." Another is the versifiers who "in building up the rhyme" accept the convention that the nightingale is a melancholy bird. They are of the tribe of wretched bards "in city pent" who in "To the Nightingale" (1795) are said to address the bird as "Sister of love-lorn Poets, Philomel." These poets "echo the conceit" of Milton's Penseroso figure in two senses: both the use of conventional figures and subjective projection (filling all things with themselves). The "youths and maidens most poetical" who dance the night away are another example of derivative versifiers. They are "poetical" in the pejorative sense of inditing conventional and artificially exaggerated effusions. Instead of listening to the sounds of nature, they rely on the conventional figuration of the female nightingale and its putative "pity-pleading strains."

Opposed to the projector of melancholy feelings, the conceited bards, and the frivolous young people is the poet who surrenders his whole spirit to nature – who has

> stretched his limbs
> Beside a brook in mossy forest-dell,
> By sun or moon-light, to the influxes
> Of shapes and sounds and shifting elements
> Surrendering his whole spirit, of his song
> And of his fame forgetful!

These lines are similar to a contemporaneous fragment of Wordsworth's.[3] But where he stresses reciprocity, a combination of giving and receiving, Coleridge emphasizes an intense but passive sensory and perceptual receptiveness to nature's "influxes." The stretching of limbs has only the passive sense of reposing, not the double sense it had in "The Eolian Harp." What one is open to in this dell is a spectrum of mild pleasures, of which lines 4–11 (the description of the natural setting in which Coleridge is speaking to William and Dorothy Wordsworth) had already provided an example. As night fell, all was "still"; in contrast to the opening of "The Eolian Harp," there was "no murmuring" and no illumination from above. But there was a glimmer in the stream, and the old bridge was mossy. Used in both passages, "mossy" is a synecdoche for the two brookside settings. Softly pleasing to the eye and to the touch, a blotch of green against a dark wettish background, moss is a relique or token of the "green earth." (It recalls the "bare branch/Of mossy apple-tree" in "Frost at Midnight," where it is in a similar micro-macro relationship to summer "greenness.") In both mossy settings, we are at a remove from the conventionally beautiful. Their *genius loci* is the self-effacing, non-egotistical poet, a channel through which the "shapes and sounds and shifting elements" of the natural world are represented in words.

The next section of "The Nightingale" foregrounds the poem's speaker and his auditors: these three night wanderers are listening to the ravishing sounds of "the merry Nightingale" whose sex is said to be male rather than female (the conventional designation). For them, the bird's notes are "delicious," and "always full of love/And joyance." The trio do not hear "pity-pleading strains" but a rhapsodic "love-chant." This is an aural parallel to what happened visually in the poem's opening lines: conventional perceptions and associations (the female nightingale as a melancholy bird) give way to a fresh apprehension. But compared to what is seen from the bridge or in the forest-dell, what is now heard in the same place has a substantial upgrading in intensity: from mossy to merry; from delicate visual particularization to encompassing aural rhapsody; from lulling tones to robust assertion; from mild passive pleasure to creative exuberance.

To invoke a favorite distinction of Coleridge's, is the cumulative difference one of degree or one of kind? Is pleasure a low form of joy, both involving "participation [in] a common spirit" (*Philosophical Lectures* 179)? As in "The Eolian Harp," the difference is connected with the shift from visual to aural apprehension of the natural world: from the silent scene of lines 1–11, the pleasure of which is prospective ("we shall find") and therefore a shade notional, to a "thick warble [of] delicious notes" – a ravishment of present sound in which duration seems suspended ("always"). Jean-Pierre Mileur reads lines 40–9 not against the opening lines of the poem, but against lines 16–22, the melancholy projections of the night-wandering solitary. He concludes that "the more the poet strains ... to convey his immediate response to the experience of the nightingale, the more recourse he must take to figurative language and projection" (for example, "love-chant," "a full soul," "as he were fearful"). As a result, "the same critique which calls into question the assertion that the nightingale is melancholy is equally destructive of Coleridge's counterassertion that nature is full of love and joyance" (49). This is an excellent point; but Mileur does not consider whether the implied author of "The Nightingale" is aware of this or not. There is no reason to think that *in propria persona* Coleridge is taken in by this sentimental illusion (as a number of traditional commentators on "The Nightingale" have been), and no reason not to regard it as simply another item in the poem's anatomy of poetic relationships to nature.

In the next section, the scene shifts to "a grove/Of large extent, hard by a castle huge," where many nightingales congregate:

> far and near,
> In wood and thicket, over the wide grove,
> They answer and provoke each other's song,
> With skirmish and capricious passagings,
> And murmurs musical and swift jug jug,
> And one low piping sound more sweet than all –
> Stirring the air with such a harmony,
> That should you close your eyes, you might almost
> Forget it was not day! On moonlight bushes,
> Whose dewy leaflets are but half-disclosed,
> You may perchance behold them on the twigs,
> Their bright, bright eyes, their eyes both bright and full,
> Glistening, while many a glow-worm in the shade
> Lights up her love-torch.

Here we have a non-projective, aesthetic perception of the nightingales' singing, which is self-sufficient and self-sustaining, and has a visual correlative in the multiple glistening of the birds' "eyes both bright and full," which is mirrored in the amorous lighting up of the glow-worms. The natural scene both echoes and reflects itself. Nature is here both subject and object, needing no subjective figurations.

Into this setting comes another night wanderer, this time an ideal figure – "a most gentle Maid" who has retained a childhood freshness of perception and a non-subjective sense of oneness with the natural world. For Mileur, she is "the self-effacing witness to nature as it exists when the impositions of human edifice/artifice [represented by the absent"great lord"and his huge dwelling] are withdrawn ... [Her] self-effacing receptiveness ... allows her to observe the nightingales without disrupting their natural behavior" (49–50). As such, one should ask (as Mileur does not) how the maid differs from the poet reclining in the mossy forest dell who is similarly self-effacing ("of his fame forgetful"). The answer is that the maid is actively a part of her setting, not an passive observer of it. She stretches her limbs in the

active sense while traversing the grove's broken pathways; he has
passively surrendered his whole spirit to Nature; her calling is higher
– she is "vowed and dedicate/To something more than Nature in the
grove." She is supernal and full; he is earthly and empty.

The second description of the birds' singing is from the point of
view of the maid. After a pause of silence,

> the moon
> Emerging, hath awakened earth and sky
> With one sensation, and those wakeful birds
> Have all burst forth in choral minstrelsy,
> As if some sudden gale had swept at once
> A hundred airy harps! And she hath watched
> Many a nightingale perch giddily
> On blossomy twig still swinging from the breeze,
> And to that motion tune his wanton song
> Like tipsy Joy that reels with tossing head.

"With one sensation": that is to say, a mirroring or rhyming of earth
and sky, a synesthetic simultaneity of sound and sight that recalls the
"one life within us and abroad" passage in "The Eolian Harp," as
does the bald use of personification at the close of the passage. It is
one of a number of figures that make the reader aware of the perceiving subject – of the gentle maid's imaginative engagement with the
"choral minstrelsy" of the nightingales.

The last figure of the poet in "The Nightingale," the final night
wanderer, is the poet's infant son, who is "capable of no articulate
sound." The infant's eyes "glitter in the yellow moon-beam," recalling the "glistening" of the "bright, bright eyes" of the nightingales as
observed by the gliding maid, and suggesting that he too is as much a
natural object as perceiving subject – that there is the same non-
subjective reciprocity between his eyes and the moon as between the
nightingales' harmonious answerings of each other's songs. The poet
describes how one night, when his "dear babe" awoke in a "most dis-
tressful mood" owing to "that strange thing, an infant's dream," he
brought his infant out into the moonlight, which at once cured his
distress. The father vows to make his son familiar with the nightingale's song so that he will grow up to associate it with natural joy, not
conventional melancholy, and then bids his friends a final farewell.

The ending is light-hearted and upbeat. Is it also unproblematic –
the fitting close of a "merry poem, recording the ecstatic triumph of
friendship" (Whalley 114)? Have the darker implications of the ending of "Frost at Midnight" been superseded? I do not believe so. For
one thing, the whole of the poem is less than the sum of its parts. The

positive future predicted for the child no more reconciles the parts of the father's meditative discourse than the same prediction did in "Frost at Midnight." For another, the high spirits of the speaker at the close of the poem seem more giddy than ecstatic – seem "Like tipsy Joy that reels with tossing head," to recall the peculiar figure (a personification used as the vehicle of a simile) used earlier in the poem to describe the unsteady perch of the nightingales on swinging twigs. The singing of these birds is one of a number subject-object relationships instanced in the poem, the very proliferation of which suggests that by the time he wrote "The Nightingale" Coleridge's thinking about symbolic perception and the one life within and abroad had become thoroughly equivocal.

Indeed, one might well wonder how long the high spirits of the poet of "The Nightingale" will last. Will nature "always" be able to provide relief from psychological distress? Can a mature poet "always" expect to find natural objects "full of love and joyance"? What will happen if Coleridge is without a beloved other – wife, intimate friends, child – on whom to bestow the gift of the one life, when there is no one present to make possible the circuit of communication that was a presupposition of the constructive imaginative activity of the conversation poems?

The answer was not long in coming. "The Nightingale" was written in April 1798; in September Coleridge left Somerset for Germany, where he spent the next eleven months. The following May he climbed the principal peak in the Hartz forest. "Lines Written in the Album at Elbingerode" describes his descent through fir groves

> Where bright green moss heaves in sepulchral forms
> Speckled with sunshine; and, but seldom heard,
> The sweet bird's song became a hollow sound;
> And the breeze, murmuring indivisibly,
> Preserved its solemn murmur most distinct
> From many a note of many a waterfall,
> And the brook's chatter; 'mid whose islet-stones
> The dingy kidling with its tinkling bell
> Leaped frolicsome, or old romantic goat
> Sat, his white beard slow waving.

The aural and visual particulars of the natural setting are acutely registered: the breeze murmurs; the brook chatters; the moss is speckled by the sunshine; the kidling is dingy; the goat's white beard waves slowly. But something is not right: the particulars are not blended or harmonized. They remain discrete; the breeze is perceived as indivisible only because of its contrast to the scene in which it is simply one of a number of disconnected items.

That is to say, no rhythm or one-life feeling integrates the particulars of the scene. The reason, Coleridge reflects, is that "outward forms … receive/Their finer influence from the Life within; – /Fair cyphers else." He might have added that the same is true of outward sounds. As Emily Dickinson remarks of the oriole's song, whether it be common or divine depends on the "Fashion of the Ear" that attires what it hears "in Dun, or fair" (#526). It is the perceiver who finds the bird's intermittent song to be hollow rather than resounding, and the other natural sounds to be dissonant rather than harmonious. It is he who supplies a sepulchral cast to the terrain.

As early as the spring of 1799, then, Coleridge had come to recognize through its absence the importance of the subjective component in perception. He had also recognized part of the reason his perception could no longer animate and unify the natural world and make it positively signify: the natural particulars were "fair cyphers … but of import vague/Or unconcerning" because on that foreign slope his English heart did not find "History or prophecy of friend, or child,/ Or gentle maid, our first and early love …" There was no loved other to raise Coleridge out of his "low and languid mood." Nor was he any longer living in Somerset, the setting of the blessed interval, a synecdoche for which was "the beautiful Fountain or natural Well at Upper Stowey":

The images of the weeds which hung down from its sides, appeared as plants growing up, straight and upright, among the water weeds that really grew from the Bottom/& so vivid was the Image, that for some moments & not till after I had disturbed the water, did I perceive that their roots were not neighbours, & they side-by-side companions. So – even then I said – so are the happy man's *Thoughts* and *Things*.   (*Notebooks* ii #2557)

By the early 1800s, the blessed interval was in the past: Coleridge was the opposite of a happy man and the distance between his thoughts and things had become unbridgeable. In the spring of 1801, he wrote to William Godwin from Keswick in the Lake District, where he had moved with his family the year before: "You would not know me –! all sounds of similitude keep at such a distance from each other in my mind, that I have *forgotten* how to make a rhyme … I look at the Mountains only for the Curves of their outlines; the Stars, as I behold them, form themselves into Triangles." Coleridge developed

two striking images of his condition (they are among the first of a
number of extraordinary prose analogies he used over the next three
decades to figure his post-poetic, post-creative being):

The Poet is dead in me – my imagination (or rather the Somewhat that
had been imaginative) lies, like a Cold Snuff on the circular Rim of a Brass
Candle-stick, without even a stink of Tallow to remind you that it was once
cloathed & mitred with Flame. That is past by! – I was once a Volume of Gold
Leaf, rising & riding on every breath of Fancy – but I have beaten myself
back into weight & density, & now I sink in quicksilver, yea, remain squat
and square on the earth amid the hurricane, that makes Oaks and Straws join
in one Dance, fifty yards high in the Element.   (*Letters* ii 714)

A year later, he described his torpid condition at greater length in
another letter – the verse epistle "A Letter to —,"[4] which in shortened
and rearranged form was published later that year as "Dejection: An
Ode." The addressee is Sara Hutchinson, the sister of Wordsworth's
wife, whom Coleridge had met in 1799, and was to love from a
distance for many years. A number of the verse letter's features recall
the conversation poems written a few years before: the evocative
evening and night skies; the stilly murmuring of a bee-hive, that
"ever-busy & most quiet Thing"; a bird's song heard as darkness
falls; the wind animating the strings of a wind harp; and the bestowal
of natural bounty on a composite figure of beloved, friend, and
"Sister." What is striking is that in each case these features have lost
their power to animate the speaker – to stimulate creative perception
and a sense of the one life. Coleridge sees but does not feel the beauty
of the heavens; the murmuring bee-hive is something remembered
from the past; he is "*vainly* woo'd" from his "heartless Mood" by the
throstle; the "dull sobbing" lute "better far were mute" (when later
in the poem its strings are "boldlier swept" it sounds first like
"a Scream/Of agony by Torture lengthen'd out" and then like the
pathetic crying of a lost child); that the absent Sara is simultaneously
gazing at the same evening sky is a "Sweet Thought … yet feebly stirs
my Heart!"
   What happened? What caused the heavy change from the blessed
interval to the state in which Coleridge felt himself cut off from
active interchange with the natural world, virtually stopped writing
poetry, and began to downgrade the importance of nature? This
change has been variously explained and it is clear that a number of
factors were involved (see Modiano *Concept* 29). One was simply
that the season of youth had ended. Genius and joy, Coleridge later
reflected, are "liveliest in youth, not from any principle in organiza-

tion but simply from this that the hardships of life, that the circumstances that have forced a man in upon his little unthinking contemptible self, have lessened his power of existing universally" (*Philosophical Lectures* 179). The hardships included chronic domestic turmoil that was only resolved by Coleridge's permanent separation from his wife and children; complications in his friendship with Wordsworth; and his hopeless love for Sara Hutchinson. There was no present or prospective love or joyance to initiate the one-life sense; rarely did Coleridge feel "that sort of stirring warmth about the Heart, which is with me the robe of incarnation of my [poetic] genius, such as it is" (*Letters* iii 5).

This was compounded by the recurrence of a "mental disease" first experienced during adolescence: the tendency to become absorbed in "abstruse researches, which exercised the strength and subtlety of the understanding without awakening the feelings of the heart" (*Biographia* i 17). In 1801, Coleridge explained to William Godwin that as a result of physical and mental distress "I have been compelled ... to seek resources in austerest reasonings – & have thereby ... denaturalized my mind" (*Letters* ii 725).[5] This denaturalization was furthered by Coleridge's increasing religious orthodoxy. As we have seen, as early as "The Eolian Harp" there were indications that he regarded the mind-nature symbiosis as connected with an infirmity in his character, a tendency to indolence and self-indulgent passivity – to being "Morbidly soft" as he described himself in "A Letter to —." By the early 1800s, guilt over his reliance on opium had intensified Coleridge's sense of himself as a weak and sinful creature needing the support of a merciful heavenly Father.

But one could argue that all of the above are as much symptoms or results of the loosening of the bond with nature as they are causes of it, and that the underlying reasons for Coleridge's loss of the one-life feeling are to be found in the deterioration of his sensory-perceptual life. As we have seen, this inevitable diminution is the subject of the Intimations Ode; it was the first part of Wordsworth's poem (stanzas 1–4) that prompted Coleridge's analysis of the epistemological basis of his condition in "Dejection." He could not hope "from outward forms to win" passion and life because their sources were within himself. It was from the "the soul itself" that illumination and sweet sounds must come. They were the outflow of "Joy":

> Joy, Lady! is the spirit and the power,
> Which wedding Nature to us gives in dower
>   A new Earth and new Heaven,
> ....

And thence flows all that charms or ear or sight,
        All melodies the echoes of that voice,
        All colours a suffusion from that light.

The sad wisdom of the Intimations Ode is that the fading of these sounds and sights is an inevitable part of the human life cycle. In Coleridge's case, the condition of "diminished impressibility from *Things*" (*Letters* ii 782) was accelerated by a precipitate decline in his physical health. Letters written between 1796 and 1806 give a great deal of information concerning his physical afflictions, which had three principal components. One was the chronic rheumatic disease which had begun in childhood. Coleridge was free of most of its symptoms during the years he lived in Somerset in the later 1790s; but in the damp climate of the Lake District his health rapidly deteriorated (see Lefebure 45–8). Another component was chronic infections in the otolaryngeal area (Rea 16–18). This condition is part of the explanation of Coleridge's lament in "Dejection" concerning the sparkling stars and the crescent moon: "I see them all so excellently fair,/I see, not feel, how beautiful they are!" The physiological dynamics of human olfaction are such that the slightest barrier between odoriferous molecules and the receptor cells at the root of the nasal cavity will entirely suppress the sense of smell. This fact is well known to persons with allergic rhinitis, nasal polyps, and other chronic sinus problems. So is the fact that with a sinus infection, taste and hearing can also be affected; sounds, for example, can become muffled and echoing. When this happens, the sensory apprehension of a bright summer day or the sky on a clear night may be greatly reduced; it can be like looking at the outside world through a plate-glass window: one sees but cannot feel the beauty of the natural world.

The third component was Coleridge's opium addiction, which by the early 1800s had become chronic. One result of this addiction is a dulling of the sensory faculties, which is most pronounced in the case of tactile sensation, including sexual sensitivity (see Schneider *Coleridge* 41–3; Fruman 164–5). In a notebook entry of 1805, Coleridge speaks of "the influence of bodily vigor and strong Grasp of Touch in facilitating the passion of Hope" (ii #2398). In another entry made four years later, this passion is conspicuous by its absence:

O! Heaven! one thousandfold combinations of Images that pass hourly in this divine Vale, while I am dozing & muddling away my Thoughts & Eyes – O let me rouse myself – If I even begin mechanically, & only by aid of memory look round and call each thing by a name – describe it, as a trial of skill in words – it may bring back fragments of former Feeling – For we can live only by feeding abroad.   (iii #3420)

Moreover, as Coleridge knew, the sense of touch was also an essential component in the visual perception of "magnitudinal sublimity" (*Notebooks* ii #2402). Without it, one could not distinguish qualitatively between sublime and mock sublime – for example between mountains and smoke from a coal-fire or the bole of a pipe. By the early 1800s, when he wrote "Apologia pro Vita Sua" and "Hymn before Sun-rise, in the Vale of Chamouni," Coleridge had lost the ability to make this distinction.

In *Biographia*, Coleridge uses the movement of a small water-insect as a figure for the creative activity of the mind in perception. In 1825, another small insect was used in a very different figuration:

Have you ever noticed the Vault or snug little Apartment which the Spider spins and weaves for itself, by spiral threads round and round, and sometimes with strait lines, so that it's Lurking-parlour or Withdrawing-room is an oblong square? This too connected itself in my mind with the melancholy truth … that as we advance in years, the World, that *spidery* Witch, spins it's threads narrower and narrower, still closing in on us, till at last it shuts us up within four walls, walls of flues and films, windowless – and well if there be sky-lights, and a small opening left for the Light from above.   (*Letters* v 414)

The light from above is that of the Christian God; it was the only possible illumination for Coleridge after the loss of the intersensory one-life illumination – the light in sound and sound-like power in light – that had informed his poetry during the blessed interval three decades earlier.

Thoreau: A Purely Sensuous Life

Thoreau began to keep a journal in 1837, when he was twenty-one. Its first entry reads: " 'What are you doing now?' he asked, 'Do you keep a journal?' – So I make my first entry to-day." The interlocutor was almost certainly Emerson, who had been keeping a journal for seventeen years and encouraging those who were coming under his influence to do the same. Thoreau kept up his journal for the next quarter century, until ill health forced him to stop some months before he died of tuberculosis in May 1862 at the age of forty-four. By that time it had become an enormous document of over two million words and the central work of his literary life.

In its earliest phase, the journal was an *omnium gatherum* of passages from Thoreau's reading, his poetry, and his thoughts. In the second phase, it became a workbook in which he drafted passages intended for essays, lectures and for the two books published during his lifetime, *A Week on the Concord and Merrimack Rivers* and *Walden*. The commercial failure of the former in 1849 caused Thoreau to reassess his literary ambitions. Shortly thereafter the journal entered its third and final phase in which he regularly recorded his detailed observations of the natural world. "Whatever things I perceive with my entire man," he wrote in 1851, "those let me record – and it will be poetry." For example, "the sounds which I hear with the consent & coincidence of all my senses these are significant & musical." Thoreau also continued to record his thoughts, but the dominant subject of the last dozen years of the journal is his "constant intercourse with nature and the contemplation of natural phenomenon," which he regarded as essential to "the preservation of [his] Moral & intellectual health" (*J* iv 28; iii 217).

An early entry speaks of "the best thought" as being "not only without sombreness – but even without morality. The universe lies outspread in floods of white light to it. The moral aspect of nature is a disease caught of man – a jaundice imported into her ... Occasionally we rise above the necessity of virtue into an unchangeable morning light" (*J i 315). In such early entries Thoreau seems to think that this higher state of consciousness is to be reached through the supersession or transcendence of the senses. In 1838, for example, he noted: "If with closed ears and eyes I consult consciousness for a moment – immediately are all walls and barriers dissipated – earth rolls from under me, and I float ... in the midst of an unknown & infinite sea ... I am from the beginning – knowing no end, no aim. No sun illumines me, – for I dissolve all lesser lights in my own intenser and steadier light" (*J i 50). In time, however, Thoreau came to realize that it was through "the coincidence of our life with the life of nature," the "mysterious relation between myself" and the particulars of the natural world, that this enhanced consciousness was attained. The key to expanded consciousness was to "Employ your senses" (*J iv 290, 468; iii 261). "We need pray for no higher heaven," he writes at the end of *A Week*,

than the pure senses can furnish, a *purely* sensuous life. Our present senses are but the rudiments of what they are destined to become. We are comparatively deaf and dumb and blind, and without smell or taste or feeling. Every generation makes the discovery, that its divine vigor has been dissipated, and each sense and faculty misapplied and debauched. The ears were made, not for such trivial uses as men are wont to suppose, but to hear celestial sounds. The eyes were not made for such grovelling uses as they are now put to and worn out by, but to behold beauty now invisible. May we not *see* God? Are we to be put off and amused in this life, as it were with a mere allegory? Is not Nature, rightly read, that of which she is commonly taken to be the symbol merely? ... What is it, then, to educate but to develope these divine germs called the senses? (382)

Because of the painstaking care with which he recorded his interactions with the natural world, it is possible to develop a detailed sensory profile of Thoreau. Touch had comparatively little value for him because there could be no distance between subject and object: "It would be better if there were but one inhabitant to a square mile, as where I live. The value of a man is not in his skin, that we should touch him." Moreover, touch was the channel of "the generative energy, which, when we are loose, dissipates and makes us unclean, [but which] when we are continent invigorates and inspires us. Chastity is the flowering of man" (*Walden* 136, 219–20). While he greatly

admired the 1856 edition of *Leaves of Grass*, Thoreau warned a correspondent that "There are 2 or 3 pieces in [Whitman's] book which are
disagreeable to say the least, simply sensual. He does not celebrate
love at all. It is as if the beasts spoke. I think that men have not been
ashamed of themselves without reason" (Harding 375).

Unlike touch, there were positive aspects to taste, the other sense
that did not allow for distance. Thoreau had on occasion "derived an
inexpressible satisfaction from … food in which appetite had no share"
– and he was "thrilled to think that I owed a mental perception to the
commonly gross sense of taste, that I have been inspired through the
palate, that some berries which I had eaten on a hill-side had fed my
genius." The reference is to the huckleberries he found growing on
Fair Haven Hill, which only retained their true flavor and "essential
part" when they grew wild and were consumed by the person who
had picked them (*Walden* 218, 173). Other berries, as well as apples,
grapes, peaches, and nuts, also provided spiritual sustenance: "I have
felt when partaking of this inspiring diet that my appetite was an
indifferent consideration – that eating became a sacrament – a method
of communion – an extatic exercise a mingling of bloods" (*J* ii 165).

But such occasions were rare and against the grain of this lower,
appetitive sense. For many years, Thoreau rarely used "animal food,
or tea, or coffee, &c." because they were "not agreeable to my imagination … I believe that every man who has ever been earnest to
preserve his higher or poetic faculties in the best condition has been
particularly inclined to abstain from animal food, and from much
food of any kind" (*Walden* 214–15). The fowls in neighboring barns
were "worth far more to me for their crowing & cackling – than for
their drumsticks & eggs." He could find no difference between the
hunter with his "taste for mud turtles & muskrats & skunks and
other such savage tid bits" and the "fine lady" who indulged "a taste
for some form of potted cheese or jelly made of a calf's foot or ancho-
vies from over the water … He goes to the mill pond – she to her preserve pot." How could they, how could Thoreau himself, "live this
slimy beastly kind of life – eating & drinking?" (*J* iii 302, 65–6).

Thoreau believed that he possessed "the sense of smell in greater
perfection than usual" and that there were "odors enough in nature
to remind you of everything, if you had lost every sense but smell"
(*J* iv 79; *J* iv 27). Certainly acute olfactory notation is abundant in the
journal: for example, "the scent of bruised pine leaves where a sled
had passed"; the "strong urine-like scent" from "a pile of red oak
recently split in the woods & now wet with rain"; the "great variety
in the fragrance of the apple blossoms." And one September night he
experienced a particularly sweet olfactory moment: "A field of ripen-

ing corn ... that has been topped with the stalks stacked up to dry – an inexpressibly dry rich sweet ripening scent. I feel as if I were an ear of ripening corn myself. Is not the whole air then a compound of such odors undistinguishable. Drying corn stalks in a field what an herb-garden" (*J iv 326, 395; iii 81; iv 48).

But the higher senses of sight and hearing were Thoreau's principal conveyors of intimations of the one life within and abroad. As a young man, he had held the traditional view of the superiority of sight:

The eye does the least drudgery of any of the senses.– It oftenest escapes to a higher employment – The rest serve, and escort, and defend it – I attach some superiority even priority to this sense. It is the oldest servant in the soul's household – it images what it imagines – it ideates what it idealizes. Through it idolatry crept in – which is a kind of *religion* ... Of five casts [castes] it is the Brahmin – it converses with the heavens ... We *see* truth – We are children of *light* our destiny is *dark*. No other sense has so much to do with the future.   (*J i 182)

This is the Emersonian eye, the organ of spiritual insight: "its axle is the axle of the soul" (*J i 155). For the young Thoreau, it was "more proper for a spiritual fact to have suggested an analogous natural one, than for the natural fact to have preceded the spiritual in our minds" (*J i 231). At this moralizing level of symbolic perception, the eye is necessarily predominant because of its ideating and idealizing power. The result is an emblematic image or (in Coleridge's phrase) loose simile that is the product of conceptual transference rather than sensory acuity. For example, "The snow falls on no two trees alike, but the forms it assumes are as various as those of the twigs and leaves which receive it. They are as it were predetermined by the genius of the tree. So one divine spirit descends alike on all, but bears a peculiar fruit in each" (*J i 239–40).

In the years of Thoreau's most intense observation of the natural world, however, the eye is not predominant. Sight and sound are equally important, and in the moments when he rises above the necessity of virtue and the moral aspect of nature, both senses are likely to be involved. The eye and the ear had close-up capabilities: "To discover a gleam in the trenches, and hear a music in the rattling of the tool we work with – is to *have* an *eye* and an *ear*" (*J i 213). But their principal superiority lay in the ability to sense what was at a distance. There was a ratio between extensiveness in space and intensiveness of feeling: as he puts it in an early entry: "To the senses that is farthest from me which addresses the greatest depth within me" (*J i 199). For

Thoreau, "the imagination require[d] a long range" (*J* xiii 17), and only sight and hearing could furnish distant sensations. In his hyperbole of 1842: "All sights and sounds are seen and heard both in time and eternity" (**J* i 400). Nine years later, when a wire for a magnetic telegraph was strung on poles along the railway line that skirted Walden Pond, he was soon recording in his journal that its vibration "reminded me ... of what finer & deeper stirrings I was susceptible ... a triumphant though transient exhibition of the truth. It told me by the faintest imaginable strain – it told me by the finest strain that a human ear can hear – yet conclusively & past all refutation – that there were higher infinitely higher plains of life – which it behoved me never to forget" (**J* iv 75–6). And in *Walden*, what is at the utmost limit of the perceptible is used to figure "the true harvest of my daily life": it is "somewhat as intangible and indescribable as the tints of morning or evening. It is a little star-dust caught, a segment of the rainbow which I have clutched" (216–17).

The ear was not only the equal of the eye. Some of Thoreau's commentators have even claimed "supremacy" for this sense "as the instrumentality of correspondence and insight" (Paul 512). The ear undoubtedly had certain advantages over the eye. For one thing, at least for the young Thoreau, sound had a restorative, renovating capability and could make an immediate physical impact on the auditor: "Nature always possesses a certain sonorousness, as in the hum of insects – the booming of ice – the crowing of cocks in the morning and the barking of dogs in the night – which indicates her sound state ... I drink in a wonderful health – a cordial – in sound." The pun is more apparent in another passage in which Thoreau declares that a test of health in persons is to determine "if their sensuous existence is sound" (**J* i 277, 274). Another advantage enjoyed by sound, a "double virtue," was that it could produce an echo, which was "to some extent an independent sound – and therein is the magic and charm of it. It is not merely a repetition of my voice – but it is in some measure the voice of the wood" (**J* i 320; iv 143).

Sound was also complemented and enhanced by its powerful opposite, silence. The stillness of an August morning seemed "deep & significant – each sound seems to come from out a greater thoughtfulness in nature – as if nature had acquired some character & mind ... I whose life was but yesterday so desultory & shallow – suddenly recover my spirits – my spirituality through my hearing." And when silence was unpunctuated by sound, as in the "monumental stillness" of a March night, the "void must be supplied by thought– It extracts thought from the beholder as the void under a cupping glass ... raises a swelling" (**J* iii 368; iv 381). Finally, sound more than sight had a something-evermore-about-to-be aspect: "I was always conscious of sounds in nature which my ears could never hear–that I caught but the prelude to a strain– She always retreats as I advance– Away and behind is she and her meaning– Will not this faith and expectation make to itself ears at length." As he notes in an entry concerning the "twittering sound of birds" in the spring dawn: "Expectation may amount to prophecy" (*J i 365; iv 415).

Thoreau was calculating in exploiting the potential of the eye and ear. In order for "the least fact or phenomenon, however familiar," to appear very different, all one had to do was to observe it "from a point a hair's breadth aside from our habitual path or routine" (J viii 44). For example, "you have only to stand on your head a moment to be enchanted with the beauty of the landscape"; the same was true of looking at a landscape through the bottom of a tumbler (*J iii 101; i 129–30). Sometimes the best vantage point was the one that showed "an indistinct prospect, a distant view, a mere suggestion" (J ix 495). Thoreau knew that reflections in water (pools and puddles as well as ponds, lakes, and rivers) could show familiar natural objects in a new way. In early November, for instance, a red oak was "a warm greenish yellow" when seen against the opposite woods; its reflection was inky black against a clear whitish sky (J x 156). Certain atmospheric conditions could also intensify visual perception. Mist, for example, "*compelled* [Thoreau] to look at near objects … My power of observation and contemplation is much increased" (J viii 14). The question was not "what you look at – but how you look & whether you see" (*J iii 355).

Or how you listened and whether you heard. "Near at hand you could fancy" the sound of a hooting owl "the most melancholy sound in Nature" and even find it "expressive of a mind which has reached the gelatinous mildewy stage in the mortification of all healthy and courageous thought … But now one answers from far woods in a strain made really melodious by distance" (*Walden* 125). And on a warm night in June, "the sense of hearing is wonderfully assisted & asserts a new dignity." Then the squeaking sound made by nighthawks high in the air was "not so fugacious going off to be lost amid the spheres but is echoed hollowly to earth – making the low roof of heaven vibrate– Such a sound is more confused & dissipated by day" (*J iii 250).

Most of Thoreau's perceptual tactics are subsumed by his strategic notion of "sauntering." To succeed "to the highest & worthiest ends" one had to abandon all specific goals; one needed to have "a genius, so to speak, for sauntering." Sauntering meant walking "so gently as to hear the finest sounds – the faculties being in repose– Your mind must not perspire" (*J iii 176, 329). Its opposite was the direct purposive scrutiny of the natural world. "I think that the man of science makes this mistake," he wrote in 1857, "and the mass of mankind along with him: that you should coolly give your chief attention to the phenomenon which excites you as something independent [of] you, and not as it is related to you. The important fact is its effect on me" (*J* x 164–5). The astronomer was "as blind to the significant phenomena – or the significance of phenomena as the wood-sawyer who wears glasses to defend his eyes from sawdust" (*J* iii 354). The woodchopper who worked in the woods for weeks or months at a time was in some respects more open to natural impressions than the naturalist and more intimately acquainted with the phenomena of nature. Not enough of the "unconscious life" of the naturalist was passed in the woods: "A man can hardly be said to be *there* if he *knows* that he is there ... The man who is bent upon his work is frequently in the best attitude to observe what is irrelevant to his work. (Mem. Wordsworth's obs. on relaxed attention)" (*J* iv 192–3).

A change in the time of day during which one sauntered could have a significant impact on what was seen and heard: "If I should reverse the usual, go forth & saunter in the woods all the forenoon then sit down in my chamber in the afternoon," Thoreau felt sure "it would be like a new season to me & the novelty of it inspire me" (*J* iii 329). A tactic he did employ regularly was sauntering in the evening and at night. During the former, "The greater stillness – the *serenity* of the air – its coolness & transparency the mistiness being condensed – are favorable to thought. (The pensive eve.)." The stillness made "every sound ... music," while the coolness condensed "the haze of noon & [made] the air transparent and the outline of objects firm & distinct. & chaste (chaste eve)." Sometimes "the pure light that attends the setting sun ... itself is the phenomenon – and no single object is so distinct to our admiration as the light itself" (*J* iv 22–3; ii 43). And one evening at Walden Pond Thoreau experienced a particularly sweet moment of sensory integration (of what he called perceiving with the entire man) and of oneness with the natural world:

This is a delicious evening, when the whole body is one sense, and imbibes delight through every pore. I go and come with a strange liberty in Nature, a part of herself. As I walk along the stony shore of the pond in my shirt sleeves, though it is cool as well as cloudy and windy, and I see nothing special to attract me, all the elements are unusually congenial to me. The bullfrogs trump to usher in the night, and the note of the whippoorwill is borne on the rippling wind from over the water. Sympathy with the fluttering alder and poplar leaves almost takes away my breath; yet, like the lake, my serenity is rippled but not ruffled. (*Walden* 129)

Because of the waning of the light, nothing attracts Thoreau's eye; the only visual notation in the passage is the fluttering of the alder and poplar leaves. But a visual image (rippling) is used to figure both the undulating serenity of his consciousness and the sound of the wind – the atmospheric channel through which other sounds (the trump of bullfrogs, the note of a whippoorwill) reach him. The mirroring of outer and inner figures the rhythmic continuum of the one life within and abroad, while the synesthetic image intimates the perceptual richness of the experience. Moreover, this figuration is itself a mirroring in different sensory modes of the unruffled haptic intensities of the beginning of the passage, where the body is described as one sense drinking in delight through every pore.

Sauntering at night offered, not a refinement of day, but something different: "Instead of the sun there are the moon & stars – instead of the wood thrush there is the whippoorwill." Fireflies replaced butterflies and instead of singing birds there was "the croaking of frogs & the intenser dream of crickets– The potatoes stand up straight – the corn grows – the bushes loom" (*J iii 92). A principal cause of nocturnal perceptual enhancement was moonlight. More valuable "for what it suggests than for what it actually is," moonlight gave a "new quality" to the natural world. In moonlight "the shadows of rocks – & trees & bushes & hills – are more conspicuous than the objects themselves"; and in certain conditions moonlight could even take "the civilization all out of the landscape" (*J iii 286, 300, 92; iv 47). Moreover, moonlight was "peculiarly favorable to reflection" in two senses. On a June night, Thoreau noted that a distant river and pond were "reflecting the light with a faint glimmering sheen ... The water shines with an inward light like a heaven on earth ... a certain glory attends on water by night. By it the heavens are related to the earth" (*J iv 86; iii 259–60). Moonlight was also "more favorable to meditation," to human reflection, than sunlight: "what a man does abroad by night requires more energy & thought – than what he is encouraged to do in the sunshine – he is more spiritual – less vegetable" (*J iii 354; iv 381).

One night in July 1851, sight and hearing collaborated to produce a more powerful sense of the one life within and abroad than the unruffled evening experience cited above:

In Baker's Orchard the thick grass looks like a sea of mowing in this weird moonlight – a bottomless sea of grass– our feet must be imaginative – must know the earth in imagination only as well as our heads. We sit on the fence, & where it is broken & interupted the fallen & slanting rails are lost in the grass (really thin & wiry) as in water. We ever see our tracks a long way behind, where we have brushed off the dew. The clouds are peculiarly wispy

wispy tonight some what like fine flames – not massed and dark nor downy –
not thick but slight thin wisps of mist – I hear the sound of Heywood's brook
falling into Fair Haven Pond – inexpressibly refreshing to my senses – it
seems to flow through my very bones.– I hear it with insatiable thirst– It
allays some sandy heat in me– It affects my circulations – methinks my
arteries have sympathy with it What is it I hear but the pure water falls within
me in the circulation of my blood – the streams that fall into my heart?– what
mists do I ever see but such as hang over – & rise from my blood– The sound
of this gurgling water – running thus by night as by day – falls on all my
dashes – fills all my buckets – overflows my float boards – turns all the
machinery of my nature makes me a flume – a sluice way to the springs of
nature– Thus I am washed thus I drink – & quench my thirst.   (*J iii 301)

As this passage develops, the scene becomes increasingly insubstantial and the boundary between inner and outer increasingly blurred.
In the moonlight, the landscape appears aqueous: the orchard is a
bottomless sea of grass; the fence is lost in the grass as in water; the
human tracks, visible because of the disturbance to the dew, look like
the wake of a vessel. While the visual elements in the scene – the dis-
appearing rails of the fence, the wispy wispy clouds – are attenuated,
the auditory elements are enhanced. Since "acoustic space implies
presence far more than does visual space," sounds heard outdoors at
night tend to "register in the imagination as presences" more than
visual particulars do (Ong 164). As the gurgling water of the
brook, which simultaneously creates and satisfies an insatiable thirst,
comes increasingly to dominate the consciousness of the observer,
the merging of inner and outer is completed. Natural and human circulation are felt to be identical; the outer becomes the amplification
of the inner.

This experience is about as intense and transporting as moments
of oneness with the natural world get in Thoreau's journal. For all
his tactics and strategy, for all his repeated concern to attain a higher,
expanded consciousness through sensory experience, the journal
describes very few experiences of an intensity that might be called
sublime. And in the last decade of his life, few if any moments comparable to the one that occurred in Baker's Orchard are recorded.
While Thoreau often gets warm, and sometimes hot, he rarely comes
to a boil.

   In attempting to explain this comparatively low energy level, commentators have called attention to two complicating factors in Thoreau's relationship to nature. One is his intense self-consciousness

and rigorous spiritual hygiene. "We are not wholly involved in Nature," he writes in the "Solitude" chapter of *Walden*: "By a conscious effort of the mind we can stand aloof from actions and their consequences." He was "sensible of a certain doubleness by which I can stand as remote from myself as from another. However intense my experience, I am conscious of the presence and criticism of a part of me, which, as it were, is not a part of me, but spectator, sharing no experience" (134–5). This self-consciousness was intensified by a strong sense of inner impurity (already instanced in his fastidiousness concerning touch and taste). As a young man, Thoreau found "an instinct in me conducting to a mystic spiritual life – and also another – to a primitive savage life." Years later, he made a not dissimilar observation: "After the era of youth is passed the knowledge of ourselves is an alloy that spoils our satisfactions ... What is this beauty in the Landscape but a certain fertility in me? I look in vain to see it realized but in my own life. If I could wholly cease to be ashamed of myself – I think that all my days would be fair" (*J ii 177; iii 124).

The other explanation calls attention to the resistance that the natural world offered to Thoreau's desires. The best-known example is the horrifying realization of nature's otherness that he experienced while descending Mount Katahdin in the Maine wilderness: "It is difficult to conceive of a country uninhabited by man ... And yet we have not seen nature unless we have once seen her thus vast and grim and drear ... for to be Vast is how near to being waste ... this was unhanselled and ancient Demonic Nature ... nature primitive – powerful gigantic aweful and beautiful, Untamed forever" (*J ii 277–8). But equally unsettling examples were found closer to home. Here, for example, is a passage in which Thoreau, like Wallace Stevens' Snow Man, is forced to have a mind of winter – to behold nothing that is not there and the nothing that is:

A cold & dark [November] afternoon the sun being behind clouds in the west The landscape is barren of objects – the trees being leafless – & so little light in the sky for variety. Such a day as will almost oblige a man to eat his own heart. A day in which you must hold on to life by your teeth ... what do the thoughts find to live on? What avails you now the fire you stole from heaven? ... Now is there nothing – not even the cold beauty of ice crystals – & snowy architecture. Nothing but the echo of your steps over the frozen ground no voice of birds – nor frogs ... The earth will not admit a spade. All fields lie fallow – Shall not your mind?   (*J iv 180–1)

Both self-consciousness and the stubbornness of natural facts are emphasized by Frederick Garber and James McIntosh in their studies

of Thoreau published during the 1970s. The former finds throughout
Thoreau's writings "differing and even contradictory assertions during the same period of time" that indicate "a stubborn, radical ambivalence in his sense of the world and himself" (103, 169). The latter
finds "programmed inconsistency," a "persistent self-qualification"
rooted in "his chief epistemological concern, the separation he felt
between mind and nature." Thoreau's "intermittent skepticism tends
to erode his faith in a combining imagination and prompts him to
look for truth in utter factuality" (11, 46, 128). It is well to remember,
however, that Garber and McIntosh both read Thoreau in the light of
the Hartman, de Man and Bloom revisionary reading of Wordsworth,
which stressed the antagonism between imagination and the natural
world and the drive of the former to overcome the latter. As a result,
these commentators might themselves be said to be programmatic in
pointing up a putative Thoreauvian equivocation.

The same might be said of Sharon Cameron's *Writing Nature: Henry
Thoreau's "Journal"* (1985), which presents Thoreau as a deconstruc-
tionist *avant la lettre*. For Cameron, the years 1850 to 1852 are crucial
because during that time Thoreau began to speculate "about a man's
relation to nature." In the journal, she contends, "the central Romantic
question – 'What is man's relation to the nature that he sees' – under-
goes drastic revision" (25, 11). The journal "proposes and subverts the
idea of correspondence. The whole of nature may be a metaphor
for the human mind, but Thoreau's formulations emphasize *failed*
attempts to make sense of the congruence." In the journal, "analogies
do not inaugurate connections between nature and the mind. They
rather call attention to the impossibility of such connection" (45, 46).
The copious naturalist detail in the journal's final phase was a "strategy for writing about nature that resists being symbolic." Metaphors
were frequently used "not to compare natural and human worlds, but
rather to expand the domain of the former, to insist on nature's infinite self-referentiality" (61, 13).

Where Cameron is deconstructive and de-idealizing, H. Daniel
Peck in *Thoreau's Morning Work* (1990) is recuperative and speaks of a
"redemptive purpose" at work in the journal. According to Peck, for
"the vertical design of Emerson's metaphysic" Thoreau substituted
"a 'horizontal' framework of perception" in which "the most characteristic object of vision is the relation between one feature of the
landscape and another." This "relational imagination" resulted in
analogies and correspondences different from what Emerson or the
younger Thoreau intended by the terms. The exhaustive cataloguing
and comparing of observations in the last phase was not the sign of
ebbing vitality. The late journal was "intensely systematic [but] not

mechanical"; it expressed "another kind of excitement: the drama of consolidation, of assembling the parts of the grand vision, of completing the picture of the world" (54, 88, 90).

Whose reading is more convincing, Cameron's or Peck's? One could equivocate, citing the former's observation that interpretation of an enormous work written over many years depends on the selection of quotations. But I am not persuaded by either reading, and believe there is a better explanatory context than the supersession of sympathizing by beholding, of vertical by horizontal. It is the Wordsworthian context that Thoreau himself repeatedly invokes in the journal. As Charles Anderson points out in *The Magic Circle of "Walden"*, Thoreau adopted the Intimations Ode as a kind of spiritual autobiography. The poem is used as a point of reference as early as 1841, when the young journal writer noted that "There is all the romance of my youthfullest moment in music. Heaven lies about us in our infancy," and as late as 1859 – the entry for 19 December on the subject of youth versus age is filled with echoes of the Ode (*J i 242; J xiii 35).

"There was a time," the first words of the Intimations Ode, were appropriated by Thoreau in a journal entry that speaks of the ravishing intensities of his early experience: "There was a time when the beauty and the music were all within, and I sat and listened to my thoughts, and there was a song in them ... I sat and listened by the hour to a positive though faint and distant music, not sung by any bird, nor vibrating any earthly harp. When you walked with a joy that knew not its own origin" (J vi 294). In his early twenties, Thoreau described his "fresh New England life" to be "as novel as green peas. The dew hangs everywhere upon the grass – and I breathe the rich damp air in slices." He had no doubt that "joy is the condition of life"; even in autumn he was "sensible of a wholly new life – which no man has lived. My faith is fed by the yellow leaf" (*J i 317, 167; ii 51). In "those youthful days," he later recalled, "the walker does not too curiously observe particulars, but sees, hears, scents, tastes, and feels only himself, – the phenomena that show themselves to him, – his expanding body, his intellect and heart. No worm or insect, quadruped or bird, confined his view, but the unbounded universe was his" (J v 75).

Nature seemed to develop as he developed and to grow up with him:

My life was extacy. In youth before I lost any of my senses – I can remember that I was all alive – and inhabited my body with inexpressible satisfaction, both its weariness & its refreshment were sweet to me. This earth was the most glorious musical instrument, and I was audience to its strains. To have such sweet impressions made on us – such extacies begotten of the breezes. I can remember how I was astonished. I said to myself – I said to others– There comes into my mind or soul an indescribable infinite all absorbing divine heavenly pleasure, a sense of elevation & expansion … This is a pleasure, a joy, an existence which I have not procured myself– I speak as a witness on the stand and tell what I have perceived.   (*J iii 305–6)

But as he grew older, Thoreau gradually ceased to be attended by this splendid vision; it eventually faded into the light of common day: "Methinks my present experience is nothing my past experience is all in all. I think that no experience which I have today comes up to or is comparable with the experiences of my boyhood– And not only this is true – but as far back as I can remember I have unconsciously referred to the experience of a previous state of existence. 'Our life is a forgetting' &c" (*J iii 305–6). The first sentence of this passage recalls "Tintern Abbey" ("For nature then … To me was all in all"). Its last phrase cites the fifth section of the Intimations Ode, which uses as a poetic postulate the Platonic myth of recollection of a previous existence. But no more than Wordsworth does Thoreau actually believe that childhood recollection of pre-existence is the explanation of the perceptual intensities of early life and fading recollection the explanation of their subsequent diminution. The reason, for which the journal provides abundant evidence, is that with the passage of time there was a weakening of Thoreau's sensory and perceptual powers.

"What is called genius," Thoreau observed in 1852, "is the abundance of life or health, so that whatever addresses the senses … each sight and sound and scent and flavor, – intoxicates with a healthy intoxication" (J iv 218–19). In 1841, he speculated that "We may grow old with the vigor of youth. Are we not always in youth so long as we face heaven. We may always live in the morning of our days" (*J i 258). Ten years later, similar speculations had become more negatively phrased: "Why should we not still continue to live with the intensity & rapidity of infants. Is not the world – are not the heavens as unfathomed as ever? Have we exhausted any joy – any sentiment?" And later in the same year a distinctly pathetic note was struck: "Remember thy creator in the days of thy youth. i.e. Lay up a store of natural influences – sing while you may before the evil days come – he that hath ears let him hear – see – hear – smell – taste – &c while these senses are fresh & pure" (*J iii 194, 323).

For Thoreau, the feeling of immortality was peculiar to the season of youth. It seemed that "at a very early age – the mind of man – perhaps at the same time with his body, ceases to be elastic … It is the transition from poetry to prose" (*J iv 265–6). And with age came a growing recognition of the difference between the human life cycle and the cycle of nature: "What means this *tragical* change which has no counterpart in nature – but is confined to the life of man – from infancy to youth – from youth to manhood – from manhood to age – while nature changes not and is never more than one year old" (*J ii 378).

In December 1851, Thoreau observed a large hawk circling the pine wood below him. In a paragraph of what he rightly called "Coleridgean thoughts," he apprehended this natural fact as a symbol of his "flights of imagination":

It flies not directly whither it is bound but advances by circles ... But the majesty is in the imagination of the beholder for the bird is intent on its prey ... It rises higher above where I stand and I see with beautiful distinctness its wings against the sky ... its inner wings within the outer – like a great moth seen against the sky. A Will-o-'the-wind. Following its path as it were through the vortices of the air. the poetry of motion – not as preferring one place to another but enjoying each as long as possible. Most gracefully so surveys new scenes & revisits the old. As if that hawk were made to be the symbol of my thought how bravely he came round over those parts of the wood which he had not surveyed – taking in new segment.– annexing new territories.   (*J iv 210–11)

But this passage is more in the nature of an envoi to symbolic perception than an celebration of it. By 1851, an elegiac quality is noticeable in the reflective passages of Thoreau's journal: in September, as in the feelings of an older man, "the year is already past and [a man] looks forward to the coming winter. His occasional rejuvenescence & faith in the current time is like the aftermath of a scanty crop ... The period of youth is past." And in April of the following year he lamented: "Too late now for the morning influence & inspiration.– The birds sing not so earnestly & joyously – there is a blurring ripple on the surface of the lake ... Once I was part and parcel of nature – now I am observant of her" (*J iv 62, 416).

Against this background, can there be any doubt what Thoreau really meant when he declared in 1854 that "We soon get through with nature. She excites an expectation which she cannot satisfy" (J vi 293)? The cause of the non-fulfillment of expectation was not in the natural world but in Thoreau – as he came to realize later in the same journal entry: "How many springs shall I continue to see the common sucker ... floating dead on our river! Will not Nature select her types from a new fount? The vignette of the year. This earth which is spread out like a map around me is but the lining of my inmost soul exposed. In me is the sucker that I see. No wholly extraneous object can compel me to recognize it. I am guilty of suckers" (J vi 294).

This passage anticipates Whitman's 1860 poem, "As I Ebb'd with the Ocean of Life": seeking natural facts that can be perceived as types or symbols of sustaining spiritual facts, both men find only watery refuse suggestive of the psychological detritus within themselves. The key antecedent text for both the Thoreau of 1854 and the Whitman of 1860 is Coleridge's "Dejection: An Ode" (the poem is alluded to by Thoreau in the only sentence in *Walden* to occur twice – as title-page epigraph and in the second chapter). Like Coleridge, Thoreau and Whitman "may not hope from outward forms to win/The passion and the life, whose fountains are within."

Thoreau knew that "he is the richest who has most use for nature as raw material of tropes and symbols with which to describe his life":

If these gates of golden willows affect me, they correspond to the beauty and promise of some experience on which I am entering. If I am overflowing with life, am rich in experience for which I lack expression, then nature will be my language full of poetry, – all nature will *fable*, and every natural phenomenon be a myth. The man of science, who is not seeking for expression but for a fact to be expressed merely, studies nature as a dead language. I pray for such inward experience as will make nature significant.   (*J* v 134–5)

But to whom or to what could Thoreau pray? What power could stop the aging process, restore elasticity, and make nature once again significant? He could remind himself to "Improve the opportunity to draw analogies. There are innumerable avenues to a perception of the truth … All perception of truth is the detection of an analogy.– we reason from our hands to our head" (**J* iv 41, 46). But knowing the paths to poetic truth was not the same as being able to traverse them.

In 1841, Thoreau drank in "a wonderful health" from the "rare soundness" of cow-bells and other natural sounds; ten years later, similar sounds "only remind me that they once said something to me, and are so by association interesting. I go forth to be reminded of a previous state of existence, if perchance any memento of it is to be met with hereabouts" (**J* i 277; iii 303). One year after he had heard ravishing intimations in the vibration of the telegraph-wire, this natural fact had lost its higher suggestiveness and become a type of inner deterioration: "I have scarcely heard one strain from the telegraph harp this season. Its strings are rusted and slackened, relaxed, and now no more it encourages the walker. I miss it much. So it is with all sublunary things. Every poet's lyre loses its tension. It cannot bear the alternate contraction and expansion of the seasons" (*J* iv 206). Even the sound of crickets, which had long been particularly evocative for Thoreau, was losing its magic. He did not cease to be drawn to the sound, but his interest was becoming scientific rather than Romantic. Through close observation, he discovered what made the crickets' sound so suggestive: it always retreated as he advanced and thus always came from a comparative distance: "Those nearest me continually cease their song as I walk so that the singers are always a rod distant" (*J iii 381). The something-evermore-about-to-be quality of the sound was thus explained. But the discovery was the result of careful observation, not of a sauntering of the ear. In Emily Dickinson's figure, it was like splitting the lark in order to find the music.

As early as 1843, Thoreau had wondered: "When nature ceases to be supernatural to a man – what will he do then? Of what worth is human life – if its actions are no longer to have this sublime and unexplored scenery?" (*J i 481). This was precisely the question addressed by Wordsworth in the closing sections of the Intimations Ode. One of his two answers is the recompense of memory: the recovery of a felt contact with "what was so fugitive," with the something living "in our embers." For Wordsworth, the thoughts of past years bring a "perpetual benediction." But Thoreau found nothing renovating or sustaining about his memories. There was only regret and nostalgia: "Ah that life that I have known!" he wrote in 1851: "How hard it is to remember what is most memorable! We remember how we itched, not how our hearts beat. I can sometimes recall to mind the quality the immortality of my youthful life – but in memory is the only relation to it." And in the following year, he wondered: "Does nothing withstand the inevitable march of time? Why did I not use my eyes when I stood on Pisgah? Now I hear those strains but seldom– My rhythmical mood does not endure– I cannot draw from it – & return to it in my thought as to a well ... Ah sweet ineffable reminiscences" (*J iii 251–2; iv 281–2).

The other Wordsworthian compensation is the replacement of the natural bond by a human bond: the soothing thoughts that spring out of human suffering; "the clouds that gather round the setting sun" (like loved ones around a deathbed) taking "a sober coloring" from an eye that hath kept watch on man's mortality. Given Thoreau's prickliness, his difficulties with friendship, his misogynist traits, and his intensely self-centered preoccupation with purity, one hardly expects to find in the journal this Wordsworthian mitigation. Thoreau's parenthetical allusion (cited above) to "Wordsworth's obs. on relaxed attention" is telling. It refers to a passage in the story of Margaret in the first book of *The Excursion* (606–19), in which the narrator describes an aspect of the psychological dynamics of his intense emotional response to "a common tale,/An ordinary sorrow of man's life,/A tale of silent suffering" (636–8). In contrast, Thoreau's concern is not with human suffering but with the best state of consciousness in which to engage the natural world.

Eventually, Thoreau came to suspect that he might be "too cold for human friendship" and that this deficiency was connected with the ruling passion of his life: "It appears to be a law that you cannot have a deep sympathy with both man & nature. Those qualities which bring you near to the one estrange you from the other" (*J iv 435). One thinks not of Wordsworth but of Wallace Stevens: "Life is an affair of people not of places. But for me life is an affair of places and that is the trouble" (Opus Posthumous 185).

If neither the past nor the human present offered abundant recompense, perhaps the future might. Occasionally in the journal there is a hopeful yearning for "a place far away – yet actual and where we have been ... reinspiring me with all the dreams of my youth." And at least once Thoreau allowed himself to wonder if "our serene moments" were "foretastes of heavenly joys gratuitously vouchsafed to us as a consolation" rather than "simply a transient realization of what might be the whole tenor of our lives" (*J iii 148, 274). But recognition of the need to live in the present remained dominant, despite the disturbing implications of a remarkable dream-like experience he had one morning in 1851. As Thoreau awakened, he seemed to vibrate to the dying strain of a musical instrument that was his own body. But with "an infinite regret" he awoke to "find myself not the thoroughfare of glorious & world-stirring inspirations – but a scuttle full of dirt – such a thoroughfare only as the street & the kennel – where perchance the wind may sometimes draw forth a strain of music from a straw" (*J iv 155).

In his later years, one sensory instrument was of sustaining value to Thoreau: his eyes. The journal for 1851 and 1852 has abundant evidence that Romantic perception of the natural world was being superseded by a different kind of perception, which was predominantly visual. (This is also noted by both Cameron and Peck.) It was as Thoreau feared it would be: "the character of my knowledge is from year to year becoming more distinct & scientific– That in exchange for views as wide as heaven's cope I am being narrowed down to the field of a microscope– I see details not wholes nor the shadow of the whole" (*J iii 380). This narrowing had a dual issue: scientific or naturalist perception on the one hand; aesthetic perception on the other. An epitome of each visual mode is found in a late essay worked up from journal material: "The Succession of Forest Trees" (1860), which is Thoreau's principal contribution to environmental studies; and

"Autumnal Tints" (1862), which is concerned with helping others to a greater appreciation of the beauty of the October foliage. In both essays there is something necessarily different from a sauntering of the eye. "It is impossible," he wrote in 1852, "for the same person to see things from the poet's point of view and that of the man of science." Some men were born with a scientific "condition of mind"; others arrived at that condition "in middle age by the decay of their poetic faculties" (*J iv 356–7). As Thoreau explains in "Autumnal Tints": "In my botanical rambles … the idea, or image, of a plant occupies my thoughts … and for some weeks or months I go thinking of it, and expecting it, unconsciously, and at length I surely see it." It requires "different intentions of the eye and of the mind to attend to different departments of knowledge! How differently the poet and the nauralist look at objects" (*Essays* 255).

Thoreau's eyesight remained acute and there are many striking visual notations in the late journal: "the cool juicy pickled cucumber green of the potatoe fields" in the July moonlight; in September, "the intense brilliancy of the red-ripe maples scattered here and there in the midst of the green oaks & hickories [was] quite charming"; a winter morning was "the time to see the woods & shrubs in their perfection wearing their snowy & frosty dress"; in the same season, pitch pines on a distant hill-side held the snow so finely that they made "the most cheerful winter scenery [when] beheld from the window" (*J iii 295; iv 111, 207, 313). One April he was delighted by "the perception of a new natural fact": when he was directly opposite the sun that was shining on a clump of dwarf Andromeda, the leaves that had previously been a greyish brown were lit up and became a "charming warm … *Indian* red color – the mellowest the ripest-red imbrowned color … It is a very interesting piece of magic" (*J iv 471, 462). And in August of 1860, while he was paddling on Walden Pond, a sudden blaze of the setting sun lit up the green leaves on the eastern shore at the same time as the sun's reflection on the water lit up the under side of the same leaves. In this double light, "the most vivid and varied shades of green were revealed. I never saw such a green *glow* before" (*J* xiv 65).

Intense looking sustained Thoreau until the end. The final entry in the journal, made in November 1861, closes with the reflection: "All this is perfectly distinct to an observant eye, and yet could easily pass unnoticed by most" (*J* xiv 346). Four years earlier, he had written the following:

The regular phenomena of the seasons get at last to be – they were *at first*, of course – simply and plainly phenomena or phases of my life. The seasons and all their changes are in me. I see not a dead eel or floating snake, or a gull,

but it rounds my life and is like a line or accent in its poem. Almost I believe
the Concord would not rise and overflow its banks again, were I not here.
After a while I learn what my moods and seasons are. I would have nothing
subtracted. I can imagine nothing added. My moods are thus periodical, not
two days in my year alike. The perfect correspondence of Nature to man, so
that he is at home in her!   (*J* x 127)

The human perceiver of this natural setting resembles Wordsworth's
leech-gatherer, a figure of resignation and endurance, more than it
does Cameron's incessant interrogator or Peck's relational redeemer.
At first, that is, during childhood, before the advent of self-
consciousness and reflection, natural phenomena and their periodical phases were all in all to Thoreau and seemed coextensive with
the phases of his life. Now, in later life, they seem so again. In the
time between, brooks and rivers had been one of Thoreau's master
tropes for the one life and for the possibility of fulfillment: "The life
in us is like the water in the river," he had written in 1850: "it may
rise this year higher than ever it was known to before and flood the
uplands – even this may be the eventful year – & drown out all our
muskrats" (*J iii 84). But in 1857, the figure of the rising water level is
not a symbol of spiritual possibility but an hyperbole indicating the
degree to which Thoreau is at home in the natural given, wishing
nothing added or subtracted. There is correspondence; but it is as between two objects – or two subjects, each of which writes the other,
the one using words, the other dead eels, floating snakes, and gulls.

SEVEN

Whitman: The Feeling of Health

"In health," Thoreau notes in his journal, "all the senses are indulged and each seeks its own gratification.– it is a pleasure to see, and to walk, and to hear – &c" (*J i 204). Walt Whitman agreed: in health, "the whole body is elevated to a state by others unknown – inwardly and outwardly illuminated, purified, made solid, strong, yet bouyant … there is no more borrowing trouble in advance. A man realizes the venerable myth – he is a god walking the earth, he sees new eligibilities, powers and beauties everywhere; he himself has a new eyesight and hearing … Merely *to move* is then a happiness, a pleasure" (1272–3). With Whitman, as with Coleridge and Thoreau, physical health and imaginative power are closely connected. At the beginning of *Song of Myself* (post-1855 version), he describes himself as "now thirty-seven years old in perfect health." In section 50 of the same poem he is at a loss for words to describe the "something" that he feels working within himself that "is not chaos or death … it is eternal life … it is happiness." Whatever the something is, it is clear that its enabling condition is physical health.[1]

One could even argue that the sprawling shapelessness of *Song of Myself* is itself the result of the poet's robust physical health. An entry in Thoreau's journal for 1841 uncannily anticipates both the content of Whitman's poem and the way it conducts itself: "there are times when we feel a vigor in our limbs – and our thoughts are like a flowing morning light … And if we were to sing at such an hour, There would be no catastrophe contemplated in our verse – no tragic element in it … It is epic without beginning or end – an eternal interlude without plot.– not subordinate one part to another, but supreme as a whole – at once – leaf and flower – and fruit" (*J i 331).

The "feeling of health" (#2) is not only a presupposition of *Song of Myself*; it is also a principal subject of the poem. In a notebook entry from the time, Whitman jotted down the idea for a "poem in which is minutely described the whole particulars and ensemble of a *first-rate healthy Human Body* – it looked into and through, as if it were transparent and of pure glass" (*Notebooks* 304). He does not seem to have composed such a poem; but *Song of Myself* has elements of it, as does another 1855 poem, "I Sing the Body Electric." In *Song of Myself*, the principal indicator of good health is sensory acuity. The notation of visual images is as sharp as in "There Was a Child Went Forth." Acute aural registrations range from natural sounds ("the katydid work[ing] her chromatic reed on the walnut-tree over the well" [#33]), through natural cum domestic ("the bravuras of birds....the bustle of growing wheat....gossip of flames....clack of sticks cooking my meals" [#26]); to urban noise ("The blab of the pave....the tires of carts and sluff of bootsoles....the clank of the shod horses on the granite floor" [#8]).

There is also abundant evidence that Whitman had a sharp and discriminating sense of smell, which remained acute even into later life. The natural descriptions in *Specimen Days* (1882), for example, often include olfactory notations. In one of them Whitman notes that "there is a scent to everything, even the snow, if you can only detect it – no two places, hardly any two hours, anywhere, exactly alike. How different the odor of noon from midnight, or winter from summer, or a windy spell from a still one" (876). In *Song of Myself*, as later, it is predominantly natural scents in which Whitman delights: "The sniff of green leaves and dry leaves, and of the shore and darkcolored sea-rocks, and of the hay in the barn" (#2); "the white roses sweet-scented and growing" (#49); "Delicate sniffs of the seabreeze....smells of sedgy grass and fields by the shore" (#36); even "The scent of these arm-pits," which is pronounced "aroma finer than prayer" (#24).

The few discrete images of taste are in the main a function of touch, the most conspicuously indulged sense in the poems of 1855–6. In a draft section of *Song of Myself*, the other senses are described as "emulous" to become as intensely feeling as touch: "Every one must be a touch. – /Or else she will ... nibble only at the edges of feeling ... Each brings the best she has,/For each is in love with touch." Touch is not only the most intense and immediate of the senses; it is even said to subsume the others:

> A touch now reads me a library of knowledge in an instant,
> It smells for me the fragrance of wine and lemon-blows,
> It tastes for me ripe strawberries and melons. –

It talks for me with a tongue of its own,
It finds an ear wherever it rests or taps,
It brings the rest around it ...   (*Notebooks* 75–6)

The sense of touch was not present in "There Was a Child," for reasons explained in chapter 1; but it is overwhelmingly present in the central 1855 poem, *Song of Myself*. Whitman is here "the caresser of life wherever moving" (#13): "the press of my foot to the earth springs a hundred affections" (#14); "Divine am I inside and out, and I make holy whatever I touch or am touched from" (#24). "Mine is no callous shell," he boasts in what has been called the "outstanding understatement in American poetry" (Rosenthal and Gall 37):

> I have instant conductors all over me whether I pass or stop,
> They seize every object and lead it harmlessly through me.

> I merely stir, press, feel with my fingers, and am happy,
> To touch my person to some one else's is about as much
>   as I can stand.   (#27)

In trying to account for this extraordinary degree of haptic sensitivity, Roger Asselineau suggests that Whitman had "a hyperesthesia of all the senses, particularly that of touch ... which is perhaps connected with the repression of his sexual instincts. He appears constantly to feel the need of rubbing himself, in his imagination, against things and against people, probably because he could not satisfy his desires otherwise"; the fable of the woman and the twenty-eight bathers in section 11 of *Song of Myself* is "a case of repression which probably was a mere transposition of his own" (13, 277n). Asselineau has a point – if it is qualified by noting that some passages celebrate the satisfaction (at least the auto-erotic satisfaction) of his desires, and that touch is presented more than once as a redemptive force. Such speculation, however, is ultimately reductive and detracts attention from the great haptic delicacy and comprehensiveness of *Song of Myself*.

In his *Notebooks*, Coleridge distinguishes several gradations in the intensity of this sensory mode. The last three in ascending order are: (*a*) "retentive power extinguishing the sense of touch, or making it mere feeling"; for example, "The Hand grasping firmly an inanimate Body – that is the one extreme of this." (*b*) touch with "retentive power"; for example, the "Lips, or the thumb and forefinger in a slight pressure." (*c*) "Touch with the sense of immediate power"; for example, "mem. vi/Riley. in acts of Es*sex*"; that is, the *membrum virile* – the phallus (i #2399). Another notebook entry elaborates on this: the erect penis is "the mutually assimilant Junction" of "*Love* & Lust"; "the vital & personal linked to & combined with the external." The passage continues (the reference seems clearly to be to the phallus): "an organ acting with what intensity of personal Life/ compare it with the Eye & Ear/then at a less distance with the Smell, still less with the Taste/less still with the diffused or concentered Touch/yet at what a distance from all these" (i #1822). In other entries Coleridge speaks of "the influence of bodily vigor and strong Grasp of Touch in facilitating the passion of Hope" (ii #2398), and of the "co-adunation [unifying] of Feeling & Sensation [as] the specific character of the sexual Pleasure: and that which renders this particular mode of bodily intercourse the apt outward Sign, Symbol, & sensuous Language of the union desired & commenced by the *Souls* of sincere Lovers" (ii #3605).[2]

Loosely using Coleridge's framework, one can sketch a qualitative typology of touch in *Song of Myself*. (*a*) *Mere feeling*: "each man and each woman of you I lead upon a knoll,/My left hand hooks you round the waist … If you tire … rest the chuff of your hand on my hip" (#46); the hand of the *accoucheur* "pressing receiving supporting" the woman during childbirth (#49). (*b*) *Touch with retentive power*: "A few light kisses….a few embraces….a reaching around of arms" (#2); "the press of a bashful hand … the touch of my lips to yours" (#19); feeling the arms of young men "on my neck as I stood, or the negligent leaning of their flesh against me as I sat" ("Crossing Brooklyn Ferry"); "to be surrounded by beautiful curious breathing laughing flesh is enough,/To pass among them..to touch any one….to rest my arm ever so lightly round his or her neck for a moment … I do not ask any more delight" ("I Sing the Body Electric").

(*c*) *Touch with immediate power*: this category divides into two parts. In the first, the *erotic*, most of the examples are instances of passive touch, of being touched rather than touching. They include "The souse upon me of my lover the sea, as I lie willing and naked" ("Bunch Poem"); lovers "Crowding my lips, and thick on the pores of my skin … Bussing my body with soft and balsamic busses" (#45); or the "curious roamer, the hand, roaming all over the body – the bashful withdrawing of flesh where the fingers soothingly pause and edge themselves" – one place of this haptic reconnaissance being "The sensitive, orbic, underlapped brothers, that only privileged feelers may be intimate where they are" ("Bunch Poem").

The second is the *phallic*. The *membrum virile* or "phallic thumb of love" ("Bunch Poem") is the dominant organ in the most extraordinary passage in *Song of Myself* (#26–29). Section 27 emphasizes the speaker's extreme haptic sensitivity and the primacy of touch in his sensorium, and stresses the importance of tactile interaction in breaking down the barriers between subject and object, self and external world: "To be in any form, what is that?/If nothing lay more developed the quahaug [a large clam] and his callous shell were enough." In the preceding section, Whitman began by announcing that he would do nothing but listen. The ensuing aural catalogue commenced with natural and domestic sounds; then came urban sounds that grew louder; and finally musical sounds with strong emotional, then erotic, pulls: "the trained soprano ... convulses me like the climax of my love-grip"; the orchestra "wrenches unnamable ardors from my breast." The vocal and orchestral music intensifies tactile sensitivity until their sounds transmogrify into an engulfing oceanic feeling: "It sails me....I dab with bare feet....they are licked by the indolent waves" (as in sections 21–22, immersion in the sea is a figure for the dominance of touch). Finally, the immersion is total: "I am ... Steeped amid honeyed morphine....my windpipe squeezed in the fakes [coils of a rope] of death." "Is it then a touch," section 28 begins,

> quivering me to a new identity,
> Flames and ether making a rush for my veins,
> Treacherous tip of me reaching and crowding to help them.
> My flesh and blood playing out lightning, to strike what is hardly
>   different from myself.
> On all sides prurient provokers stiffening my limbs,
> Straining the udder of my heart for its withheld drip,
> Behaving licentious toward me, taking no denial,
> Depriving me of my best as for a purpose,
> Unbuttoning my clothes and holding me by the bare waist,
> Deluding my confusion with the calm of the sunlight and pasture
>   fields.

There follows an extraordinary sequence full of obscure associations and displacements as inner and outer merge and consciousness becomes tactile. The "fellow-senses," having initially acted as "prurient provokers" of quivering arousal, become recessive; they are "bribed to swap off with touch, and go and graze at the edges of me." In a manuscript reading, they have "left me helpless to the torrent of touch" (*Notebooks* 76). The torrent is clearly sexual and culminates in orgasm. But what exactly is going on? Is it consensual sodomy, as Robert K. Martin seems to think? Is it anal rape, as Karl Keller conjectures? Or fellatio, as manuscript readings perhaps suggest? Or is it masturbation, as most commentators think? A reading of the figures in sensory terms is helpful. The grazing herd, the sentries who have deserted "every other part of me," and "the traitors" are all figurations of the other senses. Flames and ether rushing into the body while lightning is "playing out" from the flesh and blood suggests the conflation or merging of active and passive touch. The phallus is the "headland" by metaphor; by metonomy, it is the "red marauder" (it is engorged with blood). "I went myself first to the headland....my own hands carried me there": this surely suggests an auto-erotic act.

The passage reaches its orgasmic climax when "villain touch" – "Blind loving wrestling touch" – unclenches its floodgates. Section 29 beautifully adumbrates the orgasmic expansion of consciousness:

> Parting tracked by arriving....perpetual payment of the perpetual loan,
> Rich showering rain, and recompense richer afterward.
>
> Sprouts take and accumulate....stand by the curb prolific and vital,
> Landscapes projected masculine full-sized and golden.

The compensatory ebb-and-flow figures in the first distich suggest in the first instance the tumescent-detumescent rhythm of phallic touch; but they also recall the "respiration and inspiration" of the poet's lungs and the systole and diastole of the beating of his heart celebrated in section 2. These are all synecdochal figurations of the poet's indefatigably curious self – "Partaker of influx and efflux" (#22) – whose subject matter is "the thrust and withdrawal, the heightening and declining, the flowing and ebbing of his psychic and creative energy" (Lewis 5) as well as of his sexual energy. The second distich associates this rhythm with the natural cycle – harvest abundance after germinating rain. The urban herbage at the curbside metonymically evokes a rural landscape of fully ripened wheat; and the masculine thrust of its stalks in turn recalls the orgasmic bounty – the semen or seed – just poured out. In short, section 29 offers a condensed epitome of what Emerson called that "great principle of Undulation in nature, that shows itself in the inspiring and expiring of the breath; in desire and satiety; in the ebb and flow of the sea; in day and night ..." (62).

Sections 26–9 are one of two places in *Song of Myself* in which an allusively described sexual act triggers visionary experience. The other is found in the fifth section, but here the experience is sweetly transporting, not roughly destabilizing. In Coleridge's terms, it is more loving than lustful and thus meta-phallic: touch facilitating the passion of hope – an outward sign of spiritual union.

> Loafe with me on the grass....loose the stop from your throat,
> Not words, not music or rhyme I want....not custom or lecture, not
>   even the best,
> Only the lull I like, only the hum of your valved voice.

I mind how we lay in June, such a transparent summer morning;
You settled your head athwart my hips and gently turned over upon
     me,
And parted my shirt from my bosom-bone, and plunged your tongue
     to my barestript heart,
And reached till you felt my beard, and reached till you held my feet.

Swiftly arose and spread around me the peace and joy and knowledge
     that pass all the art and argument of the earth;
And I know that the hand of God is the elderhand of my own,
And I know that the spirit of God is the eldest brother of my own,
And that all the men ever born are also my brothers....and the women
     my sisters and lovers,
And that a kelson of the creation is love;
And limitless are leaves stiff or drooping in the fields,
And brown ants in the little wells beneath them,
And mossy scabs by the wormfence, and heaped stones, and elder and
     mullen and pokeweed.

As in sections 26–9, rhythmic sounds – here a lulling hum like "the murmur of yearning" in section 19 – initiate a shift in sensory dominance. Lying on the ground diminishes the power of the eye and in other ways leads to a loosening of the sensory stays; as the other senses recede, touch becomes dominant. It is unclear what precisely transpires when the tongue and the hands of the "you" take over. Fellatio would be not a bad guess; for one thing, "orality links vocal and sexual activity" (Nathanson 132). But the important point is that this is an instance of what Allen Ginsberg calls "friendly touch" (238). Section 5 has nothing convulsive, prurient, marauding, or predatory.

The expansion of consciousness experienced on this transparent summer morning has been compared to Emerson's "transparent eyeball" experience. But Whitman's is grounded in touch rather than in sight. The part or particle of God that he becomes is figured by his hand, not his eyeball; and it is not the visual organ that is reflected in the "leaves stiff or drooping in the fields." The onset of transparency – the fusion of inner and outer – is signalled by the shift from the past to the present tense ("And I know …"). The speaker enters a visionary, trans-temporal and trans-spatial *now* in which inner and outer perfectly mirror each other: "This is the far-off depth and height reflecting my own face," as Whitman puts it in a later section, "This is the thoughtful merge of myself and the outlet again" (#19). The last three lines describe the outlet. As visionary expansion begins to contract, sight once again becomes dominant: "limitless" is succeeded by the visual limit of what the recumbent speaker can see. What is visible is the opposite of cosmic: tiny ants and their miniature craters, mossy scabs, stones, and common weeds. But in the afterglow of his visionary experience of cosmic love, nothing is marginalized; even the weeds by the fence are lovingly particularized. They are not the phallic "sprouts … prolific and vital" of section 29, but both are woven out of the same "hopeful green stuff" as the grass that the questioning child brings the poet in the following section.

In his preface to the first edition of *Leaves of Grass*, Whitman observes that "folks expect of the poet to indicate more than the beauty and dignity which always attach to dumb real objects.…they expect him to indicate the path between reality and their souls." In discovering this path, the dominant organ of perception is not touch but sight: the "greatest poet … is a seer … the other senses corroborate themselves, but [eyesight] is removed from any proof but its own and foreruns the identities of the spiritual world" (10). Put more simply, in *Song of Myself*, "the unseen is proved by the seen" (#3).

At the center of the concern with the unseen spiritual world was the question of life after death. One poem in the 1855 edition is entirely devoted to the subject. "To Think of Time" is a meditation on temporality – on what de Man calls an authentically human destiny:

> To think of today..and the ages continued henceforward.
> Have you guessed you yourself would not continue? Have you dreaded
>   those earth-beetles?
> Have you feared the future would be nothing to you?

The poem is unsatisfactory both formally and conceptually because it breaks in two. The felt awareness of mortality is powerfully evoked in the first five sections, especially in the description of the December funeral of a stage driver. But in the sixth stanza, somber meditation abruptly gives way to assertive optimism: "What will be will be well – for what is is well … You are not thrown to the winds..you gather certainly and safely around yourself,/Yourself! Yourself! Yourself forever and ever." You were not born to be diffused but to receive identity and having received it you are "henceforth secure, whatever comes or goes"; the pattern or law is "systematic" and "eternal."

What gives rise to these assertions is simply that it is too awful to think otherwise: "We cannot be stopped at a given point.…that is no satisfaction … We must have the indestructible breed of the best, regardless of time." Once uttered, Whitman attempts to bolster these assertions by circular reasoning: if he were to "suspect death I should die now,/Do you think I could walk pleasantly and well-suited toward annihilation?" But he does walk pleasantly and well-suited and therefore, although he cannot define his destination, he knows that it must be good.

That Whitman was himself dissatisfied with these formulations is suggested by his return to the subject the next year in the masterpiece of the 1856 edition, "Crossing Brooklyn Ferry." In this poem, he adapted to his particular concern with future existence the form that M.H. Abrams denominated the greater Romantic lyric.[3] As in a number of earlier poems of this type, Coleridge's "This Lime-Tree Bower" and "Frost at Midnight" for example, symbolic perception (the relation of natural facts to spiritual facts) is the *sine qua non* of "Crossing Brooklyn Ferry." The natural facts are the particulars of the physical setting – what is seen while crossing by ferry from Brooklyn to Manhattan. These are evoked in the third section's composite panorama: the December seagulls high in the air, seeming to float with motionless wings; the reflection of the summer sky; "the fine centrifugal spokes of light round the shape of my head in the sunlit water"; the schooners, sloops, barges, steamers, lighters, steam-tugs, and hay-boats; the scalloped-edged waves in the twilight; "the fires from the foundry chimneys burning high and glaringly into the night."

The other subject is spiritual facts: "The impalpable sustenence of me from all things ... the well-join'd scheme, myself disintegrated, every one disintegrated yet part of the scheme ... The others that are to follow me, the ties between me and them." The goal of "Crossing Brooklyn Ferry" is to establish a connection between the two sets of facts. The poem's principal strategy is to address a "you" – not a "you" living in present time as in "To Think of Time" and *Song of Myself*, but a "you" living in the future – "Fifty years hence ... A hundred years hence, or ever so many hundred years hence" – who in crossing from Brooklyn to Manhattan will enjoy the very same perceptual experiences, "The glories strung like beads on my smallest sights and hearings," that Whitman did in 1856.

In the course of the poem intimacy between the present "I" and future "you" increases. In the third section, the speaker softly assures his auditor that time and space are of no avail in separating them: "I am with you" in the sense that, in looking at river and sky, in being part of a living crowd, "you" are experiencing exactly what "I" experienced. The word used to describe this degree of analogical intimacy is "similitudes" – "Just as you feel ... so I felt"; "just as you are refresh'd ... I was refresh'd." In sections 5 and 6, a more intimate connection is suggested: both "I" and "you" have felt "the curious abrupt questionings stir within." These curious feelings or "dark patches" include doubts about achievement ("The best I had done seem'd to me blank and suspicious"); "the old knot of contrariety" (a variety of moral and emotional failings); and erotic longings. In the next section, recognition of these shared intimate feelings is said to have brought speaker and addressee "closer yet."

In section 8, the speaker briefly recapitulates the perceptual similitudes of the natural setting, using the grasping of hands and being called by his "nighest name" as figures for the inner congruences. Then – it is the poem's climactic moment in more ways than one – the object of the loving embrace becomes the future "you": "What is more subtle than this," the speaker asks, "Which fuses me into you now, and pours my meaning into you?" Now there is no more "I" and "you"; there is "we":

> We understand then do we not?
> What I promis'd without mentioning it, have you not accepted?
> What the study could not teach – what the preaching could not
>   accomplish is accomplish'd, is it not?

What exactly had been promised? and what is it that can be said to have been accomplished? One key to understanding the speaker's assertion is the shift in addressee in the poem's closing section. Here the "you" is no longer the future reader of the poem: "you" are the natural facts of the physical scene – the "dumb beautiful ministers" whom "we" directly address. The section opens with a second panoramic description of the physical scene – only this time a celebratory imperative present replaces the earlier past indicative. As in Coleridge's "This Lime-Tree Bower," the change marks the shift from ordinary to visionary perception – from outlooker to participatory consciousness. What is celebrated is the fluid merging of inner and outer. The visual particulars of the scene are no longer individual glories hung on the speaker's higher senses; they are now figured as a "necessary film … envelop[ing] the soul." In another image registering the same supersession of sight by feeling/touch, the whole of the spatio-temporal continuum of "Crossing Brooklyn Ferry" is figured as an "eternal float of solution." This trope refers back to the cryptic last lines of the fifth section:

> I too had been struck from the float forever held in solution,
> I too had receiv'd identity by my body,
> That I was I knew was of my body, and what I should be I knew I should
>   be of my body.

To be struck from the float is to be born, to assume individual human form and substance. To die is to become "disintegrated"; this happens to "every one," yet every one remains "part of the scheme." Thus, there can be contact between present "I" and future "you"; indeed, such felt contact is the evidence of the existence of the "float."

Thus, by the final section the speaker has in some psychologically satisfying way come to affirm his continued future existence by means of the natural facts, the "dumb beautiful ministers" that "furnish your parts toward eternity." What is said is beautifully expressed, but what precisely is being affirmed is far from clear. The asserted relationship of natural facts to spiritual facts is not the similitude of tenor and vehicle as in simile, metaphor, and the Swedenborgian system of correspondences in which the visible is the dial-plate of the invisible. Nor is the relationship metonymic – the graduated contiguity of part to whole as with a Coleridgean symbol in which the temporal shows forth the eternal. Neither of these kinds of symbolizing would be adequate to Whitman's purpose, which is to affirm not an eternal supernatural world but rather an endless trans-natural world of perpetual floating or "crossing."

It is important to note that while the continuum – the film or float – is "impalpable," it is not wholly imperceptible. In the final stanza of "Crossing Brooklyn Ferry," what is said to be hung "About my body for me, and your body for you" are not sights and sounds but "our divinest aromas." This is not the scent of armpits but some quintessential olfactory distillation. "Unlike sight," writes F. Gonzalez-Crussi, "olfaction deals with the airy, the insubstantial, and the formless … smells often defy localization in space. Sight has regard to the actualities of space, but olfaction lives in time … Of all our senses, this is the one most closely related to time: to the past, because, better than the others, it evokes memory; to the future, because, more effectively than the others, it elicits anticipation and awakens our deepest yearnings" (71).

Bluntly put, the assertion at the end of "Crossing Brooklyn Ferry" is that natural facts *are* spiritual facts. The riddling couplet later added by Whitman to one of the 1855 poems might have been better deployed as the epigraph for "Crossing Brooklyn Ferry": "Strange and hard that paradox true I give,/Objects gross and the unseen soul are one" ("A Song for Occupations"). Anagogy is the name for the kind of symbolizing in which the duality of tenor and vehicle, signifier and signified, is overcome. Anagogic symbolism, says Northrop Frye, "is the conceivable or imaginative limit of desire, which is infinite, eternal, and hence apocalyptic. By an apocalypse I mean primarily the imaginative conception of the whole of nature as the content of an infinite and eternal living body which, if not human, is closer to being human than to being inanimate" (*Anatomy* 119).

But there is nothing apocalyptic in the biblical or Blakean sense about "Crossing Brooklyn Ferry," which is not a prophetic book but an intimate lyric communication specifically addressed to a singular "you" living in the future, on union or fusion with whom everything in the poem depends. From the point of view of "you" the reader living a hundred or hundreds of years hence, surely the only achieved "eternity" is aesthetic – the perfected verbal artwork that represents for later readers what Whitman felt at what he saw and what still is the look of things (to paraphrase Wallace Stevens' "A Postcard from the Volcano"). Despite the poem's canny assertions of the continuing existence of the "soul," it is very hard to think of "Crossing Brooklyn Ferry" as offering anything other than what Thomas Hardy called an "Idealism of Fancy: that is … an imaginative solace in the lack of any substantial solace to be found in life" (333). Certainly this was how the matter came to appear to Whitman only four years later in "Of the Terrible Doubt of Appearances":

> Of the uncertainty after all, that we may be deluded,
>
> ....
>
> That may-be identity beyond the grave is a beautiful fable only,
> May-be the things I perceive … are (as doubtless they are) only
>   apparitions.

The extraordinary differences between the poems in the 1855 and 1856 editions of *Leaves of Grass* and those added for the edition of 1860 have been variously explained. There can be little doubt that the un-happy aftermath of a homosexual love relationship was a contribut-ing factor: "Was it I who walked the earth disclaiming all except what I had in myself?" Whitman wonders in a manuscript poem: "Was it I boasting how complete I was in myself?/O little I counted the com-rade indispensable to me!" (*Manuscripts* 68). This is also the subject of one of Whitman's best-known lyrics, "I Saw in Louisiana a Live-Oak Growing," one of the twelve poems of the "Live Oak with Moss" sequence (copied into a notebook in the spring of 1859) that alludes to the love affair more directly than the forty-five *Calamus* poems of the 1860 *Leaves of Grass*, of which after reordering they became part.

> I saw in Louisiana a live-oak growing,
> All alone stood it and the moss hung down from the branches,
> Without any companion it grew there uttering joyous leaves of dark
>   green,
> And its look, rude, unbending, lusty, made me think of myself,

But I wonder'd how it could utter joyous leaves standing alone there
    without its friend near, for I knew I could not,
And I broke off a twig with a certain number of leaves upon it, and
    twined around it a little moss,
And brought it away, and I have placed it in sight in my room,
It is not needed to remind me as of my own dear friends,
(For I believe lately I think of little else than of them,)
Yet it remains to me a curious token, it makes me think of manly love;
For all that, and though the live-oak glistens there in Louisiana solitary
    in a wide flat space,
Uttering joyous leaves all its life without a friend a lover near,
I know very well I could not.

At one level, "manly love" may be taken to refer to the love of same-sex comrades or to love of a particular man. But the context of Whitman's poetic development presents another, more suggestive and resonant meaning: self-confident, independent love as opposed to unmanly love which is sentimentally dependent on another or others. The declension in meaning of the adjective in "a curious token" as compared to its deployment in "There Was a Child Went Forth" or "Crossing Brooklyn Ferry" is telling. Here "curious" means something quirky or arbitrary rather than something inciting wonder (the difference is similar to that between unmanly and manly). In *Song of Myself*, natural objects had a rich symbolic suggestiveness; but now we have a token of a token. The twig is a synecdoche for the oak, which is a metaphor for the independent and joyous poet Whitman once was. But the poet of 1860 can no longer generate (utter) joyous leaves of himself; he can only collect tokens. As such, he bears only a token resemblance to the poet of 1855–6.

Other evidence suggests that the determining factor in the change from 1855–6 to 1860 was Whitman's physical health: he simply did not feel as good at the beginning of the 1860s as he had only a few years before. In "A Hand-Mirror" (1860), for example, the speaker takes stock of his physical being: "No more a flashing eye, no more a sonorous voice or springy step"; instead, "Words babble, hearing and touch callous,/No brain, no heart left, no magnetism of sex." The flashing eye and sexual magnetism are facets of what in another poem of 1860 Whitman calls his "electric self out of the pride of which I utter poems." The reference is in part to his extraordinary tactile sensitivity. The skin "is an especially good electrical conductor"; there are those "who when they touch another feel 'a sort of electrical current' passing between them." But while some individuals "retain this sensitivity into old age, others tend to lose it in middle age" (Montagu 148). For Whitman, the diminution of this current may be

considered the equivalent of Wordsworth's loss of the visual acuity
that had made the natural world seem "apparelled in celestial light,/
The glory and the freshness of a dream" and left him toiling "In darkness lost, the darkness of the grave" (Intimations Ode).

The onset of middle age is the life-cycle term for this change.
The degree of destabilization and desolation recorded in Whitman's
poems of 1860 suggest that one should go a step further and apply
the concept of mid-life crisis. A number of other nineteenth- and
twentieth-century writers experienced a mid-life crisis that formed a
divide in their careers. Its precipitates and/or symptoms include the
feeling that, perceptually and creatively, something has fled – a loss
that makes earlier works seem like fantastications and fresh creative
achievement impossible. Wordsworth's Intimations Ode, Coleridge's
Dejection Ode, and Emerson's "Experience" are all important points
of comparison for the Whitman of 1860. So is Tolstoy's *Confession*,
which relates the great watershed in his creative and spiritual life to
irreversible bodily changes. Tolstoy recalled a time when, like the
poet of *Song of Myself*, he believed that "Everything develops, differ-
entiates, moving towards complexity and refinement and there are
laws governing its progress. You are part of a whole." During this
period he was developing physically and intellectually and it was
"natural for me to believe that there was a law governing the world,
in which I could find the answers to the questions of my life." But the
time came when he stopped growing: "I felt that I was … drying up,
my muscles were growing weaker, my teeth falling out." He realized
that "I had taken for a law something which I had discovered in
myself at a certain time of my life … it became clear to me that there
could be no law of perpetual development" (35–6).

In "As I Ebb'd with the Ocean of Life" Whitman's crisis is un-
flinchingly faced. The poem opens with the poet musing late in the
autumn day as he walks along the seashore, which since boyhood
had been a special place for him because of its analogical suggestiveness. It was the "dividing line, contact, junction, the solid marrying
the liquid – that curious, lurking something, (as doubtless every
objective form finally becomes to the subjective spirit,) which means
far more than its mere first sight, grand as that is – blending the real
and ideal, and each made portion of the other" (796). Not surpris-
ingly, then, as he wends his way along the shore Whitman is thinking
the "old thought of likenesses." He is self-consciously the poet of
Song of Myself, the "electric self seeking types."

As he walks, he is "gazing off southward" – that is, looking out
from the Atlantic coast of Long Island into the limitless expanse of sky
and ocean. But he is also hearing the continual "hoarse and sibilant"
sounds of the waves hitting the shore, which seem to be expressing

the timelessness of human suffering and isolation: "the fierce old mother [the sea] endlessly cries for her castaways." The visual correlative of these natural sounds is not the distant line of the horizon, the place where Emerson said in *Nature* a man could behold something "as beautiful as his own nature" (10). It is the harshly and sibilantly described particulars on the shore that come to compel the attention of this seeker of types. He is

> ... seiz'd by the spirit that trails in the lines underfoot,
> The rim, the sediment that stands for all the water and all the land of the
>   globe.

> Fascinated, my eyes ... dropt, to follow those slender windrows,
> Chaff, straw, splinters of wood, weeds, and the sea-gluten,
> Scum, scales from shining rocks, leaves of salt-lettuce, left by the tide ...
> ....
> I too but signify at the utmost a little wash'd-up drift,
> A few sands and dead leaves to gather,
> Gather, and merge myself as part of the sands and drift.
> ....
> I too have bubbled up, floated the measureless float, and been wash'd
>   on your shores,
> I too am but a trail of drift and debris,
> I too leave little wrecks upon you, you fish-shaped island.

These extraordinary statements demand to be read against the background of Whitman's earlier self-proclamations. The symbolic plenitude of the grass in section 6 of *Song of Myself*, for example, against the "few sands and dead leaves to gather"; the measureless float of "Crossing Brooklyn Ferry" against merging with the sands and drift; the undulating but always outwardly expanding movement of *Song of Myself* against the monotonous linearity of the miles-long trail of debris along the shore – a difference enacted in the lines of the poem, which are linear rather than undulating, prosaic rather than poetic; and the claims of the poet of *Song of Myself* to be in intimate creative contact with the "Me myself" against the energetic recantation of this presumption:

> Aware now that amid all that blab whose echoes recoil upon me I have
>   not once had the least idea who or what I am,
> But that before all my arrogant poems the real Me stands yet untouch'd,
>   untold, altogether unreach'd,
> Withdrawn far, mocking me with mock-congratulatory signs and bows,
> With peals of distant ironical laughter at every word I have written,
> Pointing in silence to these songs, and then to the sand beneath.

In section 22 of *Song of Myself*, Whitman had importuned the sea to "rock me in billowy drowse,/Dash me with amorous wet....I can repay you"; and elsewhere in the poem the earth and sea were figured as lovers. But in "As I Ebb'd," Whitman has nothing to offer anything or anyone; and there is nothing erotic about the coming together of land and sea. In the poem's third section they are figured as parents from whom the poet desperately seeks revelation. The paternal shore is beseeched to "Breathe to me while I hold you close the secret of the murmuring I envy," for (to cite the later excised line that followed in the 1860 edition) "I fear I shall become crazed, if I cannot emulate it, and utter myself as well as it" (1860: 198). But the longing for haptic intensity, the clinging to the shore/father and asking to be touched "with your lips as I touch those I love," together with the continual maternal murmuring of the sea, also suggests the desire to "merge myself as part of the sands and drift" – that is, to be steeped in a numbing substance, to return to the oceanic state of hearing/touch.

The former plea may be said to be answered in the sense that, like Wordsworth in the Intimations Ode and Coleridge in the Dejection Ode, Whitman does powerfully utter himself in his poem about no longer being a poet. But there is no engulfment, no merging. There is white space and then the poem's fourth and final section. It opens on a distinctly false note. "Ebb, ocean of life, (the flow will return)" reca- pitulates the opening of the poem which found Whitman held by his prideful self-conception as an electric self. This momentary regression to the imperative, affirmative mode of the end of "Crossing Brooklyn Ferry" suggests a nostalgia for the "the old thought of likenesses" and the float forever held in solution. But the plenitude of 1855–6 has been superseded by the perceptual realities of the 1860 shoreline, by which in the closing lines the poet's attention is once again seized:

> I mean tenderly by you and all,
> I gather for myself and for this phantom looking down where we lead,
>   and following me and mine.

> Me and mine, loose windrows, little corpses,
> Froth, snowy white, and bubbles,
> (See, from my dead lips the ooze exuding at last,
> See, the prismatic colors glistening and rolling,)
> Tufts of straw, sands, fragments,
> Bouy'd hither from many moods, one contradicting another,
> From the storm, the long calm, the darkness, the swell,
> Musing, pondering, a breath, a briny tear, a dab of liquid or soil,
> Up just as much out of fathomless workings fermented and thrown,
> A limp blossom or two, torn, just as much over waves floating, drifted at
>   random,

Just as much for us that sobbing dirge of Nature,
Just as much whence we came that blare of the cloud-trumpets,
We, capricious, brought hither we know not whence, spread out before
    you,
You up there walking or sitting,
Whoever you are, we too lie in drifts at your feet.

Who is the phantom? There are two different but not mutually exclusive possibilities. The first is "the real Me" now recognized as chimerical. Its defining feature is that it is the part of Whitman "not wholly involved in Nature" – to quote from another text of Thoreau's that seems uncannily anticipatory of a Whitman poem. "I may be either the drift-wood in the stream, or Indra in the sky looking down on it," Thoreau reflects in the "Solitude" chapter of *Walden*: "However intense my experience, I am conscious of the presence and criticism of a part of me, which, as it were, is not a part of me, but spectator, sharing no experience, but taking note of it; and that is no more I than it is you" (135). The other possibility is that the "you" is the future reader, union with whom in "Crossing Brooklyn Ferry" gave Whitman the assurance that he was not doomed to extinction. Taking the "Whoever you are" of the last line to be the reader allows for a final contrast between Whitman in 1855–6 and in 1860. In *Song of Myself* and "Crossing Brooklyn Ferry," the poet was fully in control of the poem's addressee. Here the situation is very different; the poet has as little knowledge of "you" as of "the real Me." At the end of "As I Ebb'd," the "you" is an unknown being at the feet of whom the speaker and his seashore types "lie in drifts." As Whitman reads the lines on the shore, "you" the reader read the "lines" on his page, in the words of which his failure and weakness are inscribed.

But something else is inscribed in these lines. The spiritual facts suggested by the natural facts of the shore have the same symbolic suggestiveness that they possessed in the poem's second section: randomness; contradiction; mortality; continual lament; and the shriving contrast between past plenitude and present emptiness. There is a difference, however. In the closing lines we have not terse prosaic cataloguing but copious rhythmic enumeration. For one critic, the length and tone of the passage suggest "a biding of time, a wish to prolong the lull between storms" (Larson 203). But I hear something stronger, a commitment to the natural facts. It is, to be sure, a commitment *faute de mieux*. The void has not grown luminous; but the chastened, no longer proud poet has found in the debris of the shore sufficient symbolic suggestiveness to allow him to utter himself. How impressive this effort is, and how difficult to sustain, can be gauged by comparing the end of "As I Ebb'd"

to those of two other major Whitman poems, in both of which the
sea or its figural equivalent does reveal "the secret of the murmuring
I envy."

In "Out of the Cradle Endlessly Rocking" and "When Lilacs Last
in the Dooryard Bloom'd," Whitman moves away from the silent
paternal shore toward a liquid mother who communicates a saving
message. At the climax of both poems, the sense of touch, or rather
Whitman's distinctive amalgam of hearing/touch, resumes its dominance. We have already noted this collocation in the key expansion
of consciousness experiences in *Song of Myself*, in which rhythmic or
musical sounds, what Tenney Nathanson nicely calls an "archaic
fluidity activated by voice" (132), trigger visionary ecstasy.

In "Out of the Cradle," engulfment in operatic sound begins with
the pyrotechnics of the poem's overture, which shows how a curious
boy absorbs and vicariously participates in experiences. The mature
poet's imaginative act – adumbrated in the overture – recapitulates
the child's imaginative act. Like "As I Ebb'd," the opening of this
poem includes an explicit back reference to 1855–6: "I, chanter of
pains and joys, uniter of here and hereafter." The chanter is the poet
of *Song of Myself*; the uniter is the visionary of "Crossing Brooklyn
Ferry." But in 1860 the subject is not "now" or "forever"; it is a remi-
niscence. The implications of this difference are most sharply seen in
the contrasting accounts of how the person becomes the poet. In *Song
of Myself*, the figuring of poetic incarnation emphasized fulfillment
and plenitude: the fusion of the ordinary self with "the real Me"
or "my soul," with sexual climax as the trigger of expanded consciousness and heightened perception. In contrast, the fable of poetic
incarnation in "Out of the Cradle" offers a loss-based explanation.
Listening both to the unmanly crooning of the lovelorn he-bird, and
to its undertone, the incessant moaning of the sea, the boy experiences a tremendous emotional release. In a moment of empathetic
identification, he becomes "the outsetting bard": "now in a moment I
know what I am for, I awake/ … Never more the cries of unsatisfied
love be absent from me." The boy becomes the poet the moment he
recognizes that loss and unfulfillment are both his subject matter and
his fate: his awakened songs will be fueled by "the fire, the sweet hell
within,/ The unknown want, the destiny of me."

At the climax of "Out of the Cradle," the boy/poet wonders if
"the sweet hell within" will burn forever unquenched and if so
whether he will be able to bear it. "O give me the clew!" he cries, "O if

I am to have so much, let me have more!" In the "Clef Poem" of 1856, the clew (or clef) was that "A vast similitude interlocks all" – including "All identities that have existed or may exist on this globe." In "Out of the Cradle" the clew is a musical clef or key: the "low and delicious word death" whispered by the sea in mantric repetition. It offers a merging and engulfing in which the fire will be quenched and identity obliterated:

> … edging near as privately for me rustling at my feet,
> Creeping thence steadily up to my ears and laving me softly all over,
> Death, death, death, death, death.

In sensory terms, both he-bird and boy/poet are suffering from touch-deprivation, a need that originates in infancy. In the womb the fetus is surrounded by, is steeped in, amniotic fluid; it also feels the systole and diastole of the maternal heartbeat and experiences the mother's motions as a gentle rocking. After birth, this condition is replicated outside the womb: swaddling increases tactile stimulation and engulfing; lulling, humming sounds recall the maternal heartbeat, which is often mimed in an infant's first sounds (mama, papa); and cradle-rocking approximates the floating sensation. Against this sensory background, the appositeness of the later-added, often-lamented, penultimate line of the poem becomes clear:

> That strong and delicious word which, creeping to my feet,
> (Or like some old crone rocking the cradle, swathed in sweet garments,
>   bending aside,)
> The sea whisper'd me.

In the climactic revelation of "When Lilacs Last in the Dooryard Bloom'd," death is once again imaged as a maternal liquidity in which the synesthetic richness of infantile feeling/touch is recovered. But the Lincoln elegy conducts itself in a manner very different from that of "Out of the Cradle" and offers a much richer orchestration of its themes. Three natural objects dominate the poem: star, lilac, and bird. The "great star early droop'd in the western sky in the night" is Hesper, the evening star (the planet Venus when seen in the western sky). It is an elegiac trope of long standing (see, for example, the four-line Greek lyric attributed to Plato that Shelley used as the epigraph for *Adonais*). But the star also has a personal meaning for the American elegist. The drooping star with the countenance full of woe that Whitman saw in Washington in March 1865 came to be associated by him with the death the following month of President Lincoln, "the sweetest, wisest soul of all my days and lands." At the limit of visual perception, the star functions as a determinate symbol (or in de Man's sense an allegory) of the dead leader.

The lilac, blooming in April, has "heart-shaped leaves of rich green, [and] many a pointed blossom rising delicate." A sprig from it, ritually bestowed in section 6, is the funereal offering (another elegiac convention), the token of the poet's grief. In perceptual terms, the lilac is proximate sight plus scent ("the perfume strong I love," the "mastering odor"). Figurally, as the poem opens out geographically from "the dooryard fronting an old farm-house near the white-wash'd palings" to the continental expanse of America, "the varied and ample land," the lilac "blooming perennial" becomes a synecdochal symbol of natural process and cyclic renewal ("ever-returning spring"). The third of the poem's trio of natural facts is the solitary hermit-thrush, whose song comes from "the swamp in the dimness." Here, the sensory mode is first hearing then hearing/touch. Since the bird speaks for himself, it is perhaps best considered not as a figure of speech, but as a character in a psychodrama representing an awareness in the dark depths of the speaker's being – of the "knowledge of death" that finally supersedes "the thought of death."

The sensory and perceptual movement of "Lilacs" is, then, from distanced sight, through proximate sight and scent, to hearing and hearing/touch, and finally (as we shall see) to non-perceptual insight; from star to lilac to bird's song to vision. The movement from the dominance of the lilac to the dominance of the thrush also recapitulates Whitman's development from 1855 to 1865. As the lilac "With every leaf a miracle" recalls the natural supernaturalism of *Song of Myself*, so the solitary singing bird recalls the he-bird of "Out of the Cradle" – the "singer solitary, projecting me." As in that poem, the turning point of "Lilacs" comes when "the voice of my spirit tallied the song of the bird." It is in its climactic vision of a Civil War battlefield that "Lilacs" finally goes beyond "Out of the Cradle."

On the thematic level, the star is the "thought of death" (the death of Lincoln); it is associated with "black murk" and "the long black trail" of the funeral journey of the murdered President's corpse through the cities draped in black. This awareness is internalized as "the harsh surrounding cloud that will not free my soul" that keeps Whitman from tallying with the song of the bird. Because of its consolatory and renovative potential, the lilac and what it symbolizes also detains the speaker. The description of the diurnal movement of the sun in section 12 invites an analogy between the phases of a human life and the phases of the day. Each part of the non-linear pattern is welcome and fulfilling, including the inevitable arrival of "the welcome night and the stars," while something more than acceptance is offered by the repeatedly emphasized timelessness of natural process: the "ever-returning spring"; "the endless grass"; "the trees prolific"; the growing wheat, "every grain from its shroud in the dark-brown fields uprisen," with its nearly explicit suggestion of a corresponding human triumph over the temporal. And in section 11, to adorn the walls of "the burial-house of him I love" the poet selects "Pictures of growing spring and farms and homes ... With the fresh herbage under foot." Implicit here is what "Crossing Brooklyn Ferry" made explicit: natural wonders furnish their parts for eternity, for the soul.

In 1865, however, this is not the last word. The "beautiful fable" of 1856 is alluded to, but it is not believed. In "Lilacs," Whitman does not succumb to the temptation (in de Man's words) "for the self to borrow ... the temporal stability that it lacks from nature" (197). The pill of an authentically human destiny is swallowed – but it is heavily coated with sugar. Whitman finally hears the bird's song, "liquid and free and tender," after he has "fled forth to the hiding receiving night ... Down to the shores of the water, the path by the swamp in the dimness." As Helen Vendler has noted, while in the periodic stanzas of the rest of the poem long lines and long sentences that drop to a conclusion are "the embedded syntactic figure for the temporality of all life and action," the rhythm of the death carol is "not periodic. Rather, like the waves of the ocean ... it is recursive, recurrent, undulant, self-reflexive, self-perpetuating"; it expands "into oceanic and cosmic space" ("Reading" 145–46).

The drooping star in the sky, the burgeoning land and swelling sun are all apprehended visually; the dark swamp is not seen but heard and felt. There is no perception of objects by a subject, but a merging, an engulfment. In the death carol, all is soothing and soft: "Lost in the loving floating ocean of thee,/Laved in the flood of thy bliss O Death." This is haptic absorption, a "nestling close" in the "sure-enwinding arms of cool-enfolding death." It is a version of being steeped amid honeyed morphine and squeezed in the fakes of death. This black hole absorbs into it the sunlit world celebrated in the earlier sections of the poem: "the sights of the open landscape and the high-spread sky ... And life and the fields ... the myriad fields and the prairies wide." It also sucks in earlier texts of Whitman: the "objects and knowledge curious" of "There Was a Child"; the "life and joy" and "the dense-pack'd cities" of *Song of Myself*; "the teeming wharves and ways" of "Crossing Brooklyn Ferry"; "The ocean shore and the husky whispering wave" of "Out of the Cradle."

As in *Song of Myself*, immersion in touch brings an expansion of consciousness: "the sight that was bound in my eyes unclosed,/ As to

long panoramas of visions." But the vision of section 15 is very different from that of sections 5 and 29 of *Song of Myself*. There is no sense
of experiential immortality or of sprouts prolific and vital; and the
other senses are not heightened, but curtailed – sight is blinkered and
hearing entirely suppressed:

> And I saw askant the armies,
> I saw as in noiseless dreams hundreds of battle-flags,
> Borne through the smoke of the battles and pierc'd with missiles I saw
>   them,
> And carried hither and yon through the smoke, and torn and bloody,
> And at last but a few shreds left on the staffs, (and all in silence,)
> And the staffs all splinter'd and broken.
>
> I saw battle-corpses, myriads of them,
> And the white skeletons of young men, I saw them,
> I saw the debris and debris of all the slain soldiers of the war,
> But I saw they were not as was thought,
> They themselves were fully at rest, they suffer'd not,
> The living remain'd and suffer'd, the mother suffer'd,
> And the wife and the child and the musing comrade suffer'd,
> And the armies that remained suffer'd.

In the first stanza, seeing "askant" means not seeing soldiers pierced
with missiles and torn and bloody; one sees only the battle flags and
their staffs. It is these, not the limbs and bones of the soldiers, that are
"all splinter'd and broken." Seeing "askant" also means seeing from
a great distance. The second stanza cuts from the shredded flags and
splintered staffs to corpses "fully at rest" and white skeletons, not a
few but "myriads," including in this temporal as well as spatial panorama "all the slain soldiers of the war." This increase in visual distance has a blurring and numbing effect. At the distance necessary for
panoramic vision, nothing hurts or disturbs. Moreover, to continue
the cinematic analogy, the scene is filmed without sound; it is a noiseless battle. In the account of the naval battle in *Song of Myself* aural
imagery was used to give a powerful sense of the suffering of the
wounded and dying: "The hiss of the surgeon's knife and the gnawing teeth of his saw,/The wheeze, the cluck, the swash of falling
blood....the short wild scream, the long dull tapering groan" (#36).
The suppression of sound here has exactly the opposite effect. It acts
as a *cordon sanitaire* between the viewer and the horror of war.

Vendler has called attention to Whitman's "profound de-Christian-
izing" of the elegiac form in "Lilacs," the plot of which she describes

as the attempt "to find, in the language of perception, an equivalent for transcendence" ("Reading" 145, 136). But the poem's plot can be described another way – a preferable way for readers like myself who consider "Lilacs" a magnificent poem but find the death carol and the vision it evokes unwholesome – who prefer the Whitman of "As I Ebb'd," compelled to recognize himself in the debris on the shore, to the anaesthetized vision of seeing "the debris of all the slain soldiers of the war." In Charles Feidelson's formulation, the symbolic objects in the poem "behave like characters in a drama, the plot of which is the achievement of a poetic utterance" (22). This self-reflexive aspect of the elegy is conspicuous in sections 4, 10 and 16, which make explicit the poem's re-enactment of the problem explored in both "Out of the Cradle" and "As I Ebb'd": the problem of how to utter oneself, how to turn pain and suffering into poetry. At the end of the elegy, the completed utterance is foregrounded. A farewell to the poem's symbols is followed by the assurance that each and all of them have nonetheless been kept, and then by the offering of the completed poem to the memory of its subject:

> and this for his dear sake,
> Lilac and star and bird twined with the chant of my soul,
> There in the fragrant pines and the cedars dusk and dim.

The poem is not only the funereal offering of the poet Whitman (as the lilac sprig was of the grieving Whitman within the poem); it is also his version of the crucial substitution – not that but this – which is the turning point in the movement of elegy from loss to recompense. To say this is virtually to say that the ultimate consolation in "Lilacs" is the creative activity of the mind – the making of metaphors and other figures. The completed poem, and not simply the two most extraordinary of its component parts, is the principal consolation for the loss that initially held the poet powerless and inarticulate.

In Whitman's later poetry, as has often been noted, the Romantic visionary was largely superseded by the public bard programmatically celebrating democracy, America and the spiritual evolution of mankind.[4] The shift from private to public was already marked by 1873, when at the age of fifty-three Whitman suffered a paralytic stroke and left Washington an invalid, moving to Camden, New Jersey, to live with one of his brothers. The stroke was the beginning of two decades

of sharply curtailed physical activity and failing physical health –
subjects to which he often referred in his letters, his prefaces and
afterwords to editions of *Leaves of Grass*, and sometimes in his poems.

When Richard Maurice Bucke visited Whitman in 1880, however,
he noted that the senses of the sixty-one-year-old poet remained
"exceptionally acute, his hearing especially so," and that his "favorite occupation seemed to be strolling or sauntering about outdoors
by himself, looking at the grass, the trees, the flowers, the vistas of
light, the varying aspects of the sky, and listening to … all the hundreds of natural sounds. It was evident that these things gave him a
feeling of pleasure far beyond what they give to ordinary people"
(216, 220). The literary result of these saunterings were the "Nature-
notes 1877–'81" (collected in *Specimen Days*), which consist of numerous passages of "spontaneous" natural description written "on the
spot" (690, 807). In these notes, "all the senses, [that is] sight, sound,
smell, [are] delicately gratified" (876).[5]

In two self-reflexive passages of the "Nature-notes," Whitman
made extremely interesting observations on his new way of perceiving the external world:

The *emotional* aspects and influences of Nature! I, too, like the rest, feel these
modern tendencies (from all the prevailing intellections, literature and
poems,) to turn everything to pathos, ennui, morbidity, dissatisfaction,
death. Yet how clear it is to me that those are not the born results, influences
of Nature at all, but of one's own distorted, sick or silly soul. Here, amid this
wild, free scene, how healthy, how joyous, how clean and vigorous and
sweet! (813–14)

[Even in the presence of a magnificent July dawn, he felt] not the weight of
sentiment or mystery, or passion's ecstasy indefinable – not the religious
sense, the varied All, distill'd and sublimated into one, of the night just
described. Every star now clear-cut, showing for just what it is, there in the
colorless ether. The character of the heralded morning, ineffably sweet and
fresh and limpid, but for the esthetic sense alone, and for purity without
sentiment. (826)

The "modern tendencies" described in the first passage are the dark
side of the common nineteenth-century assumption that (in Francis
Jeffrey's formulation) "the very essence of poetry … consists in the
fine perception and vivid expression of that subtle and mysterious
Analogy which exists between the physical and the moral world"
(474). The second passage rejects the other *raison d'être* of symbolic
perception: the sense sublime of natural phenomena symbolizing

the transcendent. Instead, the older Whitman looks at nature without subjective projection. Looking naively rather than sentimentally, he finds a tonic freshness and health and a purity without sentiment.

"Nature-notes," then, records Whitman's partial recovery of the aesthetic mode of perception of the child who went forth every day. But unlike the child, the older Whitman is self-conscious and reflective and thus aware of the symbiotic bond between himself and what he perceives:

there comes a time ... when one feels through his whole being, and pronouncedly the emotional part, that identity between himself subjectively and Nature objectively which Schelling and Fichte are so fond of pressing. How it is I know not, but I often realize a presence here – in clear moods I am certain of it, and neither chemistry nor reasoning nor esthetics will give the least explanation. All the past two summers it has been strengthening and nourishing my sick body and soul, as never before.   (809)

Friedrich Schelling and Johann Fichte were proponents of *Naturphilosophie*, the doctrine that all phenomena, including the human self, are organically related and maintained in being by a force energized by the opposition of polar powers. The doctrine may be regarded as a philosophical cum scientific amplification of the Romantic sense of the one life within and abroad. The weeds mentioned at the end of the passage recall the elder and mullen and pokeweed enumerated at the end of the representation of expanded consciousness in section 5 of *Song of Myself*. But the differences between the two passages are more telling than the similarities. In the latter, the "delicious medicine" (809) is not the elixir of touch but the less intoxicating objects of the senses of sight, sound and smell. As a result, there is reciprocity but not merging, invigoration but not ecstasy.

One July evening, however ("the night just described" referred to in a passage above), Whitman had an experience different in kind from those described in the other "Nature-notes":

from a little after 9 till 11 the atmosphere and the whole show above were in [a] state of exceptional clearness and glory ... A large part of the sky seem'd just laid in great splashes of phosphorous. You could look deeper in, farther through, than usual; the orbs thick as heads of wheat in a field. [There was] a curious general luminousness throughout to sight, sense, and soul ... There, in abstraction and stillness ... the copiousness, the removedness, vitally, loose-clear-crowdedness, of that stellar concave spreading overhead, softly absorb'd into me, rising so free, interminably high, stretching east, west, north, south – and I, though but a point in the center below, embodying all.

As if for the first time, indeed, creation noiselessly sank into and through me its placid and untellable lesson ... the visible suggestion of God in space and time – now once definitely indicated, if never again. The untold pointed at – the heavens all paved with it.   (825)

The elemental Wordsworthian grandeur of the sky, particularly its unusual depth, perceived by a combination of sight and feeling/ touch (here called "sense"), triggers an expansion of consciousness experience. In Whitman's terminology it is "the religious sense [of] the varied All, distill'd and sublimated into one" (826); in the cognate terms used elsewhere in this study, it is the sublime sense of the infinite symbolized by the finite – "the visible suggestion of God in space and time."

Was the one-life medicine, which on one extraordinary occasion rose to definite transcendent intimations, sufficient to reconcile the aging poet to his temporal destiny, which had been his antagonist in 1855–6 and his suffocating savior in "Out of the Cradle" and "Lilacs"? Two short poems of natural description, written a few years before Whitman's death in 1892 at the age of seventy-two, suggest that the correct answer is *yes* and *no*. In "Twilight," the recognition of mortality is explicit:

> The soft voluptuous opiate shades,
> The sun just gone, the eager light dispell'd – (I too will soon be gone, dispell'd,)
> A haze – nirwana – rest and night – oblivion.

This is Whitman's last poetic registration of longing to be merged, steeped, squeezed, floated, laved, enwound, enfolded in some numbing oceanic continuum. In the other poem, "A Prairie Sunset," the recognition of mortality (here implicit) prompts a different reaction:

> Shot gold, maroon and violet, dazzling silver, emerald, fawn,
> The earth's whole amplitude and Nature's multiform power consign'd
>   for once to colors;
> The light, the general air possess'd by them – colors till now unknown,
> No limit, confine – not the Western sky alone – the high meridian –
>   North, South, all,
> Pure luminous color fighting the silent shadows to the last.

In *Song of Myself*, Whitman had described his response to a spectacular daybreak: "The air tastes good to my palate ... / Something I cannot see puts upward libidinous prongs, / Seas of bright juice suffuse heaven." The "dazzling and tremendous" sunrise would "kill" him, he says, if he could not meet it as an equal, "could not now and always send sunrise out of me" (#24–25). But this abounding egotism and figural exuberance, an epitome of the alpha point of his poetic career, was now four decades in the past. "A Prairie Sunset" is an epitome of the omega point. The aged poet is not competing with the spectacular sunset, as the younger poet did with the dawn; in tandem with the setting sun, he is fighting the silent shadows to the last.

EIGHT

Dickinson:
The Glimmering Frontier

"The act of imagination," Emerson declares, "is ever attended by pure delight. It infuses a certain volatility and intoxication into all Nature. It has a flute which sets the atoms of our frame in a dance." An essential aspect of this delight is the poet's ability to see "the same sense in things so diverse"; this gives "a pure pleasure ... we find a charm in the metamorphosis" ("Poetry" 18, 25). Perhaps the first poet that this description brings to mind is Emily Dickinson: the way her linguistic and metaphorical exuberance infuses volatility into nature is one of the most immediately arresting features of her work. Examples abound: the stars – "the wampum of the night" that only God can count (#128); the lightning – an "electric Moccasin" passing over "a strange Mob of panting Trees" (#1593) or, in another figuration, "a yellow Fork/From Tables in the sky/By inadvertent fingers dropt" (#1173); the atmosphere after a summer thunderstorm: "Nature was in an Opal Apron,/Mixing fresher air" (#1397); the falling snow that "sifts from Leaden Sieves [and] powders all the Wood" (#311); the mushroom as a love child – the "surreptitious scion/Of Summer's circumspect" (#1298); the darting hummingbird visible only in his vanishing: "A route of Evanescence/With a revolving Wheel –/A resonance of Emerald –/A Rush of Cochineal" – "evanescence" here referring both to the bird's quick exit and, in the ornothological sense, to the luminous sheen of its feathers (#1463).

A well-known Dickinson poem, #448 ("This was a Poet"), describes a fundamental aspect of her poetic practice: she is a "Discloser," a person of extraordinary sensory and perceptual acuity who distills the "Attar" – the essential freshness and vividness – from natural objects. Other poems say or suggest the same thing: that Dickinson's poetry is the outflow of a special gift or endowment – a bolt of lightning or "waylaying Light" that "founds the Homes and decks the Days" and imposes obligation: "Advocate the Azure/To the lower Eyes –/ He has obligation/Who has Paradise" (#1581, #1348). It used to be axiomatic that this endowment was an essential characteristic of Dickinson's creative genius.[1] But in the late twentieth century this is no longer the case. As a description of her poetic practice, most commentators would privilege poem #675, which offers a different account of the distillation of the "Attar." In this poem the extraction of poetry from experience is compared to flower pressing: in both cases the attar or "Essential Oils" are "not expressed by Suns – alone –/It is the gift of Screws." That is to say, poetic power is the result of suffering and deprivation rather than a positive endowment. According to another poem, poets learn "the Transport by the Pain": they are the amanuenses or "duller scholars/Of the Mysterious Bard" deep within whose "ceaseless Carol" of anguish they transcribe (#167).

Much current critical emphasis falls not on sensation and perception, but on Dickinson's internal states and psychological struggles. David Porter, for example, quotes a poem in which the speaker is looking at her reflection in a mirror:

> Like Eyes that looked on Wastes –
> Incredulous of Ought
> But Blank – and steady Wilderness –
> ....
> Just Infinites of Nought –
> As far as it could see –
> So looked the face I looked upon –
> She looked itself – on Me –   (#458)

Porter correctly says that this poem epitomizes one of Dickinson's fundamental subjects: "the nebulous, irrational opacity that subsists beyond knowledge" (35). Like many of her poems, the subject of #458 is the "Center," the inner landscape of the poet rather than the external world. Its source is not sensory-perceptual acuity but a keen sense of loss, absence, and emptiness, which in one poem is figured as the mind being "Contented as the Eye/Upon the Forehead of a Bust –/ That knows – it cannot see" (#305). In these poems, sensation and perception tend to be present only in the vehicles of metaphors or similes. Not infrequently the dominant senses are touch and taste – for example "Icicles upon my soul/Prickled Blue and Cool" (#768; and see #510). And the image of a female being molested by a male is the vehicle of several metaphorical figures: the "ghastly Fright" in #512 that caresses the hair and sips from the lips of the defenseless female; the incoming tide in #520 that "made as He would eat me up"; and the "Agony" that drew nearer and nearer until it "Toyed coolly with the final inch/Of your delirious Hem" (#414).

Porter laments that so few of Dickinson's poems are about "what it is exactly to knead dough, put your hands in soil, smell flowers, walk in grass, feel water in your hand" (116). But the reason for this is not that all of Dickinson's poetry is autogenetic and non-referential; it is rather that touch and taste are not the senses that dominate in her experiences of the external world. Nor is the sense of smell, though there are occasional notations of odors, usually flowers and plants, and a few figurative uses of scent, as in #448 and #675. The lower senses were of limited use to a female poet of the New England middle class whose point of natural observation was often the window of her second-floor room in her father's house. Nor for someone in chronically poor health, who seems, on the basis of circumstantial evidence, to have suffered from anorexia (see H.K. Thomas). The images of shivering and freezing cited above, for example, suggest the hypothermia that is one of the symptoms of this illness, and in the poems are numerous images of the rejection of food, the definitive symptom.

In an early letter, Dickinson writes: "I do not care for the body, I love the timid soul, the blushing, shrinking soul" (#39). The observation posts of this particular soul were the higher senses of sight and sound. Dickinson's visual acuity has already been instanced; the notations and figurations of what she heard are equally acute and as freshly rendered. One reason for (or effect of) the dominance of eye and ear is Dickinson's perceptual and temperamental predisposition to be affected by the more imperceptible aspects of the natural world – instantaneous motion, evanescence, transience, diurnal and seasonal change. It is the eye and ear that detect and register these changes: both the close-up and the distant – the hummingbird's evanescence and the spectacular sights and sounds of midsummer electrical storms (the subject of a number of poems) – and both the rapid and the gradual: the sudden appearance of the mushroom ("the Elf of Plants … Vegetation's Juggler" [#1298]) and the bursting out of the natural world in early summer ("Bright Flowers slit a Calyx/And soared upon a Stem" [#606]), as well as the gradual changes of the seasons wonderfully caught in the time-lapse cinematography of poems #342 ("It will be Summer – eventually") and #1540 ("As imperceptibly as Grief").

Another reason for the dominance of eye and ear is the stimulus to contemplation and speculation afforded by distance. A spectacular evening sunset is given "To Contemplation – not to Touch" (#1241); what is distant and ungraspable, what is "beyond the hope of touch" (#1691), has mystery and suggestiveness. The "Tint" (one of the "impalpable Array" of sunset colors) that she "cannot take – is best," even though its "Graspless manners – mock us" (#627). In the same way, the "Far Psalteries of Summer –/Enamouring the Ear/They never yet did satisfy" are "Remotest – when most fair" (#606). To want to touch is to be a "Sceptic Thomas," to be like the disciple who refused to believe in the resurrection of Christ until touching his wounds gave irrefutable proof. To "split the Lark" in the attempt to discover the secret of its song would be a "Scarlet Experiment": it would still the song and kill the singer (#861).

The many poems recording the particulars of Dickinson's intense visual and aural interaction with the natural world are poems of the "Circumference" rather than of the "Center." Their subjects are the interaction of consciousness/imagination with the natural world and the symbolic potential of natural facts – especially as they relate to the "Redoubtablest" of subjects: "Where go we –/Go we anywhere/Creation after this?" (#1417). Dickinson wrote some rhetorically impressive poems that insist that this life and this world are all that there is and are sufficient – for example #1408 ("The Fact that Earth is Heaven"), #370 ("Heaven is so far of the Mind"), and #1741 ("That it will never come again"); their gist is encapsulated in a remark made in one of her letters: "I was thinking, today … that the 'Supernatural,' was only the Natural disclosed – Not 'Revelation' – 'tis – that waits/ But our unfurnished eyes" (#280). Other poems assert that it is better to be uncertain than to be certain: "It's finer – not to know –/If Summer were *an Axiom* –/What sorcery had *Snow*?" (#191); "In insecurity to lie/Is Joy's insuring quality" (#1434); "How Human Nature dotes/ On what it cant detect./The moment that a Plot is plumbed/Its meaning is extinct" (#1417).

But these poems are the exceptions. The rule is that throughout Dickinson's poetry there is a predisposition to want to believe, an eager openmindedness as to the possibility of supernatural revelation, coupled with an equally strong predisposition to resist substituting the wish for the fact. She is rarely guilty of following the cynical advice ironically offered in her poem on the disappearance of God in the nineteenth century – that an *ignis fatuus* (the flickering phosphorescent light sometimes seen over marshes and swamps and thus a deceptive attraction) is better "Than no illume at all" (#1551). But how is one to gain knowledge or assurance of the existence of a state that is "By Ear unheard,/Unscrutinized by Eye" (#160)? In one poem she argues that "What I see not, I better see –/Through Faith" than through "my Hazel Eye" (#939). But this is an exceptional thought. For Dickinson, the abiding answer was that intimations of what is beyond the senses come through the eye and the ear. Before going on to scrutinize her scrutiny of these intimations, we must first inquire further into the particular quality and mode of operation of these senses in her poetry.

Emily Dickinson had a serious eye problem: like her mother and sister, she suffered from exotropia – that is, she was wall-eyed. This can be determined from ophthalmological analysis of the one extant photograph of her, taken when she was seventeen or eighteen. The symptoms of exotropia are eyestrain, blurring of vision, headaches, and photophobia ("great discomfort from bright lights ... sunlight in particular"):

For most patients with *exotropia*, the onset is close to birth, but initially this deviation is often intermittent ... With time, this deviation becomes more constant, usually first for distance vision, and later for near vision as well. The progression may be slow; a person may reach age thirty or later before developing a constant *exotropia*. Ironically, when this deviation is intermittent, a person may have the most pronounced symptoms, because when this deviation becomes constant, some suppression of vision usually develops in the deviating eye to prevent double vision.   (Wand and Sewall 403–4)

In order to receive medical treatment from a distinguished specialist, Dickinson lived away from Amherst in a Cambridgeport boarding house run by her cousins for more than half of both 1864 and 1865. It is not clear whether during these stays she was operated on (the standard treatment in severe cases). It is certain that "during this dismal time the trouble with her eyes precluded much writing" (Sewall *Life* 636). In a letter of early 1865, Dickinson sounds upbeat about her eyes, even though "the snow-light offends them, and the house is bright" (#302). But in a letter written much later, she recalls that "Some years ago I had a woe, the only one that ever made me tremble. It was a shutting out of all the dearest ones of time, the strongest friends of the soul – BOOKS. The medical man said avaunt ye tormentors, he also said 'down, thoughts, & plunge into her soul.' He might as well have said, 'Eyes be blind,' 'heart be still.' So I had eight months of Siberia" (Sewall *Lyman* 76).

It is easy to imagine the fear and apprehension that serious eye illness or the anticipation of it would have caused a reclusive woman of literary interests who read widely and wrote verse and letters almost daily. This fear undoubtedly contributed to Dickinson's psychological turmoil during the early 1860s, her most intense creative period (see Sewall *Life*, 605–7). The evidence in the poetry is compelling. A number of Dickinson's poems either are about her eye illness or use this affliction as a figure for a psychological condition. #574 ("My first well Day – since many ill"), for example, seems to be about an experience of visual incapacitation lasting the length of a summer (see Guthrie 18). The subject of #258 is a "certain Slant of light" experienced on winter afternoons that "oppresses" – an "affliction" or "Heavenly Hurt" that leaves no external mark but makes an "internal difference." Charles Anderson allows the poem only a "figurative meaning," saying that it does not belong in the category of nature poems (*Emily* 216). But if we remember Dickinson reporting in a letter that the glare off snow hurt her eyes, the poem can be read at a literal level – as describing a physical affliction that has psychological repercussions.

In another poem, #327 ("Before I got my eye put out"), the literal level is patent. The poem states that because of an ocular affliction the speaker's sense of sight has been hypersensitized and as a result looking directly at the expanse of the natural world – including noon – would strike her dead. In the last stanza, the speaker concludes that it is safer not to look at all but rather to guess about the places others can see. In the context of Dickinson's life and poetry, it is easy to posit other levels of meaning – for example, "feminine constraint" (McNeil 104). But while there are several possible tenors, it is the vehicle that dominates the poem.

If a number of commentators have recognized the effects of exotropia on Dickinson's life, very few have considered its connection with either her creative practice or poetic vision. Even those who have gone into the question of Dickinson's illness (Sewall, Wand and Sewall, Wolff) have not considered how it might have affected her perception of the external world, and hence the creative activity of her mind. Certainly Dickinson herself saw the connection. "Don't put up my Thread and Needle," poem #617 begins,

> I'll begin to Sew
> When the Birds begin to whistle –
> Better Stitches – so –
>
> These were bent – my sight got crooked –
> When my mind – is plain
> I'll do seams – a Queen's endeavor
> Would not blush to own –
>
> Hems – too fine for Lady's tracing
> To the sightless Knot –
> Tucks – of dainty interspersion –
> Like a dotted Dot –

On the literal level, this poem is about a serious eye condition that for the time being makes sewing impossible. On another level, the poem concerns the relationship between the poet's sight or vision and her poetic texts. The "sightless knot," as Helen McNeil has noted, "is a brilliant instance of the kind of linguistic condensation which it represents: Dickinson's poems knot meanings together so skilfully that the technique is invisible. The tucks – compressions and ellipses – are signatures of a Dickinson work" (159). So is the metrical and grammatical unconventionality that are figured as stitches that have become "bent" or "zigzag" (as they are called in a later stanza).

Another example of the connection between Dickinson's exotropia and her creative practice concerns the photophobia that is a characteristic feature of the illness. For Dickinson, who in one poem speaks of a person eager for the close of a "too bright" day (#878), the intense light of the sun at noon could not be tolerated. In a number of her poems this sun is portrayed as overpowering – so much so that in their *Madwoman in the Attic* Sandra Gilbert and Susan Gubar identify the sun in Dickinson's poetry as a figure for the patriarchal (600). This was picked up on by Wendy Barker, who made it the subject of an entire monograph. In her reading of Dickinson's poetry, the sun and daylight represent "male energy, male power" (2). Barker is not satisfied with a physiological explanation for Dickinson's "frequent association of light with pain" because it ignores the "pervasiveness and complexity of [her] metaphorical associations and their correspondences to similar metaphors occurring in the works of other [female] writers" (4).

Certainly there is some evidence for Barker's case – for example the well-known letter of June 1852 in which the transition from bride to wife is likened to "flowers at morning, *satisfied* with the dew" as compared with "those same sweet flowers at noon with their heads bowed in anguish before the mighty sun" (#93). But Barker can be reductive, as in her reading of the four lines of #1190:

> The Sun and Fog contested
> The Government of Day –
> The Sun took down his Yellow Whip
> And drove the Fog away –

This piece is identified not as "another charming 'nature poem' [but] rather, one of Dickinson's most succinct criticisms of patriarchy." Since "fog is a female image, an entity composed of individual particles of dew," the lashing of the sun, which has "long been associated with the phallus," represents "a cruel act of male power" (70–1).[2]

The truth of the matter is that in Dickinson's poetry the sun has a number of non-literal meanings. In some poems, it can stand for the site of the Christian afterlife: "'Heaven' has different Signs – to me –/ Sometimes, I think that Noon/Is but a symbol of the Place" (#575). Other poems, as Elisa New points out, recall "an old tradition that takes the sun for the Son; its illumination for his Revelation" (155). In still others, it is a figure for eternity in the sense of a condition of ecstatic transcendence – when "Consciousness – is Noon":

> There is a Zone whose even Years
> No Solstice interrupt –
> Whose Sun constructs perpetual Noon
> Whose perfect Seasons wait –   (#1056)

It is also used as a figure for the directly apprehended, unmediated truth. Poem #1129, for example, takes on an added resonance once the reader is aware of Dickinson's ocular sensitivity.

> Tell all the Truth but tell it slant –
> Success in Circuit lies
> Too bright for our infirm Delight
> The Truth's superb surprise
> As Lightning to the Children eased
> With explanation kind
> The Truth must dazzle gradually
> Or every man be blind –

The "superb surprise" of Truth is imaged as the direct light of a sun-surrogate – bolts of lightning which are "too bright" for the "infirm Delight" of the poet and her audience. If one is not to be blinded, the truth must be revealed indirectly; in Dickinson's oxymoron, it must "dazzle gradually." The same contrast between seeing aslant and seeing directly is picked up again in another poem, the subject of which may be taken to be the perceptual advantages of Dickinson's affliction:

> Must be a Woe –
> A loss or so –
> To bend the eye
> Best Beauty's way –
>
> But – once aslant
> It notes Delight

> As difficult –
> As Stalactite
>
> A Common Bliss
> Were had for less ...   (#571)

Dickinson's photophobic woe is the physiological basis of her perceptual preference, not for the harsh light of noon, but for the prismatic hues of dawn and, especially, evening, the times of day when "the sunlight must travel through a much greater thickness of atmosphere, the particles in which, by scattering and absorption, filch from the white sunlight some of its constituent colours, so that only certain colours remain, and those generally warm ones" (Lockyer and Lockyer 57). Indeed, one may wonder whether without her affliction Dickinson would have realized what a challenging poetic subject sunsets were. According to #291, the pictorial skills of Guido, Titian, and Domenichino were unequal to the task of successfully rendering them. Another poem suggests that to succeed in doing so would be to attain artistic fame: the person who "could reproduce the Sun"

> At period of going down –
> The Lingering – and the Stain – I mean –
>
> When Orient have been outgrown –
> And Occident – become Unknown –
> His Name – remain –   (#307)

Thoreau observed that "we never tire of the drama of sunset"; each day one looks "with fresh curiosity to see what new picture will be painted there – what new panorama exhibited – what new dissolving views" (*J iv 242). This was certainly the case with Dickinson. Her *oeuvre* contains more than forty renderings of the metamorphosis of day into night.[3]

Sunsets were not simply a congenial subject for the display of Dickinson's exuberant powers of invention. Coleridge had wondered "What is it that makes the silent *bright* of the Morning vale so different from that other silence & bright gleams of late evening? Is it in the mind or is there any physical cause?" (*Notebooks* i #789). In Dickinson's case, the correct answer is the former. The sun is "Fairer through Fading" (#938) because "To disappear enhances" (#1209); "going out of sight in itself has a peculiar charm" (*Letters* #471). She would "rather recollect a setting/ Than own a rising sun" because "in going is a Drama/Staying cannot confer" (#1349). Moreover, sunsets are tinctured with "Night's possibility" (#106) – the possibility of vision or "Amber Revelation" (#552). "By a departing light," she observes in poem #1714,

> We see acuter, quite,
> Than by a wick that stays.
> There's something in the flight
> That clarifies the sight
> And decks the rays.

The possibilities suggested by sunsets are seen rather than heard; but Dickinson's ear is capable of apprehensions equal in suggestiveness to those of the eye. Indeed, her aural apprehensions tend to be more intense in that they were involuntary and immediate. As D.H. Lawrence noted: "we really have no choice of what we hear. Our will is eliminated. Sound acts direct, almost automatically, upon the affective centres. And we have no power of going forth from the ear. We are always and only recipient" (58). Several poems contain examples of this aural vulnerability and defenselessness (for example #891). Another speaks of the inexplicable and overpowering combination of joy and anguish with which she responds to the sound of birds on "a Summer morning/Before the Quick of Day": the birds "stab my ravished spirit/With Dirks of Melody" (#1420). And in poem #1764, the penetration of a spear rather than simply of a dirk is the figure for the effect of hearing the dawn sound of birds at the beginning of spring:

> The saddest noise, the sweetest noise,
>   The maddest noise that grows, –
> The birds, they make it in the spring,
>   At night's delicious close.
>
> Between the March and April line –
>   That magical frontier
> Beyond which summer hesitates,
>   Almost too heavenly near.
>
> It makes us think of all the dead
>   That sauntered with us here,
> By separation's sorcery
>   Made cruelly more dear.

It makes us think of what we had,
  And what we now deplore.
We almost wish those siren throats
  Would go and sing no more.

An ear can break a human heart
  As quickly as a spear,
We wish the ear had not a heart
  So dangerously near.

The unusual (for Dickinson) metrical regularity and the invariably full rhymes (also unusual) give this poem a pronounced, even insistent, cadence that mimes its subject – the racket that birds make in the spring dawn. The effect of the noise is to reduce perceptual consciousness to a single sense. Heard at dawn on the equinoctial line between winter and spring, the noise makes one think of the plenitude of summer that already seems tantalizingly close – "too heavenly near." At the same time, one is made to think of heaven in the sense of a world beyond to which one hopes departed loved ones have gone. As Dickinson observes in another poem, "The Triumph of the Birds/When they together Victory make" is one of the signs of "the Place/That Men call 'Paradise'" (#575).

Part of the associative connection between the birds' sound and "the dead/That sauntered with us here" is that the contemporaneous liminal moments in the natural world (dawn and the vernal equinox) bring powerfully to mind the threshold between life and death. But since what lies beyond is figured as heaven, why is the heart pierced as if by a spear by the birds' sound? Because, as Dickinson puts it in another late poem, "Parting is all we know of heaven,/ And all we need of hell" (#1732). The difference between the natural and the human thresholds is the difference between white magic and black magic – between something "magical" in the deliciously transporting sense and the "sorcery" that bewitches, as sailors in the *Odyssey* were bewitched by the sirens, the women-birds whose singing drew them to their deaths.

What is the poet of acute sensitivity to do – wish for less intense aural perceptions? That would be to wish not to feel deeply and therefore not to be a poet. Moreover, for Dickinson it would be to deny herself access to another, more reflective, level of aural consciousness. In a late poem, Robert Browning speaks of "the purged ear apprehend[ing]/Earth's import" ("Prologue" to *Asolando*). In several poems, Dickinson similarly speaks of a special power of this sensory mode. In poem #733, the spirit is called "the Conscious Ear" and is distinguished from the "smaller Ear/Outside the Castle." The former can hear "Reportless Measures" that are a "suspective – stimulus" (#1048) and – to cite another poem – can experience "a lonesome Glee [that] sanctifies the Mind" in overhearing a bird from afar (#774).

In another poem, one of Dickinson's finest, the sound of unseen crickets has a similar power:

> Further in Summer than the Birds
> Pathetic from the Grass
> A minor Nation celebrates
> Its unobtrusive Mass.
>
> No Ordinance be seen
> So gradual the Grace
> A pensive Custom it becomes
> Enlarging Loneliness.
>
> Antiquest felt at Noon
> When August burning low
> Arise this spectral Canticle
> Repose to typify
>
> Remit as yet no Grace
> No Furrow on the Glow
> Yet a Druidic Difference
> Enhances Nature now   (#1068)

When August is "burning low" in New England, a late summer soft-ness and "Glow" to the light, together with other natural effects like the sound of crickets, give the time of year a hauntingly suggestive quality. Nathaniel Hawthorne's evocation of this special time, in his preface to *Mosses from an Old Manse* (1846), closely anticipates Dickinson's:

There is no other feeling like what is caused by this faint, doubtful, yet real perception, if it be not rather a foreboding, of the year's decay – so blessedly sweet and sad, in the same breath. …

[T]he song of the cricket … may be called an audible stillness; for, though very loud and heard afar, yet the mind does not take note of it as a sound; so completely is its individual existence merged among the accompanying characteristics of the season. [In August, summer still seems at its height] – and yet, in every breath of wind, and in every beam of sunshine, we hear the whispered farewell, and behold the parting smile, of a dear friend. …. A pen-sive glory is seen in the far, golden gleams, among the shadows of the trees.

The flowers – even the brightest of them, and they are the most gorgeous of the year – have this gentle sadness wedded to their pomp, and typify the character of this delicious time, each within itself.   (1142–3)

But there are telling differences between the two renderings. Where Hawthorne paints a composite picture, and personifies and generalizes, Dickinson concentrates on a particular perceptual aspect of the time of year. The emotion evoked in her poem is not explicitly named; it is stranger and more difficult to express than the sweet sadness so well conveyed by the ripe fullness of Hawthorne's post-prandial prose. Dickinson's emphasis is not on the natural moment finding an echo in every bosom, but on the way in which the auditor's "loneliness" is enlarged by a sharpened sense of the foreignness of the natural world. This is figured by the alien rituals – those of the Druids and of Roman Catholics, the Mass being the religious service of the Irish-Catholic immigrants to New England (see Eberwein "Calvinist" 76).

The first version of Dickinson's poem was much less concentrated (see Franklin 553–4 for a transcription). It had seven stanzas rather than four: the first two are virtually identical with those of the final version; the next three describe the crickets' sound ("audibler at dusk," no difference of "cadence or of pause," of indeterminate cessation). The final two stanzas are:

> The earth has many keys –
> Where melody is not
> Is the unknown peninsula
> Beauty is nature's fact.
>
> But witness for her land
> And witness for her sea
> The cricket is her utmost
> Of elegy to me.

Here the experience is generalized ("many keys") and thus dissipated; banality is not avoided (the cricket gets her vote for superior elegiac sound effects); and a portentous allusion – "the unknown peninsula" is Hamlet's "undiscover'd country, from whose bourn/No traveller returns" [iii 1.79–80] – brings into the poem a speculative concern with the future.

In the final version, the entire emphasis is on the present moment – on the enhanced "now." There is no looking before or after and therefore nothing to adulterate or break the present intensity of apprehension. In another Dickinson poem, crickets are described as sent by the

"Typic Mother" to epitomize the seasonal change: their murmuring is "The Revelations of the Book/Whose Genesis was June" (#1115). If there is a typological suggestion in #1068, it is certainly not the silver lining found by one critic: "the speaker's mind [has] been visited from beyond circumference by a natural manifestation of grace that enables the poet to accept the coming death of the year in expectancy of renewal" (Eberwein *Strategies* 191). What is typified is exactly what the poem says is typified: not renewal in the future but "Repose" in the present – in a strangely enhanced moment in which the enlarged loneliness of the perceiver has merged with the primordial natural strangeness that had caused the subjective expansion. But the present repose of #1068 is not oblivious of impermanence. No grace has been taken away from the natural moment, there is no furrow on the glow: *yet*, as in Keats's "To Autumn," there is an unvoiced premonition of future diminution that does not diminish, but rather adds to, the intensity of the present experience.

In #1068 the ear is the key sense in the poet's enhanced conscious-ness; in other poems it is the eye. Dickinson (unlike Thoreau) makes no qualitative distinctions between the sensitive registrations of the ear and those of the eye. It might be observed that visual intimations tend to elicit a more reflective response than aural ones, while the latter carry a stronger emotional charge. But more than once strong visual impressions are synesthetically described in aural terms: the light in spring that almost speaks to the poet (#812); the slant of winter sun-light that oppresses like the heaviness of cathedral music (#258); the prism that "never held the Hues,/It only heard them play" (#1602). And in #673, visual and aural perceptions supply equally transporting intimations of a celestial "diviner thing":

> 'Tis this – in Music – hints and sways –
> And far abroad on Summer days –
> Distils uncertain pain –
> 'Tis this enamors in the East –
> And tints the Transit in the West –
> With harrowing Iodine –
>
> 'Tis this – invites – appalls – endows –
> Flits – glimmers – proves – dissolves –
> Returns – suggests – convicts – enchants –
> Then – flings in Paradise –

As the plethora of verbs in the last stanza of poem #673 suggests, Dickinson's aural and visual intimations of a "diviner thing" were fleeting and unstable. She longed for clear and unequivocal signs or symbols of the transcendent – of what one poem calls "Compound Vision –/Light – enabling Light –/The Finite – furnished/With the Infinite" (#906). The opening stanza of this poem, however, says that only "through an Open Tomb" – that is, only by the experience of dying – can this definitive symbolic perception be gained. The human condition is one of uncertainty and scepticism: one lives in a terrestrial "House of Supposition" speculating about heavenly mansions that are "never quite disclosed/And never quite concealed"; one tries to reach "The Glimmering Frontier that/Skirts the Acres of Perhaps," but the "timid life of Evidence/Keeps pleading – 'I don't know'" (#696, #1173).

A principal cause of Dickinson's uncertainty is her awareness of the inevitable subjective component in perception: "The Outer – from the Inner/Derives its Magnitude –/'Tis Duke, or Dwarf, according/As is the Central Mood" (#451). Just as every day has two lengths, its "absolute extent/And Area superior/By Hope or Horror lent," so eternity will seem "Velocity or Pause" depending on the earthly character of the individual (#1295). This is as true for the ear as for the eye: the oriole's singing may be common or divine depending on the predisposition of the hearer (#526); the sun "is gay or stark/According to our Deed" (#878). Another tendency to subjective distortion is found in the imagination itself. One can imagine a plenitude – "Certainties of Sun –/Midsummer – in the Mind" – so intensely that the long-pondered vision "So plausible becomes/That I esteem the fiction – real –/The Real – fictitious seems" (#646).

At other times, the problem is with the heart's tendency to cloud the mind, as in Dickinson's lovely Indian summer poem:

> These are the Days when Birds come back –
> A very few – a Bird or two –
> To take a backward look.
>
> These are the days when skies resume
> The old – old sophistries of June –
> A blue and gold mistake.
>
> Oh fraud that cannot cheat the Bee –
> Almost thy plausibility
> Induces my belief.

Till ranks of seeds their witness bear –
And softly thro' the altered air
Hurries a timid leaf.

Oh Sacrament of summer days,
Oh Last Communion in the Haze –
Permit a child to join.

Thy sacred emblems to partake –
Thy consecrated bread to take
And thine immortal wine!   (#130)

The poem's stanza form and rhyme scheme are those of "the most
lyrical of hymn meters, *aabccb*, the so-called Common Particular.
Both the movement and the meaning of the poem call for a division
into three double stanzas instead of the six as printed" (Anderson
Emily 147). The three sections are further demarcated by the two
apostrophes, "Oh fraud" and "Oh sacrament." The second is the
only metrically regular of the three sections, suggesting a balance
between the attitudes to natural fact in the other two. The first
describes Indian summer, which seems like early summer – but only
seems. The discriminating perceiver knows that it is a "mistake" to
think that the blue and gold of the October sky means the return of
June, just as she knows that the blue and gold of early summer were
themselves "sophistries" in that they seemed to encourage belief in
their permanence.

Nonetheless, in the second section the plausibility almost induces
"belief." Almost, but not quite. The natural facts of October – seeds
being blown through the air, leaves falling to the ground when the
stillness of the air is altered by the slightest breeze: these "bear
witness" to the fact that June is long gone. But the third section has
another reversal. There is no disagreement about what the natural
facts are; but a different reading of their signification allows the
poem to end in a haze of Christian symbols. The second attitude is
that of a believing or credulous child, not that of a knowing bee. We
now have not fraud but sacrament; not apian nectar but immortal
wine; not scattered seeds and withered leaf but consecrated bread.
The stasis at the end of #130 might seem a version of poem #1068
("Further in Summer"), but the two poems are quite different. If
#1068 recalls Keats's "To Autumn," #130 looks forward to Robert
Frost's Indian summer poem "October" (from his first volume *A
Boy's Will*), whose daydreamy speaker has a heart "not averse to

being beguiled" and would fain lay an ineffectual finger on the spoke of Time's great wheel.

   Despite her epistemological self-awareness, Dickinson never doubted the authenticity of her "Heavenly Moments" (#393) or "ecstatic instant[s]" (#125) – for example, that "something in a summer's noon – /A depth – an Azure – a perfume –/Transcending ecstasy" (#122). But these moments or instants were infrequent and fortuitous; most of the time they were known through their absence – were experienced only prospectively or retrospectively. The former condition is instanced in poem #812:

> A Light exists in Spring
> Not present on the Year
> At any other period –
> When March is scarcely here
>
> A Color stands abroad
> On Solitary Fields
> That Science cannot overtake
> But Human Nature feels.
>
> It waits upon the Lawn,
> It shows the furthest Tree
> Upon the furthest Slope you know
> It almost speaks to you.
>
> Then as Horizons step
> Or Noons report away
> Without the Formula of sound
> It passes and we stay –
>
> A quality of loss
> Affecting our Content
> As Trade had suddenly encroached
> Upon a Sacrament.

March, as Dickinson says in another poem, "is the Month of Expectation" (#1404). In this poem, a certain quality to the morning light in early spring stirs a deep-seated longing in the speaker. The light seems a companionable form or answering other: it waits for us, reveals the furthest limits of the visible, and "almost speaks." *Almost* is the pivotal word (as in #130). Its importance is highlighted by the absence of the expected *b* rhyme at the end of the third stanza, which enacts the breaking of the one-life illusion. This vernal light passes "Without the Formula of sound" (it doesn't speak), and in doing so affects "Content" in two senses: it leaves one both dissatisfied rather than satisfied, and empty rather than full.

The transience of ecstatic moments and the subsequent discontent are the subjects of numerous poems: as certainly as "A Grant of the Divine" comes, it "Withdraws – and leaves the dazzled Soul/In her unfurnished Rooms" (#393). In poem #430, the speaker recalls the assurance she had once felt that "Difference – had begun" and that her life "would never be Common – more"; but "suddenly – my Riches shrank –/A goblin – drank my Dew." She had to put back on the "The Sackcloth … The Frock I used to wear." Whatever happened, she wonders, to "my moment of Brocade –/My – drop – of India?" And in poem #1257, the ephemeral nature of human fulfillment contrasts with the timeless flitting of the butterflies and bees:

> Dominion lasts until obtained –
> Possession just as long –
> But these – endowing as they flit
> Eternally belong.
>
> How everlasting are the Lips
> Known only to the Dew –
> These are the Brides of permanence
> Supplanting me and you.

The contrast here is primarily sexual. The ephemeral natural creatures pollinate the flowers and thus contribute to the regenerative processes of the natural world. In our pursuits, on the other hand, me and you desire to possess and to dominate. Butterflies and bees do not take or appropriate to themselves; they endow rather than possess. In doing so they seem a part of the continuum of nature – they eternally belong to it. The flowers (their petals figured as lips) are reproductive without being impregnated: they are unravished brides like Keats's Grecian urn and similarly permanent or timeless in comparison to all breathing human passion. Human possession, on the other hand, is lasting only in anticipation.

Despite their elusive nature, however, the longing for the "Moments of Dominion/That happen on a Soul" cannot be mastered. One reason is that such moments are highly addictive; they leave the soul "with a Discontent/Too exquisite – to tell" (#627). One poem describes the condition of those "lonesome for they know not What." They are figured as "Eastern Exiles" from Paradise who once strayed beyond "the Amber line" on the eastern horizon and ever since have vainly striven to climb the "purple Moat" on the now western horizon and so return to the place they know only through its absence (#262).[4]

The other reason the longing for "Moments of Dominion" cannot be mastered is that for Dickinson they seem the predestined or pre-programmed goal of human existence. In #1099, a poem that in tandem with #1257 illustrates the figural versatility of natural facts in her poetry, this encoding is symbolized by the butterfly's development:

> My Cocoon tightens – Colors tease –
> I'm feeling for the Air –
> A dim capacity for Wings
> Demeans the Dress I wear –
>
> A power of Butterfly must be –
> The Aptitude to fly
> Meadows of Majesty implies
> And easy Sweeps of Sky –

Like the butterfly emerging from its cocoon, humans seem endowed with the potential for reaching higher things. The "Aptitude to fly" of itself "implies" (in the variant reading of "concedes" that I have adopted) a celestial plenitude. "So," the poem concludes,

> I must baffle at the Hint
> And cipher at the Sign
> And make much blunder, if at last
> I take the clue divine –

The remaining poems I want to consider instance or comment on what Robert Weisbuch calls Dickinson's analogical poetics (11), her frequently baffled perceptual search for divine clues. For "ecstatic need," as she puts it in poem #1101, "Liquor at the Lip" is superior to "Liquor in the Jug," But for someone who cannot, or cannot always, get the cork out, the only other way of slaking this thirst are "Apprehensions" (#797) or analogical inferences. The hint or sign in poem #1241 is a sunset:

> The Lilac is an ancient shrub
> But ancienter than that

The Firmamental Lilac
Upon the Hill tonight –
The Sun subsiding on his Course
Bequeathes this final Plant
To Contemplation – not to Touch –
The Flower of Occident.
Of one Corolla is the West –
The Calyx is the Earth –
The Capsules burnished Seeds the Stars –
The Scientist of Faith
His research has but just begun –
Above his synthesis
The Flora unimpeachable
To Time's Analysis –
"Eye hath not seen" may possibly
Be current with the Blind
But let not Revelation
By theses be detained –

The quotation in the last quatrain is from 1 Corinthians: "Eye hath
not seen, nor ear heard, neither have entered into the heart of man,
the things which God hath prepared for them that love him" (2:9).
The poem contrasts scientific knowledge, which is dependent on the
input of eye and ear, with "Revelation." In contemplating the lilac
sunset, the botanist uses a taxonomy in which the macro is considered in terms of the micro. The proportion play is ingenious but the
result is reductive: for this scientist, the spectacular sunset is merely
a firmamental shrub. For the "Scientist of Faith" – the Rationalist,
the Unitarian, the Higher Critic – earthbound criteria also obtain. For
him, all transcendent notions are ultimately rooted in or projected
from the human need for a sky-god. Opposed to both scientific syn-
theses – the botanical and the theological – is the view that the Flower
of Occident is beyond temporal analysis; it is not a finer-toned repetition of the terrestrial but a "Revelation" – a showing forth in perceptible form of something transcendent. The conclusion of the poem,
however, does not affirm that tonight's sunset is such a revelation;
it rather suggests that a showing forth of the transcendent cannot be
"detained" (apprehended) by "theses" or by any of the other tools of
rational analysis.

The conclusion to poem #797 is similarly measured. The poem's
first three stanzas are a fanciful exercise in proportion play: what the
speaker sees and smells from her window is perceived as a small-scale
world. This exercise becomes more serious in the fourth and fifth

stanzas when perceptual attention centers on what is heard when the
wind blows through the pine:

> Of its Voice – to affirm – when the Wind is within –
> Can the Dumb – define the Divine?
> The Definition of Melody – is –
> That Definition is none –
>
> It – suggests to our Faith –
> They – suggest to our Sight –
> When the latter – is put away
> I shall meet with Conviction I somewhere met
> That Immortality –

Is there, the speaker wonders, an invisible or supernatural dimension
to the world outside the window? Can the dumb (the pine tree)
"define the Divine" – that is, can a natural fact symbolize the transcendent? When the wind is within, it would seem that the tree can
do so; after all, the definition of the wind's sound, its melody, is that it
has no definition. The definition (the meaning) of "Melody" is that
it is not de-finite: it has no fixed or quantifiable limits. It is infinite,
and as such a suggestive figuration of something beyond the natural.

The fifth stanza has another allusion to 1 Corinthians: "When I was
a child, I spake as a child, I understood as a child, I thought as a
child; but when I became a man, I put away childish things" (13:11).
When the speaker has put away the visual game of figuring the pine
tree as a globe she will meet "That Immortality" of which the wind
was a symbol. But she will presumably be able to do so only because
she has earlier "play[ed] at Paste –/Till qualified, for Pearl," as Dickinson puts it in another poem. When the real thing is met, we drop
the imitation "and deem ourself a fool" – but we could not have
learned to identify the real thing without the prior play with simulacra (#320).

The confidence in this stanza is prospective; it is succeeded in the
last stanza by a return to a lightly suggestive:

> Was the Pine at my Window a "Fellow
> Of the Royal" Infinity?
> Apprehensions – are God's introductions –
> To be hallowed – accordingly –

Fellows of the British Royal Society are scientists. Dickinson is not a
scientist of Faith; she is a connoisseur of the "Apprehensions" – the

divine intimations or revelations that are (in a variant of the poem's final line) "Extended inscrutably."

Poems #797 and #1241 are upbeat and confident; but they are also cagey in what they suggest. Their principal thrust is to make possibility possible. The caution with which they conduct themselves is understandable in the light of the powerful counterstatements found in numerous other poems. Some of them describe an initial confidence being undermined. In poem #501 the subsidence is brilliantly enacted:

> This World is not Conclusion.
> A Species stands beyond –
> Invisible, as Music –
> But positive, as Sound –
> It beckons, and it baffles –
> Philosophy – dont know –
> And through a Riddle, at the last –
> Sagacity, must go –
> To guess it, puzzles scholars –
> To gain it, Men have borne
> Contempt of Generations
> And Crucifixion, shown –
> Faith slips – and laughs, and rallies –
> Blushes, if any see –
> Plucks at a twig of Evidence –
> And asks a Vane, the way –
> Much Gesture, from the Pulpit –
> Strong Hallelujahs roll –
> Narcotics cannot still the Tooth
> That nibbles at the soul –

The most positive point in the poem is the period at the end of its first line; after that, each image contributes to the undermining of the initial declaration. This gradual process follows the stages of "Crumbling" as analysed by Dickinson in poem #997: it is not "an instant's Act" but rather "Devil's work/Consecutive and slow –/Fail in an instant, no man did/Slipping – is Crash's law." The invisible "Species" ("sequel" in a variant reading) seems susceptible of aural apprehension (as in #797); but this simultaneously beckons emotionally and baffles intellectually. Philosophy has to play dumb: it "dont know." "Sagacity" – experientially rather than conceptually grounded knowledge of what is beyond this world – can only be gained "at the last" by going through the "Riddle" of dying. In the past, men have heroically endeavored to reach the beyond; women have agitated themselves towards the same end. In their Sunday congregations, conventional Christians receive powerful rhetorical and choral reinforcement of their belief in a sequel to this world. But in the sardonic final lines, all of these efforts are glossed as pain-killers that cannot still the gnawing doubt that there may be no sequel to this world.

Poem #501 satirizes more than conventional religious belief. The marvelous figure of Faith as a well-bred, self-conscious young woman trying to do the proper thing in distressing circumstances is also a self-parody of Dickinson's own tendency to analogical inquiry. The wind, which as any weather vane indicates bloweth where it listeth, is the same force that is credited with being able to "define the Divine" in #797; and in her speculative poems many "twigs" are tentatively plucked. In #742, the twigs belong to "Four Trees – upon a solitary Acre" in an otherwise barren place. The most striking feature of this poem is the spareness of both subject and its representation. The randomly situated trees on a bare acre suggest no proprietorial purpose, aesthetic or practical: the trees have to maintain themselves. They have the morning sun and the wind in their branches, and they have a figure/ground relationship to the earth. But what does their perceiver have? The last stanza shows the perceiving mind moving in a familiar direction – towards inference and analogy. Of what spiritual fact might this natural fact be the symbol? Do the four trees have a relationship to their third nearest neighbor (God)? What witness "is Theirs" unto the whole of which they are a part? What evidence do they give of a providential purpose or plan? The one-word answer to all these questions – "Unknown" – is utterly and unequivocally agnostic.

"Unknown" is also a key word in #1202. The poem's subject is a natural process – the work of the frost. Its first three stanzas are playfully descriptive, emphasizing the stealth and cunning of a "never seen" force – a "Stranger" that is felt to be "hovering round" remote villages. But "search effaces him/Till some retrieveless Night … The Garden gets the only shot/That never could be traced." There follows a stanza of generalization on this natural process:

> Unproved is much we know –
> Unknown the worst we fear –
> Of Strangers is the Earth the Inn
> Of Secrets is the Air –

In this nicely turned but unexceptional piece of worldly wisdom, the operation of the frost is the vehicle of a didactic figure, the tenor of which is the uncertainty and contingency of human life – that we can be adversely affected by forces that we cannot trace or begin to understand.

The poem does not end here, however. There is, so to speak, another final stanza:

> To analyze perhaps
> A Philip would prefer
> But Labor vaster than myself
> I find it to infer.

This is a great deal more interesting. Its basis is the familiar Dickinsonian distinction between scientific knowledge and inference. In John's Gospel, when Jesus says "I am the way, the truth, and the life: no man cometh unto the Father, but by me," Philip replies: "Lord, shew us the Father, and it sufficeth us." Jesus answers: "Have I been so long time with you, and yet hast thou not known me, Philip? he that hath seen me hath seen the Father … Believest thou not that I am in the Father, and the Father in me? the words that I speak unto you I speak not of myself: but the Father that dwelleth in me, he doeth the works" (14:6–10). We now have an implicit analogy in which the lethal effects of the frost's secret ministry are to the unseen, traceless stranger causing them (the frost itself) what Jesus is to his invisible Father. But the frost is known only through its effects – indeed, it does not exist apart from its effects. Consequently, a Philippean or scientific attempt to distinguish between them would yield only a notional and not a real distinction.

Besides, anyone with common sense and some experience of the New England climate can infer with confidence that frost is the cause of the seasonal destruction of gardens. The reader of Dickinson's poem can be equally confident that frost is not on the speaker's mind when inference is described as a vaster labor than she can perform. As the biblical allusion attests, she is thinking about supernatural inference – about the relationship of visible facts to invisible facts. The scientific mistake is to analyse – to employ rational thinking in a sphere where symbolic perception is called for. But it would be equally a blunder to try to infer the existence of a loving heavenly Father from the killing operation of the frost. Such analogical reflection would lead instead to a Hardyesque vision of cosmic malignity, like that found in poem #1624:

> Apparently with no surprise
> To any happy Flower
> The Frost beheads it at its play –

> In accidental power –
> The blonde Assassin passes on –
> The Sun proceeds unmoved
> To measure off another Day
> For an Approving God.

Better no illume at all than the *ignis fatuus* of the frost.

In the last analogical meditation I want to consider, the illumination is celestial:

> The Moon upon her fluent Route
> Defiant of a Road –
> The Star's Etruscan Argument
> Substantiate a God –
>
> If aims impel these Astral Ones
> The ones allowed to know
> Know that which makes them as forgot
> As Dawn forgets them – now –   (#1528)

In another Dickinson poem, the moon is figured as a female stranger, "A Lady in the Town" who seems "engrossed to Absolute –/With shining – and the Sky" and shows no "Concern/For little Mysteries/ … /As harass us – like Life – and Death –/And Afterward – or Nay" (#629). In this poem, the same celestial quality of utter unconcern for sublunar beings is more cryptically and powerfully intimated. "Etruscan" may be taken to mean strangely mysterious and awe-inspiring (like "Antiquest" and "Druidic" in #1068). But the allusion is more pointed. Little is known of the Etruscans, the pre-Roman inhabitants of Italy. Their inscriptions, written in the Greek alphabet and therefore legible, are transcribed from a mysterious tongue related to no known language group and are thus undecipherable. Thus, the stars shining in the night sky may seem natural facts symbolizing and substantiating a God, just as the moon's graceful movement through the heavens may seem fluent in the secondary sense of inscribing a message for terrestrial readers. But one cannot know what is being said because one does not know the language of the spheres.

The problem implicit in "Etruscan" is made explicit in the opening line of the second stanza – "If aims impel these Astral Ones." But agnostic uncertainty is not the conclusion of this poem, as it is of other Dickinson poems. The conditional phrase is immediately followed by a powerfully negative statement that erases possibility and replaces it with negative certainty. This reading presupposes two crucial determinations. The first is to read the last two lines as an analogical proposition in which the "them" in the penultimate line refers to "The Ones allowed to know" and the "them" in the final line to "these Astral Ones" – the moon and stars. Even if the celestial characters are legible and do figure a God, the ones allowed to read them only "know" (have knowledge of) something utterly oblivious of them (like the Northern Lights in #290), something that makes them as insignificant, as forgotten, as the light of the rising sun makes the stars and the moon.

The second determination concerns the identity of "The Ones allowed to know." There are two possibilities. The privileged ones might be taken to be the dead – those, and those alone, who have the sagacity that comes with having gone through the "Riddle" (#501). A collective example would be the Etruscan race, who by failing to communicate with succeeding races have become a forgotten people. In this reading, the poem's closing statement becomes simply a version of the Christian commonplace that Time like an ever-rolling stream bears all its sons away, making them forgotten as a dream that dies at the break of day. The alternative reading is more chilling: "The ones allowed to know" are Romantic seers like Emily Dickinson with the gift of symbolic perception, who are committed to the principle that natural facts are the symbols of spiritual facts – that as Ishmael puts it in chapter 99 of *Moby-Dick*, "some certain significance lurks in all things, else all things are little worth, and the round world itself but an empty cipher." In this reading, at the end of #1528 all that these privileged seers have learned is that, like the vanished stars and moon, they too will be extinguished.

In reading and thinking about the speculative poems of Emily Dickinson, where should the final emphasis fall – on the negative or the positive? There is poem #761:

> From Blank to Blank –
> A Threadless Way
> I pushed Mechanic feet –
> To stop – or perish – or advance –
> Alike indifferent –
>
> If end I gained
> It ends beyond
> Indefinite disclosed –
> I shut my eyes – and groped as well
> 'Twas lighter – to be Blind –

But a late prose statement implies something very different: "Tis a dangerous moment for any one when the meaning goes out of things and Life stands straight – and punctual – and yet no content(s) (signal) come(s). Yet such moments are. If we survive them they expand us" (*Letters* iii 919).

I would say that despite the numerous poems describing terrible moments where the meaning goes out of things and no signal comes, the ultimate impression conveyed by Dickinson's poetry is that the journey is worthwhile even if there can be no arrival. "Wonder," the poet says in #1331, "is not precisely Knowing / And not precisely Knowing not"; a person "has not lived who has not felt" this "beautiful but bleak condition." A better image of Dickinson's analogical quest than a seeker moving from blank to blank is the traveller in #1450:

> The Road was lit with Moon and star –
> The Trees were bright and still –
> Descried I – by the distant Light
> A Traveller on a Hill –
> To magic Perpendiculars
> Ascending, though Terrene –
> Unknown his shimmering ultimate –
> But he indorsed the sheen –

As in #1528, the night scene is illuminated by the moon and stars; the speaker is just able to make out in the distance the figure of a traveller on a hill. That this is a figure of the poet is suggested in the third line: "Descried I –" can be read as "I saw there myself (or a figure of myself)." Although the traveller is "Terrene," not celestial, he is moving towards, and seems drawn upwards by, a magical illumination. The specific goal or destination is "unknown" and there is no suggestion that the earthbound traveller will ever arrive at a "shimmering ultimate." But the poem does affirm that the traveller's presence authenticates (endorses) the illuminated scene (metonymically figured by the sheen), giving it a focal point and a value it would not otherwise possess, just as the unknown shimmering ultimate gives a focus, a direction and a value to the longing for a disclosure of the beyond.

Afterword:
Two Victorian Seers

How useful is sensory-perceptual contextualization for the study of other nineteenth-century poets? It is difficult to generalize. In my view, it would not be useful to follow up William Michael Rossetti's observation that "a marked peculiarity in Browning's eyes – one of them long-sighted, the other short-sighted" – illustrates "the quality of his mind" or mental vision (299n). Pursuing the implications of Lionel Trilling's observations on Keats's sensory profile is another matter. Trilling notes that while in Wordsworth "virtually the only two sense-faculties of which he takes account are seeing and hearing" and "the matter of the senses' experience passes very quickly into what Wordsworth calls the 'purer mind'," in Keats there is "no distinction of prestige among the senses, and to him the sensory, the sensuous and the sensual were all one … Eating and the delicacies of taste are basic and definitive in his experience and in his poetry … Sense cannot be left behind" (13–14).

There are also the cases of Tennyson and Hopkins. I want to conclude with brief discussions of these two poets because they show the usefulness of sensory-perceptual contextualization for post-Romantic poets, even for those who exhibit an antipathy to symbolic perception. Tennyson's severe myopia was the physiological basis of his equivocal attitude to symbolic perception and his reliance in his speculative poetry on intuition rather than sensory-perceptual experience. In his journals and poetry, Hopkins attempted to perceive the natural world intensely but objectively, without subjective distortion. But two of his very finest poems are exceptions to this rule. And the shape of his creative career has more in common with that of Wordsworth, Coleridge, Thoreau, and Whitman than has been recognized.

In 1892, the year of his death, Tennyson reaffirmed his belief that "God *is* love, transcendent, all-pervading! We do not get *this* faith from Nature or the world … We get this faith from ourselves, from what is highest within us" (H. Tennyson i 314). In understanding Tennyson's life-long insistence on this point, the place to begin is with the most conspicuous feature of his sensory profile. "The shortness of his sight, which was extreme, tormented him always," James Knowles recalled: "When he was looking at any object he seemed to be smelling it … at my first visit to him he warned me, as I left, to come up and speak to him whenever I next met him, 'for if not,' he said, 'I shouldn't know you though I rubbed against you in the street'" (Page 88). This report comes from a friend of later years; but Tennyson was just as myopic in youth. As a Cambridge undergraduate, for example, he "customarily read only with a monocle or reading-glasses, with the book held close to the end of his nose." He also used a monocle at meals because he was "unable to see to eat without it" (Martin *Tennyson* 93).

The need to peer closely at what was within a limited focal range helps account for the detailed particularity of Tennyson's natural descriptions. John Stuart Mill notes of his early poems that "the delineation of outward objects … is, not picturesque, but … statuesque; with brilliancy of colour superadded. The forms are not, as in painting, of unequal degrees of definiteness; the tints do not melt gradually into each other, but each individual object stands out in bold relief, with a clear decided outline" (Jump 89). In Valerie Pitt's formulation, Tennyson had "cloistered vision": because of the isolation of "visual details from the things with which they would be associated in a normal field of vision," he seems in his poetry "to move in a world of over-emphasised detail so precisely stated that it appears fantastic to normal vision" (21–2).

Tennyson's shortsightedness also helps to account for other conspicuous features of his sensory-perceptual life. For one thing, as Patrick Trevor-Roper notes in his study of *The World through Blunted Sight*, Tennyson's extreme myopia was the reason "his epithets often have a tactile quality – like the 'wrinkled sea', which recalls the poems written by the truly blind" (32). For another, when one sense is defective, another sense will sometimes acquire a compensatory acuteness. Zola, for example, who was also severely shortsighted, had a highly developed sense of smell. In Tennyson's case, the compensatory sense was hearing – or so he believed. His hearing "was exceptionally keen," Knowles recalled, "and he held it as a sort of compensation for his blurred sight; he could hear 'the shrieks of a bat', which he always said was the test of a quick ear" (Page 88).

Myopia also explains the vagueness of the poet's distanced perspectives – the frequency with which material phenomena lose their outline and fade into shadow. Tennyson told an astronomer friend that "without spectacles the two stars of the Great Bear forming the pointers appeared to him as two intersecting circular disks" (Lockyer and Lockyer 31). Another friend reported "that the moon, without a glass, seemed to him like a shield across the sky" (H. Tennyson i 512). As Pitt has noted: "sharpness of detail belongs only to the foreground of Tennyson's descriptions, more distant objects appear with a kind of mysterious generality: landscape takes on a haziness like a landscape in the half light, and seems like the country of a dream or a fantasy." Tennyson's world, "physically and emotionally, is a world without middle distance where the near is detailed, intimate and striking, and the distant unreal, ungraspable, and vague" (22).

The absence of middle distance in Tennyson's visual field has important implications for the status of symbolic perception in his poetry. At the close-up extreme we have this brief reflective lyric:

> Flower in the crannied wall,
> I pluck you out of the crannies,
> I hold you here, root and all, in my hand,
> Little flower – but *if* I could understand
> What you are, root and all, and all in all,
> I should know what God and man is.   (ii 693)

If, could, should: Tennyson is too close to the flower for it to function as an instrument in apprehending the supernatural. It cannot be a Coleridgean metonymic symbol, like the flowery meadow in the middle distance described in the *Statesman's Manual*, because there is no continuum or whole of which it can be perceived to be a part. In Tennyson's view,

> … any man that walks the mead,
>   In bud or blade, or bloom, may find,
> According as his humours lead,
>   A meaning suited to his mind.   (ii 56)

At the other extreme is "The Higher Pantheism":

> The sun, the moon, the stars, the seas, the hills and the plains –
> Are not these, O soul, the Vision of Him who reigns?
>
> Is not the Vision He? though He be not that which He seems?
> Dreams are true while they last, and do we not live in dreams?
>
> Earth, these solid stars, this weight of body and limb,
> Are they not sign and symbol of thy division from Him.
> ....
> And the ear of man cannot hear, and the eye of man cannot see;
> But if we could see and hear, this Vision – were it not He?   (ii 706)

The material dissolve at the extreme limits of the phenomenal gives rise to cosmic ruminations and a pretty taste for sparadox. But the result is no more conclusive and no more satisfying than Tennyson's musings on the tiny flower. Celestial facts are equally unhelpful as indicators or examples of spiritual facts.

No wonder, then, that throughout his career Tennyson insisted on a distinction between knowledge, which is dependent on the experience of the senses, and a higher faculty that is not empirically based and that he usually calls wisdom. The former is "earthly of the mind," the latter "heavenly of the soul" (ii 436). Assurance of the existence of transcendent entities can only be gained through inner experience – the "heat of inward evidence" (i 585). Knowledge is "the swallow on the lake/That sees and stirs the surface-shadow there" but cannot penetrate beyond the surface (iii 140). Nor can sensory and perceptual experience help to "fight the fear of death" (ii 435). All too often, what the senses discover in the phenomenal world are not tokens of transcendence but "outward signs" of mortality (i 584). At other times, there seems to be a radical discontinuity between external phenomena and the individual human life: "will one beam be less intense," the still small voice asks the tormented speaker of "The Two Voices," "When thy peculiar difference/Is cancelled in the world of sense?":

> Not less the bee would range her cells,
> The furzy prickle fire the dells,
> The foxglove cluster dappled bells.   (i 573–4)

Hopkins is the Victorian poetic seer who most closely approximates Ruskin's anti-Romantic ideal of perception without subjective distortion. As an Oxford undergraduate of eighteen, Hopkins reported that he was sketching "a good deal." He described the point of view of his drawings as "Ruskinese" and went on to explain: "I have particular periods of admiration for particular things in Nature; for a certain time I am astonished at the beauty of a tree, shape, effect etc, then when the passion, so to speak, has subsided, it is consigned to my treasury of explored beauty, and acknowledged with admiration and interest ever after, while something new takes its place in my enthusiasm" (*Further Letters* 202). The same point of view is found in the journal that Hopkins intermittently kept from 1866 to 1875. The most striking aspect of the many renderings of natural phenomena in the journal is their impersonality. Hopkins does not allow his moods or thoughts to be associated with his perception of nature and even seems intent on promoting the self-sufficiency of the object of perception and demoting the contribution of the perceiver to the perceptual act. For example, in passages where he is closely scrutinizing a natural object Hopkins tends to employ a dangling participle or detached modifier "in such a way as to blur the distinction between the human observer and the surrounding physical world" (Martin *Hopkins* 204).

This syntactic equivocation is one manifestation of Hopkins' complex sensibility. On the one hand, his senses were acute and exquisitely discriminating. In a journal entry of May 1871, for example, he notes of the bluebells he had held in his hand that they seemed "made to every sense" and then shows this in a long passage of detailed description (*Journals* 209). On the other hand, from an early age, Hopkins had a rigorous scruple concerning his body and kept his senses under strict control. His poem "The Habit of Perfection," written in 1866, is a catalogue of sensory mortification: silence is asked to "sing to me" and beat upon his ear; his eyes will be closed in order to find "the uncreated light"; the palate, "the hutch of tasty lust," is encouraged to welcome "fasts divine" and the nostrils to content themselves with what the censers send forth from the sanctuary; and the hands and feet are similarly addressed.

Despite these severities, the journal entries for the late 1860s and early 1870s show that Hopkins allowed himself a good deal of visual pleasure. "What you look hard at," he notes, "seems to look hard at you" (*Journals* 204). This intense interaction brought numerous aesthetic frissons indicated by terms like "melodious," "beautiful," "graceful," and "charming." The journal even shows a Thoreauvian awareness of how the circumstances and tactics of the perceiver could

affect the intensity of perception. For example, in looking hard at natural objects Hopkins needed to be alone: "Even with one companion
ecstasy is almost banished: you want to be alone and to feel that, and
leisure – all pressure taken off" (*Journals* 182).

In time, aesthetic perception modulated into a more disciplined
intellectual scrutiny of natural phenomena. But to call the natural
observations in the journal scientific would be misleading. Hopkins'
ruling passion is his perception of "natural objects as active, autonomous beings in the continuous process of self-creation" (Frederick
96). Looking hard at objects in attempting to capture their uniqueness, their informing principle of organization, and their process of
self-creation, led Hopkins to coin the terms "inscape" and "instress."
The former is the distinctive sense-perceived pattern or inner form of
a natural object. The latter is the term for the unifying force in the
object, the energy that sustains the pattern: "all things are upheld by
instress and are meaningless without it" (*Journals* 127). In this sense,
instress is ultimately a supernatural force. But the term is also used
by Hopkins to connote "that impulse *from* the 'inscape' which acts on
the senses and, through them, actualizes the inscape in the mind
of the [perceiver] … Instress, then, is often the *sensation* of inscape"
(Gardner xxi).

That is to say, instress has both an objective and a subjective
aspect: it is both a quality of an object or a presupposition of its
existence and an aspect of the interaction between perceived and
perceiver. In its latter aspect, instress resembles Coleridge's primary
imagination – "the living Power and prime Agent of all human Perception" (*Biographia* i 304). For Hopkins, both subject and object
share in the possession of the energy of instress: there is "a stem of
stress between us and things," a complementarity, a rhyming or mirroring, a "canon … of feeling" (*Journals* 127, 135). (A canon is a musical piece with different parts taking up the same subject successively
in strict imitation.) But the instress "which unmistakeably distinguishes and individualises things" is "not imposed outwards from
the mind as for instance by melancholy or strong feeling" (*Journals*
215). We are not, that is to say, dealing with examples of the pathetic
fallacy. It is rather the case that (as Hopkins put it in "Hurrahing
in Harvest") "These things, these things were here and but the
beholder / Wanting."

In the late 1870s, Hopkins gave up his journal and returned to
writing poetry after having abstained from metrical composition for
eight years because he believed it incompatible with his religious
vocation. This occurred during the period when he was stationed at

St Beuno's, a Jesuit house in a lovely natural setting in north Wales. Hopkins later described his three years there as his "salad days" (*Bridges* 163), and one may equally well appropriate Coleridge's term and describe this time as a "blessed interval" during which his poetic faculties expanded in tandem with his intensified sense of the beauty of natural facts.

During this period, Hopkins wrote about one-third of all his mature poetry, including the famous series of nature poems which celebrate the particulars of the natural world in the continuous process of being themselves. One indication of this perceived plenitude is the mirroring or rhyming of one part of the natural world by another: "As kingfishers catch fire, dragonflies draw flame"; "Thrush's eggs look little low heavens" ("Spring"); skies are "of couple-colour as a brinded cow" ("Pied Beauty"); the stars in the night sky resemble (*inter alia*) "Flake-doves sent floating forth at a farmyard scare" ("The Starlight Night"). As in Coleridge's conversation poems, synesthetic imagery is another sign of the intense reciprocity of inner and outer, of the rhythm in Hopkins' poetic perception of the natural world. In "Spring," the song of the thrush "Through the echoing timber does so rinse and wring/The ear, it strikes like lightnings to hear him sing" (rinse and wring are tactile verbs, lightning a visual image). Just as the trees do, these figures amplify and enhance the bird's song.

As is well known, what helped persuade Hopkins of the appropriateness of these poetic celebrations was his discovery a few years previously of the thought of the medieval theologian Duns Scotus, a key aspect of which is encapsulated in "As kingfishers catch fire":

> Each mortal thing does one thing and the same:
>   Deals out that being indoors each one dwells;
>   Selves – goes itself: *myself* it speaks and spells,
> Crying *What I do is me: for that I came.*

Scotus gave, so to speak, a Catholic imprimatur to Hopkins' intense sensory-perceptual apprehension of nature. In the nature poems the relationship between the particularized beauty of the natural world and his Christian supernatural beliefs is repeatedly proclaimed. The essential difference between Hopkins' apprehension of the natural world and that of the Romantic subjects of this study was pinpointed by Marshall McLuhan: his "is literally a sacramental view of the world since what of God there is he does not perceive or experience but takes on faith" (82). Most of Hopkins' nature poems presuppose a belief in what is being celebrated rather than represent the discovery of a relationship between seen and unseen. These poems are rhetorical rather than meditative, allegorical rather than symbolic. Thus, for all its greater intensity, there is no difference in intention and theme between Hopkins' wonderful curtal sonnet "Pied Beauty" and another well-known Victorian doxology, Mrs Alexander's "All things bright and beautiful."

I agree with Seamus Heaney that Hopkins' nature poems are more interesting when they do not simply celebrate and declare the supernatural infusion of the natural, but when they represent or re-enact the intense apprehension of a natural fact. I would further urge that the most interesting of these poems are those with a self-reflexive element, when one is made aware that the "fine delight" of perceptual apprehension "fathers thought" ("To R.B.") – that it is the trigger of the creative activity of mind that has resulted in the poem. It is useful to remember that as used by Hopkins "inscape" and "instress" can refer to both natural objects and aesthetic objects – paintings and sketches, musical compositions, and poems. Just as Hopkins' notion of the subjective aspect of the instress of natural objects resembles Coleridge's primary imagination, so too the instress of a poem may be likened to Coleridge's secondary imagination, which is "identical with the primary in the *kind* of its agency, and differing only in *degree*, and in the *mode* of its operation" (*Biographia* i 304).

Both degrees or modes of the creative activity of mind are inscribed in two of Hopkins' very finest poems, "The Windhover" and "Spelt from Sibyl's Leaves." The former, Heaney recognizes, is "an extended mime of the process described in the sonnet to Bridges, an anatomy of the movement of inspiration and illumination" (96). In the octet, the speaker represents his recent perception of the flight of a kestrel:

> I caught this morning morning's minion, king-
> > dom of daylight's dauphin, dapple-dawn-drawn Falcon, in
> > > his riding
> > Of the rolling level underneath him steady air, and
> > > striding
> High there, how he rung upon the rein of a wimpling wing
> In his ecstasy! then off, off forth on swing,
> > As a skate's heel sweeps smooth on a bow-bend: the hurl
> > > and gliding
> > Rebuffed the big wind. My heart in hiding
> Stirred for a bird, – the achieve of, the mastery of the
> > thing.

The kestrel is drawn to his hunting by the dawn light: it "patrols the lower air, 30–50 feet up, in great level loops," effortlessly riding the air currents (MacKenzie 379). The bird also hovers by flying against the wind at the wind's own speed and thus in the dawn light seems drawn in another sense – etched against the sky.

The octet also etches the intensity of the poet's apprehension of the windhover: he has not simply seen the bird; he has "caught" it. His heart has been powerfully "stirred" by the bird's showing forth of itself, enacting its being. The attribution of "ecstasy" to the wind-hover is a hypallage or transferred epithet; the emotion belongs to the speaker and not the bird, who is hungry, not ecstatic. This figure, a perfect example of what Ruskin termed the pathetic fallacy, can also be associated with the activity of the secondary imagination. The bird's dealing out of his being has prompted Hopkins' tongue to fling out broad his distinctive poetic being, to declare and utter him-self through the composition of the poem. The windhover is also "drawn" in a third sense: it is inscribed in Hopkins' words and exu-berant figures – the equestrian and skating imagery, the imagery of royalty and its Christian connotations.

For the predatory kestrel, one hover in eight "results in a stoop – a slow, gentle, fairly steep descent on its prey, wings held high above the back" (MacKenzie 379). Its dive is described in the first half of the poem's sestet:

> Brute beauty and valour and act, oh, air, pride, plume, here
>   Buckle! and the fire that breaks from thee then, a billion
> Times told lovelier, more dangerous, O my chevalier!

As the bird's flight changes from a glide to a more dangerous-seeming downward swoop, its wings buckle in a V- or plough-shape. "Buckle" refers to both a visual aspect of the bird's descent and the fusion of subject and object. The bird's dive causes a quantum leap ("a billion/Times") in the perceiver's intensity of apprehension; this is registered in the change from "caught" in the past tense to "Buckle" in the present tense with imperative undertones. The em-phatic "here" also locates the buckling together of subject and object in the creative present of its representation. Similarly, while at the perceptual level "the fire that breaks from thee then" may be taken to be the now visible russet underside of the kestrel (against the light of the dawn, any color in the bird would have been obliterated), it also functions as a transferred epithet, a figure both for rapturous appre-hension and creative kindling – the "strong/Spur, live and lancing like the blowpipe flame" ("To R.B.") – that impregnates the mind with the seed of the poem.

The final tercet offers ground-level analogies or mirrorings of the aerial buckling (it is the level of a self-mortifying Jesuit poet-priest whose emotions and feelings were usually kept under severe control):

> No wonder of it: sheer plod makes plough down sillion
> Shine, and blue-bleak embers, ah my dear,
> Fall, gall themselves, and gash gold-vermilion.

The sheer plod of the plough in its quotidian employment causes both its cutting blade and the overturned earth to "shine"; the embers of a fire break into brilliant color as they fall from a grate. Both images may also be taken to refer to "The Windhover" as well as to the flight of the windhover, just as the Latin word *versus* can mean both a line of verse and the turning of a plough at the end of a furrow. Like plough and earth, poet and bird are both made to shine in the poem. The gash of gold-vermilion is a figure for the luminosity of the spectacular sonnet that has broken forth from the initial monochrome apprehension of its subject.

These things are in "The Windhover" but have not always been beheld. Paul Mariani's explanation is that the "religious significance" in the poem – Christ's incarnation, his stooping to take on human form – "is so continually bursting through the natural scene that many commentators have spent most of their time on the secondary meaning without grounding it in the perceptual world" (111). The ground of the poem is the natural ecstasy of an intense perceptual apprehension; the figural amplification adds to the poem's resonance but is not its enabling condition or *raison d'être*. One might even wonder whether without its subtitle ("to Christ our Lord"), added nearly seven years after the poem's composition, religious readings would ever have gained such currency.[1]

The perceptual basis of "Spelt from Sibyl's Leaves" has also been obscured – in this case by commentators who present the poem as a tripartite Ignatian meditative exercise on the Day of Judgement, when Christ will separate "one from another, as a shepherd divideth his sheep from the goats" (Matthew 25:32). In the copiously annotated Clarendon edition of Hopkins' poems, for example, Norman MacKenzie glosses the poem's title only with the assertion that it derives from the requiem hymn "Dies Irae" (which speaks of the Day of Judgement as "Teste David cum Sibyllo") and the suggestion that there are reminiscences of the sixth book of Virgil's *Aeneid*. But the title explicitly mentions the leaves of the Sibyl, as neither the hymn nor Virgil's epic does. Why, one wonders, couldn't the title equally well be taken to allude to Coleridge's *Sibylline Leaves*, the 1817 collection of his poems, two of which are in fact cited in MacKenzie's notes to Hopkins' poem? And where is the essential information that the title specifically alludes to the Sibyl's practice of writing her prophecies on leaves placed at the entrance to her cave?

"Spelt from Sibyl's Leaves" is better read not as a dogmatic *aide-mémoire* but as a Romantic lyric concerning natural facts and spiritual facts, that represents the activity of the primary imagination. In this reading, the natural fact of the fall of night prompts an overpowering intimation of mortality, just as autumn (the evening of the year) does in another Hopkins poem, "Spring and Fall," the subject of which is the inner-outer rhyming of the child Margaret and the falling leaves. The leaves in this poem are also natural facts symbolically perceived as figures (oracles) of mortality:

> Heart, you round me right
> With: Our evening is over us; our night whelms, whelms, and will
>   end us.
> Only the beakleaved boughs dragonish damask the tool-smooth
>   bleak light; black,
> Ever so black on it. Our tale, O our oracle!

At the end of the poem, an apocalyptic element is unquestionably present – but too much has been made of it. The vision of Hell is the vehicle of a metaphorical figure, the tenor of which is the speaker's *timor mortis*. This is the explanation of what troubled one commentator about the poem – that while it asserted that man had an ultimate choice between right and wrong, "in the tone and direction of the poem there is no hope" (Schneider *Dragon* 166). There is no hope because the site of the poem's ending is not an eschatological *there* but a psychological *here*. It is in the poetic present, in the poem itself, and not in the Hell of an imagined future that "selfwrung, self-strung, sheathe- and shelterless, thoughts against thoughts in groans grind."

There is another figurative dimension to the leaves: they may be taken to refer to Hopkins' own poems and the tale they tell. His unpublished poems are sibylline leaves in the same sense that that Coleridge used the figure in his collection of 1817: "in allusion to the fragmentary and widely scattered state in which [the poems] have been long suffered to remain" (*Poems* ii 1150). The tale that is cryptically spelt out is that, like the evening sky, the "dapple" of Hopkins' poems "is at an end." There will be no more energetic celebrations of the "skeined stained veined variety" of the natural world. With an exception or two, verbal and descriptive exuberance is not found in the late poetry.

In a letter of 1879, Hopkins told Robert Bridges: "Feeling, love in particular, is the great moving power and spring of verse and the only person that I am in love with seldom, especially now, stirs my heart sensibly and when he does I cannot always 'make capital' of it, it would be a sacrilege to do so" (*Bridges* 66). God, who had been accessible through the natural world during the years at St Beuno's, seemed to have withdrawn a sense of himself from Hopkins, to have become a *Deus absconditus*. I suggest that there is a perceptual explanation of this sense of desertion – that God, so to speak, stayed where he was, while Hopkins lost the ability to contact him "sensibly," that is, through the senses.

By the end of the 1870s, Hopkins, who had been in poor physical health most of his adult life, had become aware of diminished sensory acuity. In reflecting on "the loss of taste, of relish for what once charmed us," he notes that "insight is more sensitive, in fact is more perfect, earlier in life than later and especially towards elementary impressions: I remember that crimson and pure blues seemed to me spiritual and heavenly sights fit to draw tears once; now I can just see what I once saw, but can hardly dwell on it and should not care to do so" (*Correspondence* 38).[2] What replaced this diminution of the external senses was a sharpened proprioceptive sense, the sense of himself. In an extraordinary passage from his retreat notes for August 1880, Hopkins notes:

Nothing else in nature comes near this unspeakable stress of pitch, distinctiveness, and selving, this selfbeing of my own … to me there is no resemblance: searching nature I taste *self* but at one tankard, that of my own being. The development, refinement, condensation of nothing shews any sign of being able to match this to me or give me another taste of it, a taste even resembling it.

One may dwell on this further. We say that any two things however unlike are in something like. This is the one exception: when I compare my self, my being-myself, with anything else whatever, all things alike, all in the same degree, rebuff me with blank unlikeness.   (*Sermons* 123)

Given this felt sense of the absolute uniqueness of his own being, there could no longer be any rhyming or mirroring of inner or outer in Hopkins' perception of natural objects. All that could be feelingly experienced was the taste of himself:

I am gall, I am heartburn. God's most deep decree
Bitter would have me taste; my taste was me;
Bones built in me, flesh filled, blood brimmed the curse.

These lines from "I wake and feel the fell of dark" posit a providential cause of Hopkins' condition ("God's ... decree"). The poem's next line, however, adumbrates an internal rather than an external explanation: "Selfyeast of spirit a dull dough sours." That is, Hopkins' spiritual or creative yeast, the leavening agent for his whole being and a *sine qua non* of perceptual intensity, had gone bad, souring the "dull dough" ("selfstuff" in a variant reading) of the body.

"All things," Hopkins wrote in 1881, "are charged with love, are charged with God and if we know how to touch them give off sparks and take fire, yield drops and flow, ring and tell of him" (*Sermons* 195). Like Coleridge, Hopkins lost the sense of feeling/touch. He could still see (though less acutely) the objects of the natural world; but he was seldom able to feel them – and thus he was unable both to find God in the natural world and to conceive poetically. "[W]hat is life without aim, without spur, without help?" he wrote a year before his death at the age of forty-four: "All my undertakings miscarry: I am like a straining eunuch" (*Sermons* 262). The reference is to poetic creation – the spur and the images of insemination both reappear in his last poem, the self-reflexive "To R.B." At St Beuno's, Hopkins had flung out broad his robust poetic signature. Now in "lagging lines" of verse he laments that he lacks "the one rapture of an inspiration" and can no longer celebrate "The roll, the rise, the carol, the creation."[3]

In a letter of 1886, Hopkins had taken vigorous exception to a correspondent's low opinion of Wordsworth's Intimations Ode, For Hopkins, the poem had an "extreme value"; indeed, it registered a liminal moment in human history. Through the ages there had been a very few men who had "*seen something* ... human nature in these men saw something, got a shock ... in Wordsworth when he wrote that ode human nature got another of those shocks, and the tremble from it is spreading. This opinion I do strongly share; I am, ever since I knew the ode, in that tremble" (*Correspondence* 147–8).[4] For Hopkins, as for Wordsworth, Coleridge and Thoreau, "the radiance which was once so bright" faded and disappeared because he lost the ability to perceive it.

Notes

1 In Dorothy Emmet's terms, the perceptual mode is that of a higher level of the "adverbial mode [of] integral feeling," an "aesthetic seeing" in which the perceiver is concerned "not only with differentiating contents but with enjoying the integral feeling conveyed by the composition as a whole" (42). Helen Vendler describes the end of "There Was a Child" as one in which the viewer experiences "the sensuality of perception" in an "aesthetic present" ("Placing" 25).

2 Traditional classifications of the senses are surveyed in Louise Vinge's *The Five Senses*. On the influence of Newton's *Opticks*, see Marjorie Hope Nicolson's *Newton Demands the Muse*. Raimonda Modiano's "Coleridge's Views on Touch and Other Senses" usefully summarizes the historical background and brings together many of Coleridge's scattered comments on the senses.

CHAPTER 2

1 Another gloss on the Coleridge passage is found in section 32 of *Song of Myself*; there Whitman speaks of animals as "bring[ing] me tokens of myself....they evince them plainly in their possession. // I do not know where they got those tokens, / I must have passed that way untold times ago and negligently dropt them." Lewis Hyde comments: "Natural objects – living things in particular – are like a language we only faintly remember. It is as if creation had been dismembered sometime in the past and all things are limbs we have lost that will make us whole if only we can recall them." Whitman's sympathetic perception of objects, says Hyde, "is a remembrance of the wholeness of things" (174).

2 Humphry House usefully summarizes the key points in this important distinction: "the *strength of impression* of external nature on the mind is the

essential starting-point"; nature has "her own *proper* interest irrespective of a secondary act of application to moralised human life"; and this proper interest "derives from the dual fact that everything (including a human being), while having its own life, yet shares in the common life of all" (54).

3 My account of the pathetic fallacy is indebted to George Landow and Patricia Ball. On the changing relationship between object and emotion in the nineteenth century, see Ball, Josephine Miles, Zelda Boyd, and Carol Christ (*Victorian and Modern Poetics*).

4 In *Moby-Dick* (1851), for example, Ahab and Ishmael, both of whom are committed to the search for the higher spritual facts symbolized by natural facts, succumb at moments to a horrifying suspicion: "sometimes I think there's naught beyond," says the former in chapter 36, condensing into a phrase what Ishmael reflects on at length in "The Whiteness of the Whale" (chapter 42): that the spiritual fact corresponding to the natural fact of whiteness is "a colorless, all-color of atheism from which we shrink"; that "by its indefiniteness … shadows forth the heartless voids and immensities of the universe, and thus stabs us from behind with the thought of annihilation."

CHAPTER 3

1 See Griggs's note in *Letters* ii 865; Griggs also calls attention to Coleridge's borrowings from Bowles's "Coombe Ellen."

2 In the change from day to night, the eye switches from the dominance of one type of retinal light receptor to another – from color sensitive cones, which are located in the small central area of the retina (the fovea) where incoming light is received, to rods, which are sensitive to a much lower threshold of light, offer poor spatial resolution and are slower processing (see Kandel et al. 402).

3 If lights of different hues but the same intensity are shone into the eyes, some will look brighter than others. This can be charted on a graph known as the spectral luminosity curve; the colors in the middle of the spectrum – green and yellow – are the brightest. This is of great practical importance in connection with distress signals or markers, which is why the buoy's light is green.

4 For a complementary view, see Nicholas Ruddick's excellent discussion of synesthesia in Emily Dickinson's poetry. He argues that "similes and metaphors with an intersensory texture have been used with varying degrees of success by most poets of all ages," that attempting to distinguish between clinical and literary synesthesia causes "an enormous amount of confusion," and that the term should be dropped from the critical vocabulary. Critics "interested in the language of poetry could

then concentrate on the problem of whether or not each intersensory image – regardless of hierarchical reference, source, destination and so on – is, in its context, vivid, spontaneous and effective" (77).

CHAPTER 4

1 These instances suggest that one of Wordsworth's characteristic creative modes involved "a continuing reinterpretation not only of what he had already experienced, but especially of what he had already written" (Eakin 390; see Wolfson and Stoddard). Obvious examples are those reflecting the post-1805 movement away from Romantic naturalism toward Christian supernaturalism. In the 1805 *Prelude* (ii 428–30), for example, Wordsworth comments as follows on himself at the age of seventeen:

> Wonder not
> If such my transports were, for in all things
> I saw one life, and felt that it was joy.

In the 1850 *Prelude* (ii 409–14), this becomes:

> Wonder not
> If high the transport, great the joy I felt,
> Communing in this sort through earth and heaven
> With every form of creature, as it looked
> Towards the Uncreated with a countenance
> Of adoration, with an eye of love.

2 Earlier commentators made similar arguments. In 1944, for example, J.C. Smith wrote that it was "an open question" whether the Wordsworthian sublime "was simply an extraordinary heightening (hyperaesthesia) of the senses of sight and hearing … or some mode of perception transcending sense" (13). And in 1959, David Ferry found two views of nature in Wordsworth, the sacramental and the mystical. In the latter, nature "can be nothing else than purely and simply an obstruction" between the poet and "direct contact with the eternal Presences. Nature must therefore be destroyed, obliterated absolutely" (32).

3 The handful of tactile notations in the *Prelude* include the following. In book i the poet describes himself as having once been "soothed by a sense of touch/From the warm ground"; it had "balanced" him when his thinking had reached a vertiginous pitch (89–90). And in book iv the account of a summer night spent in dancing, gaiety and mirth as part of "a festal company of maids and youths"includes this splendid notation:

> here and there
> Slight shocks of young love-liking interspersed
> That mounted up like joy into the head,
> And tingled through the veins.   (324–7)

CHAPTER 5

1 Coleridge's conversation poems have received much critical attention. In
   my view, the best commentator has been Kathleen Wheeler, from whose
   The Creative Mind in Coleridge's Poetry I learned a great deal. In the main,
   my readings are congruent with hers. Both are Coleridgean in the sense
   that they work from authorial premises about the mind and its opera-
   tions; both are opposed to deconstructive readings like those by Tilottama
   Rajan and Jean-Pierre Mileur, which proceed from Derridean and de
   Manian premises. But there are significant differences in emphasis
   between Wheeler's treatment and mine. She is primarily concerned with
   Coleridge's "creative theory of mind" (150), with his strategies to encourage the reader's more active engagement with the text of the poems, and
   with "theoretical implications about the nature of art and imagination"
   (90). Thus, in her book Wheeler devotes chapters to "The Ancient Mariner" and "Kubla Khan" as well as to "The Eolian Harp," "This Lime-Tree
   Bower," and "Frost at Midnight." I concentrate on sensory-perceptual
   dynamics, on representations of the operation of the primary imagination,
   and on discriminating among degrees and kinds of perception. Consequently I examine in detail "The Nightingale," which Wheeler does not
   consider.

2 This positive thrust is emphasized in the additional lines of the poem's
   original ending, which describe the icicles as being

> Like those, my babe! which ere tomorrow's warmth
> Have capp'd their sharp keen points with pendulous drops,
> Will catch thine eye, and with their novelty
> Suspend thy little soul; then make thee shout,
> And stretch and flutter from thy mother's arms
> As thou wouldst fly for very eagerness.

   The contrast between infant and parent is nicely conveyed by "flutter,"
   which adumbrates the contrast between the former's enchanted eager-
   ness in the daylight and the meditatively vexed father who makes the
   midnight fluttering of a film on his grate "a toy of Thought." The cancel-
   lation of this charming passage does not gainsay the positive thrust of the
   last stanza insofar as the child is concerned; but it does throw into relief
   the equivocal resonances of the stanza for the adult speaker.

3 Here is the Wordsworth passage:

> There is creation in the eye,
> Nor less in all the other senses; powers
> They are that colour, model, and combine
> The things perceived with such an absolute
> Essential energy that we may say
> That those most godlike faculties of ours

> At one and the same moment are the mind
> And the mind's minister. In many a walk
> At evening or by moonlight, or reclined
> At midday upon beds of forest moss,
> Have we to Nature and her impulses
> Of our whole being made free gift, and when
> Our trance had left us, oft have we, by aid
> Of the impressions which it left behind,
> Looked inward on ourselves, and learned perhaps,
> Something of what we are.   (*PW* v 343–4)

4 The text for quotations from "A Letter to —" is that in *Letters* ii 790–98.

5 The next year Coleridge explained to a correspondent that when he tried "to force myself out of metaphysical trains of Thought" through poetic composition, he would "beat up Game of far other kind – instead of a Covey of poetic Partridges with whirring wings of music, or wild Ducks *shaping* their rapid flight in forms always regular (a still better image of verse) up came a metaphysical Bustard, urging it's slow, heavy, laborious, earth-skimming Flight, over dreary & level Wastes" (*Letters* ii 814).

CHAPTER 7

1 In referring to the speaker of *Song of Myself* as Whitman, I do not mean to suggest that in every physical particular the "I" of the poem is identical with its author. The difference between the physical health of the "mythic Whitman persona" and that of "Whitman's flesh-and-blood self" (3) is discussed in Harold Aspiz' *Walt Whitman and the Body Beautiful*. Aspiz also shows that Whitman's interest in the body and the physiological and medical lore of his time informs the first editions of *Leaves of Grass*. In another cultural study, *Healing the Republic: The Language of Health and the Culture of Nationalism in Nineteenth-Century America*, Joan Burbick discusses the "biodemocracy" of the early editions of *Leaves of Grass*, in which "the healthy body [is] the perfect 'natural symbol' for the nation" – a figuration that presupposes Whitman's "ability to represent the felt sensations of the healthy body in poetic language" (116–30). In a note (322–3n), Burbick usefully summarizes other recent work on Whitman and the body.

2 Coleridge's typology anticipates the discoveries of modern neurological science. For example, (*a*) "retentive power extinguishing the sense of touch" describes the loss of salience that is the result of sustained contact between animate and inanimate objects. When neurons are in a constant state of stimulation from the same identifiable source, after a short interval they will stop transmitting the 'on' message. An everyday example is the rapidity with which one forgets about the clothes one is wearing.

Their touch becomes a "mere feeling" of presence. Concerning (*b*), "touch with retentive power": areas like the lips and fingertips are exceptionally receptive and contain a much greater density of highly specialized touch neurons than a less sensitive area like the back. There are surface receptors and subcutaneous receptors; in each case some of the receptors are quickly adapting and some slowly adapting. Their co-presence accounts for the "retentive" quality of tactile impressions in these areas.

3 "Crossing Brooklyn Ferry" closely approximates Abrams' paradigm of poems that "present a determinate speaker in a particularized, and usually a localized, outdoor setting, whom we overhear as he carries on, in a fluent vernacular which rises easily to more formal speech, a sustained colloquy, sometimes with himself or with the outer scene, but more frequently with a silent human auditor, present or absent. The speaker begins with a description of the landscape … [a meditative movement of mind is evoked] which remains closely intervolved with the outer scene. [At the poem's climax, the speaker has an insight or realization.] Often the poem rounds upon itself to end where it began, at the outer scene, but with an altered mood and deepened understanding which is the result of the intervening meditation" (*Breeze* 76–7).

4 The qualitative implications for Whitman's poetry were summarized by Wallace Stevens: "It is useless to treat everything in Whitman as of equal merit. A great deal of it exhibits little or none of his specific power. He seems often to have driven himself to write like himself. The good things, the superbly beautiful and moving things, are those that he wrote naturally, with an extemporaneous and irrepressible vehemence of emotion" (*Letters* 871).

5 Here are two examples:

June 19th, 4 to 6[:30] p.m. – Sitting alone by the creek … the wild flageolet-note of a quail near by – the just-heard fretting of some hylas down there in the pond – crows cawing in the distance – a drove of young hogs rooting in soft ground near the oak under which I sit – some come sniffing near me, and then scamper away, with grunts. And still the clear notes of the quail – the quiver of leaf-shadows over the paper as I write … the swift darting of many sand-swallows coming and going, their homes in the neighboring marl-bank – the odor of the cedar and oak, so palpable, as evening approaches – perfume, color, the bronze-and-gold of nearly ripen'd wheat – clover-fields, with honey-scent – the well-up maize, with long and rustling leaves – the great patches of thriving potatoes, dusky green, fleck'd all over with white blossoms – the old, warty, venerable oak above me – and ever, mix'd with the dual notes of the quail, the soughing of the wind through some near-by pines.   (787)

... 9th [March]. – A snowstorm in the morning, and continuing most
of the day. But I took a walk over two hours ... amid the falling
flakes. No wind, yet the musical low murmur through the pines,
quite pronounced, curious, like waterfalls, now still'd, now pouring
again ... Every snowflake lay where it fell on the evergreens, holly-
trees, laurels, &c., the multitudinous leaves and branches piled,
bulging-white, defined by edge-lines of emerald – the tall straight
columns of the plentiful bronze-topt pines – a slight resinous odor
blending with that of the snow.   (876)

CHAPTER 8

1 In reading and thinking about Dickinson's poetry, I have found the following commentators particularly helpful: Charles Anderson; Northrop
   Frye; Robert Weisbuch; Joanne Feit Diehl; Helen McNeil; Cynthia Griffin
   Wolff; E. Miller Budick; Jane Donahue Eberwein; and Gary Lee Stonum.
2 Another example of feminist over-reading of Dickinson's sun imagery is
   Margaret Homans' analysis (203–5) of #106 ("The Daisy follows soft the
   Sun"); see Elisa New's excellent rebuttal (155–6).
3 They include: ships of purple unloading opal bales on the banks of a
   yellow sea (#265, #266); a sapphire farm with opal cattle (#628); the
   "largest Fire ever known" consuming an "Occidental Town" (#1114);
   armies and navies in battle (#152, #1174, #1642); a dying peacock (#120);
   the finale of that master entertainer, "the Juggler of Day" (#228); the
   "Firmamental Lilac," its corolla the west, its calyx the earth, its seeds the
   stars (#1241); the "Lady of the Occident" undressing herself (#716); and
   the housewife sweeping "with many-colored Brooms" and leaving shreds
   of color behind (#219).
4 The same exile is more starkly described in poem #1382:

> In many and reportless places
> We feel a joy –
> Reportless, also, but sincere as Nature
> Or Deity –
>
> It comes, without a consternation –
> Dissolves – the same –
> But leaves a sumptuous Destitution –
> Without a Name –
>
> Profane it by a search – we cannot
> It has no home –
> Nor we who having once inhaled it –
> Thereafter roam.

CHAPTER 9

1 On "The Windhover" I have found F.X. Shea, Thomas P. Harrison,
  Paul L. Mariani, and Michael Sprinker particularly helpful.
2 One of the "structural changes" involved in the aging of the eye is the
  "*senile yellowing*" of the optic lens. This causes "low tone colors, such as
  blues, greens, violet, and pastels to fade" (Brant 162). In her detailed
  study of Emily Dickinson's use of color, Rebecca Patterson notes that the
  "most curious aspect of her color system after 1865," when she was in her
  mid 30s, was "the dulling and fading of her palette" (137).
3 In the lagging lines of "Work without Hope," one of his last poems,
  Coleridge had poignantly documented his loss of the one-life feeling:

> All Nature seems at work. Slugs leaves their lair –
> The bees are stirring – birds are on the wing –
> ....
> And I the while, the sole unbusy thing,
> Nor honey make, nor pair, not build, nor sing,

  At the end of one of Hopkins' last poems, "Thou art indeed, just, Lord,"
  the same pathetic recognition is recorded in closely similar images:

> See, banks and brakes
> Now, leavèd how how thick! lacèd they are again
> With fretty chervil, look, and fresh wind shakes
> Them; birds' build – but not I build; no, but strain,
> Time's eunuch, and not breed one work that wakes.

4 Lawrence Kramer shows how the Intimations Ode "stands like a horizon
  behind a whole array of Romantic and post-Romantic poems" (315). In his
  survey, Coleridge's Dejection Ode, Shelley's "Hymn to Intellectual
  Beauty," Tennyson's *In Memoriam*, Arnold's "The Scholar Gypsy," and
  Browning's "Prologue" to *Asolando* are the primary examples. Other
  nineteenth-century texts that show the Ode's extraordinary influence
  include: the fifth chapter of John Stuart Mill's *Autobiography*; Arthur
  Henry Hallam's letter of 17 April 1831 to Emily Tennyson; and
  J.A. Froude's *Nemesis of Faith* (118). The importance of the Ode in Newman's thinking is discussed by Thomas Vargish (100–2). For both John
  Ruskin and Thomas Hardy, the poem was an essential point of reference
  over many years.

  Shocks continue to be felt, as Philip Larkin attested: "Poetry can creep
  up on you unawares. Wordsworth was almost the price of me once. I was
  driving down the M1 on a Saturday morning: they had this poetry slot on
  the radio, 'Time for Verse': it was a lovely summer morning, and someone
  suddenly started reading the Immortality ode, and I couldn't see for tears
  … I don't suppose I'd read the poem for twenty years, and it's amazing
  how effective it was when one was totally unprepared for it" (53).

Works Cited

Abrams, M.H. *The Correspondent Breeze: Essays in English Romanticism*. New York: Norton, 1984.

– *Natural Supernaturalism: Tradition and Revolution in Romantic Literature*. New York: Norton, 1971.

Anderson, Charles R. *Emily Dickinson's Poetry: Stairway of Surprise*. New York: Holt, Rinehart, 1960.

– *The Magic Circle of "Walden"*. New York: Holt, Rinehart, 1968.

Aristotle. *On Poetry and Style*. Trans. G.M.A. Grube. New York: Liberal Arts, 1958.

Aspiz, Harold. *Walt Whitman and the Body Beautiful*. Urbana: University of Illinois Press, 1980.

Asselineau, Roger. *The Evolution of Walt Whitman: The Creation of the Book*. Cambridge: Harvard University Press, 1962.

Ball, Patricia. *The Science of Aspects: The Changing Role of Fact in the Work of Coleridge, Ruskin and Hopkins*. London: Athlone, 1971.

Barker, Wendy. *Lunacy of Light: Emily Dickinson and the Experience of Metaphor*. Carbondale: Southern Illinois University Press, 1987.

Benzon, William. "Metaphoric and Metonymic Invariance: Two Examples from Coleridge." *Modern Language Notes* 96 (1981): 1097–1105.

Blake, William. *Poetry and Prose*. Ed. David V. Erdman. New York: Doubleday, 1965.

Blasing, Mutlu Konuk. *American Poetry: The Rhetoric of its Forms*. New Haven: Yale University Press, 1987.

Bloom, Harold. *The Visionary Company: A Reading of English Romantic Poetry*. Rev. ed. Ithaca: Cornell University Press, 1970.

Boyd, Zelda. "What a Poet Sees: A Study of the Aesthetic Theories of Mill, Carlyle, Ruskin, and Arnold." Diss., University of Michigan, 1971.

Bradley, A.C. "Wordsworth." *Oxford Lectures on Poetry*. London: Macmillan, 1909.

Brant, Barbara A. "Sensory Functioning." *Nursing Care in an Aging Society.* Ed. Donna M. Corr and Charles A. Corr. New York: Springer, 1990.

Browning, Robert. *Poems.* Ed. John Pettigrew. 2 vols. New Haven: Yale University Press, 1981.

Bucke, Richard Maurice. *Cosmic Consciousness: A Study of the Evolution of the Human Mind.* New York: Dutton, 1969.

Budd, Malcolm. "Belief and Sincerity in Poetry." *Pleasure, Preference and Value: Studies in Philosophical Aesthetics.* Ed. Eva Schaper. Cambridge: Cambridge University Press, 1983.

Budick, E. Miller. "The 'Fraud That Cannot Cheat the Bee': The Dangers of Sacramental Symbolism." *Emily Dickinson and the Life of Language: A Study in Symbolist Poetics.* Baton Rouge: Louisiana State University Press, 1985.

Burbick, Joan. "Biodemocracy in *Leaves of Grass.*" *Healing the Republic: The Language of Health and the Culture of Nationalism in Nineteenth-Century America.* Cambridge: Cambridge University Press, 1994.

Burke, Edmund. *A Philosophical Enquiry into the Origin of our Ideas of the Sublime and Beautiful.* Ed. Adam Phillips. Oxford: Oxford University Press, 1990.

Cameron, Sharon. *Writing Nature: Henry Thoreau's "Journal".* Chicago: University of Chicago Press, 1989.

Chandler, James K. "Romantic Allusiveness." *Critical Inquiry* 8 (1982): 461–87.

Christ, Carol T. *The Finer Optic: The Aesthetic of Particularity in Victorian Poetry.* New Haven: Yale University Press, 1975.

– *Victorian and Modern Poetics.* Chicago: University of Chicago Press, 1984.

Coleridge, Samuel Taylor. *Biographia Literaria.* Vol. 7 of *Collected Works.* Ed. James Engell and Walter Jackson Bate. 2 vols. London: Routledge, 1983.

– *Complete Poetical Works.* Ed. Ernest Hartley Coleridge. 2 vols. Oxford: Clarendon, 1957.

– *The Friend.* Vol. 4 of *Collected Works.* Ed. Barbara Rooke. 2 vols. London: Routledge, 1969.

– *Lectures 1808–1819 on Literature.* Vol. 5 of *Collected Works.* Ed. R.A. Foakes. 2 vols. London: Routledge, 1987.

– *Letters.* Ed. Earl Leslie Griggs. 6 vols. Oxford: Clarendon, 1956–71.

– *Notebooks.* Ed. Kathleen Coburn. 4 vols. London: Routledge, 1957–1990.

– *Philosophical Lectures.* Ed. Kathleen Coburn. New York: Philosophical Library, 1949.

– *The Statesman's Manual. Lay Sermons.* Vol. 6 of *Collected Works.* Ed. R.J. White. London: Routledge, 1972.

Collins, Philip. "Tennyson In and Out of Time." *Studies in Tennyson.* Ed. Hallam Tennyson. London: Macmillan, 1981.

de Man, Paul. "Intentional Structure of the Romantic Image." *Romanticism and Consciousness: Essays in Criticism*. Ed. Harold Bloom. New York: Norton, 1970.

– "The Rhetoric of Temporality." *Blindness and Insight: Essays in the Rhetoric of Contemporary Criticism*. 2nd ed. Minneapolis: University of Minnesota Press, 1983.

De Quincey, Thomas. *Recollections of the Lakes and the Lake Poets*. Ed. David Wright. Harmondsworth, England: Penguin, 1970.

Derrida, Jacques. "Structure, Sign and Play in the Discourse of the Human Sciences." *The Structuralist Controversy: The Language of Criticism and the Science of Man*. Ed. Richard Macksey and Eugenio Donato. Baltimore: Johns Hopkins University Press, 1970.

Dickie, Margaret. *Lyric Contingencies: Emily Dickinson and Wallace Stevens*. Philadelphia: University of Pennsylvania Press, 1991.

Dickinson, Emily. *The Complete Poems of Emily Dickinson*. Ed. Thomas H. Johnson. Boston: Little, Brown, 1960.

– *Letters*. Ed. Thomas H. Johnson. 3 vols. Cambridge: Harvard University Press, 1958.

– *Poems*. Ed. Thomas H. Johnson. 3 vols. Cambridge: Harvard University Press, 1955.

Diehl, Joanne Feit. *Dickinson and the Romantic Imagination*. Princeton: Princeton University Press, 1981.

Dostoevsky, Fyodor. *The Idiot*. Trans. Alan Myers. Oxford: Oxford University Press, 1992.

Dupriez, Bernard. *A Dictionary of Literary Devices: Gradus A-Z*. Trans. Albert P. Halsall. Toronto: University of Toronto Press, 1991.

Durr, R.A. *Poetic Vision and the Psychedelic Experience*. Syracuse: Syracuse University Press, 1970.

Eakin, Sybil S. "The Spots of Time in Early Versions of *The Prelude*." *Studies in Romanticism* 12 (1973): 389–405.

Eberwein, Jane Donahue. "Emily Dickinson and the Calvinist Sacramental Tradition." *Emerson Society Quarterly* 33 (1987): 67–81.

– *Emily Dickinson: Strategies of Limitation*. Amherst: University of Massachusetts Press, 1985.

Ellis, David. *Wordsworth, Freud and the Spots of Time*. Cambridge: Cambridge University Press, 1985.

Emerson, Ralph Waldo. *Essays and Lectures*. Ed. Joel Porte. New York: Library of America, 1983.

– "Poetry and Imagination." Vol. 8 of *Complete Works*. Ed. Edward Waldo Emerson. Boston: Houghton Mifflin, 1904.

Emmet, Dorothy. "The Character of Perceptual Experience." *The Nature of Metaphysical Thinking*. London: Macmillan, 1961.

Empson, William. "Sense in the *Prelude.*" *The Structure of Complex Words.* London: Chatto, 1951.

Engell, James. "Imagining into Nature: 'This Lime-Tree Bower My Prison'." *Coleridge, Keats, and the Imagination: Romanticism and Adam's Dream.* Ed. J. Robert Barth and John L. Mahoney. Columbia: University of Missouri Press, 1990.

Engen, Trygg. *The Perception of Odors.* New York: Academic Press, 1982.

Feidelson, Charles. *Symbolism and American Literature.* Chicago: University of Chicago Press, 1953.

Ferry, David. *The Limits of Mortality: An Essay on Wordsworth's Major Poems.* Middletown: Wesleyan University Press, 1959.

Frank, Joseph. *Dostoevsky: The Years of Ordeal, 1850–1859.* Princeton: Princeton University Press, 1983.

Franklin, R.W. "The Manuscripts and Transcripts of 'Further in summer than the birds'." *Papers of the Bibliographic Society of America* 72 (1978): 552–60.

Frederick, Douglas. "The Prose Style of Landscape Description in the Journals of Gerard Manley Hopkins." Diss., Catholic University of America, 1986.

Freud, Sigmund. *Civilization and its Discontents.* Ed. James Strachey. London: Hogarth, 1979.

Frost, Robert. *Collected Poems, Prose, & Plays.* Ed. Richard Poirier and Mark Richardson. New York: Library of America, 1995.

Froude, J. A. *The Nemesis of Faith.* London: Libris, 1988.

Fruman, Norman. "Creative Process and Concealment in Coleridge's Poetry." *Romantic Revision.* Ed. Robert Brinkley and Keith Hanley. Cambridge: Cambridge University Press, 1992.

Frye, Northrop. *Anatomy of Criticism: Four Essays.* Princeton: Princeton University Press, 1957.

– "Emily Dickinson." *Fables of Identity: Studies in Poetic Mythology.* New York: Harcourt Brace, 1963.

Garber, Frederick. *Thoreau's Redemptive Imagination.* New York: New York University Press, 1977.

Gardner, W.H. Introduction to *Poems and Prose of Gerard Manley Hopkins.* Harmondsworth, England: Penguin, 1985.

Gatta, John. "Whitman's Revision of Emersonian Ecstasy in *Song of Myself.*" *Walt Whitman Here and Now.* Ed. Joann P. Krieg. Westport, CT: Greenwood Press, 1985.

Gibson, James J. *The Senses Considered as Perceptual Systems.* Boston: Houghton Mifflin, 1966.

Gilbert, Sandra M. and Susan Gubar. "A Woman–White: Emily Dickinson's Yarn of Pearl." *The Madwoman in the Attic: The Woman Writer and the Nineteenth-Century Literary Imagination.* New Haven: Yale University Press, 1979.

Gill, Stephen. *William Wordsworth: The Prelude*. Cambridge: Cambridge University Press, 1991.

Ginsberg, Allen. "Allen Ginsberg and Walt Whitman." *Composed on the Tongue*. Ed. Jim Perlman et al. Minneapolis: Holy Cow Press, 1981.

Gonzalez-Crussi, F. *The Five Senses*. New York: Vintage, 1991.

Gregory, R.L. *Eye and Brain: The Psychology of Seeing*. 3rd ed. New York: McGraw-Hill, 1978.

Guthrie, James. " 'Before I got my eye put out': Dickinson's Illness and its Effects on her Poetry." *Dickinson Studies* 42 (1982): 16–21.

Hall, Donald. "Ezra Pound: An Interview." *Paris Review* 28 (1962): 22–51.

Harding, Walter. *The Days of Henry Thoreau: A Biography*. Princeton: Princeton University Press, 1982.

Hardy, Thomas. *The Life and Work of Thomas Hardy*. Ed. Michael Millgate. London: Macmillan, 1985.

Harrison, Thomas P. "The Birds of Gerard Manley Hopkins." *Studies in Philology* 54 (1957): 448–63.

Hartman, Geoffrey H. *Wordsworth's Poetry, 1787–1814*. New Haven: Yale University Press, 1971.

Haven, Richard D. *Patterns of Consciousness: An Essay on Coleridge*. Amherst: University of Massachusetts Press, 1969.

Hawthorne, Nathaniel. *Tales and Sketches*. Ed. Roy Harvey Pearce. New York: Library of America, 1987.

Hazlitt, William. *Complete Works*. Ed. P.P. Howe. 21 vols. London: Dent, 1930–4.

Heaney, Seamus. *Preoccupations: Selected Prose 1968–1978*. London: Faber & Faber, 1980.

Helsinger, Elizabeth K. *Ruskin and the Art of the Beholder*. Cambridge: Harvard University Press, 1982.

Hiley, David R., James F. Bohman, and Richard Shusterman, eds. *The Interpretive Turn: Philosophy, Science, Culture*. Ithaca: Cornell University Press, 1991.

Homans, Margaret. *Woman Writers and Poetic Identity: Dorothy Wordsworth, Emily Brontë, and Emily Dickinson*. Princeton: Princeton University Press, 1980.

Hopkins, Gerard Manley. *The Correspondence of Gerard Manley Hopkins and Richard Watson Dixon*. Ed. Claude Colleer Abbot. London: Oxford University Press, 1955.

– *Further Letters*. Ed. Claude Colleer Abbot. 2nd ed. London: Oxford University Press, 1956.

– *Journals and Papers*. Ed. Humphry House and Graham Storey. London: Oxford University Press, 1959.

– *Letters to Robert Bridges*. Ed. Claude Colleer Abbot. London: Oxford University Press, 1955.

– *Poetical Works.* Ed. Norman H. MacKenzie. Oxford: Clarendon, 1990.

– *Sermons and Devotional Writings.* Ed. Christopher Devlin, S.J. London: Oxford University Press, 1959.

Hopkins, R.H. "Coleridge's Parody of Melancholy Poetry in 'The Nightingale: A Conversation Poem, April 1798'." *English Studies* 49 (1968): 436–41.

House, Humphry. *Coleridge.* London: Hart-Davis, 1953.

Howes, David, ed. *The Varieties of Sensory Experience.* Toronto: University of Toronto Press, 1991.

Huxley, Aldous. *The Doors of Perception and Heaven and Hell.* London: Chatto, 1972.

Hyde, Lewis. *The Gift: Imagination and the Erotic Life of Property.* New York: Random House, 1983.

James, William. *The Varieties of Religious Experience.* Ed. Martin E. Marty. Harmondsworth, England: Penguin, 1985.

Jay, Martin. *Downcast Eyes: The Denigration of Vision in Twentieth-Century French Thought.* Berkeley: University of California Press, 1993.

– "The Rise of Hermeneutics and the Crisis of Ocularcentrism." *Poetics Today* 9 (1988): 307–26.

Jeffrey, Francis. Review of Felicia Hemans's poems. *Contributions to the Edinburgh Review.* Philadelphia: A. Hart, 1852.

Johnston, Kenneth R. "The Idiom of Vision." *New Perspectives on Coleridge and Wordsworth.* Ed. Geoffrey H. Hartman. New York: Columbia University Press, 1972.

Jonas, Hans. "The Nobility of Sight: A Study in the Phenomenology of the Senses." *The Phenomenon of Life: Toward a Philosophical Biology.* New York: Harper, 1966.

Juhasz, Suzanne. *The Undiscovered Continent: Emily Dickinson and the Space of the Mind.* Bloomington: Indiana University Press, 1983.

Jump, John D., ed. *Tennyson: The Critical Heritage.* London: Routledge & Kegan Paul, 1967.

Kandel, Eric R., James H. Schwartz and Thomas M. Jessell, eds. *Principles of Neural Science.* 3rd ed. New York: Elsevier, 1991.

Keats, John. *Letters.* Ed. Hyder Edward Rollins. 2 vols. Cambridge: Harvard University Press, 1958.

Keller, Karl. *The Only Kangaroo among the Beauty: Emily Dickinson and America.* Baltimore: Johns Hopkins University Press, 1979.

Kirkham, Michael. "Metaphor and the Unitary World: Coleridge and Henry Vaughan." *Essays in Criticism* 37 (1987): 121–34.

Kramer, Lawrence. "The Intimations Ode and Victorian Romanticism." *Victorian Poetry* 18 (1980): 315–35.

Landow, George. *The Aesthetic and Critical Theories of John Ruskin.* Princeton: Princeton University Press, 1971.

Larkin, Philip. *Required Writing: Miscellaneous Pieces 1955–82*. London: Faber & Faber, 1983.

Larson, Kerry C. *Whitman's Drama of Consensus*. Chicago: University of Chicago Press, 1988.

Lawrence, D.H. "The Five Senses." *Fantasia of the Unconscious*. London: Martin Secker, 1930.

Leavis, F.R. *Revaluation: Tradition and Development in English Poetry*. London: Chatto & Windus, 1962.

Lefebure, Molly. *Samuel Taylor Coleridge: A Bondage of Opium*. London: Gollancz, 1974.

Lewis, R.W.B. "Walt Whitman: Always Going Out and Coming In." *Trials of the Word*. New Haven: Yale University Press, 1965.

Lifton, Robert Jay and Eric Olson. *Living and Dying*. New York: Praeger, 1974.

Lockyer, Sir Norman and Winifred L. Lockyer. *Tennyson as a Student and Poet of Nature*. London: Macmillan, 1910.

MacKenzie, Norman H. Commentary to *Poetical Works*, by Gerard Manley Hopkins. Oxford: Clarendon, 1990.

Mariani, Paul L. *A Commentary on the Complete Poems of Gerard Manley Hopkins*. Ithaca: Cornell University Press, 1970.

Marks, Lawrence E. *The Unity of the Senses: Interrelations among the Modalities*. New York: Academic Press, 1978.

Martin, Robert Bernard. *Gerard Manley Hopkins: A Very Private Life*. New York: Putnam, 1991.

– *Tennyson: The Unquiet Heart*. Oxford: Clarendon, 1980.

Martin, Robert K. "Whitman's *Song of Myself*: Homosexual Dream and Vision." *Partisan Review* 42 (1975): 80–96.

McFarland, Thomas. "Involute and Symbol in the Romantic Imagination." *Coleridge, Keats, and the Poetic Imagination: Romanticism and Adam's Dream*. Ed. J. Robert Barth and John L. Mahoney. Columbia: University of Missouri Press, 1990.

McIntosh, James. *Thoreau as Romantic Naturalist: His Shifting Stance toward Nature*. Ithaca: Cornell University Press, 1974.

McLuhan, Herbert Marshall. "The Analogical Mirrors." *Hopkins: A Collection of Critical Essays*. Ed. Geoffrey H. Hartman. Englewood Cliffs, NJ: Prentice-Hall, 1966.

McNeil, Helen. *Emily Dickinson*. London: Virago, 1986.

Mellor, Anne K. "On Romantic Irony, Symbolism and Allegory." *Criticism* 21 (1979): 217–29.

Melville, Herman. *Letters*. Ed. Merrell Davis and William H. Gilman. New Haven: Yale University Press, 1960.

– *Moby-Dick or, the Whale*. Ed. Charles Feidelson. Indianapolis: Bobbs-Merrill, 1964.

– *Pierre or, the Ambiguities*. Ed. Henry A. Murray. New York: Hendricks House, 1962.

Merleau-Ponty, M. *The Primacy of Perception and Other Essays*. Ed. James M. Edie. Evanston: Northwestern University Press, 1964.

Miles, Josephine. *Pathetic Fallacy in the Nineteenth Century: A Study of the Changing Relation between Object and Emotion*. New York: Octagon, 1965.

Mileur, Jean-Pierre. *Vision and Revision: Coleridge's Art of Immanence*. Berkeley: University of California Press, 1987.

Miller, James E. *A Critical Guide to "Leaves of Grass"*. Chicago: University of Chicago Press, 1957.

Miyagawa, Kiyoshi. "Sound and Vision in Wordsworth's Poetry." *Studies in English Literature* (Tokyo). English number (1981): 25–42.

Modiano, Raimonda. *Coleridge and the Concept of Nature*. Tallahassee: Florida State University Press, 1985.

– "Coleridge's Views on Touch and Other Senses." *Bulletin of Research in the Humanities* 81 (1978): 28–41.

Montagu, Ashley. *Touching: The Human Significance of the Skin*. New York: Columbia University Press, 1971.

Nathanson, Tenney. *Whitman's Presence: Body, Voice and Writing in "Leaves of Grass"*. New York: New York University Press, 1992.

New, Elisa. *The Regenerate Lyric: Theology and Innovation in American Poetry*. Cambridge: Cambridge University Press, 1993.

Nichols, Ashton. "The Epiphanic Trance: Why Tennyson is Not a Mystic." *Victorian Poetry* 24 (1986): 131–48.

Nicolson, Marjorie Hope. *Newton Demands the Muse: Newton's "Opticks" and Eighteenth Century Poets*. Princeton: Princeton University Press, 1946.

Ogden, John T. "The Power of Distance in Wordsworth's *Prelude*." *PMLA* 88 (1973): 246–59.

O'Malley, Glenn. "Literary Synesthesia." *Journal of Aesthetics and Art Criticism* 15 (1957): 391–411.

Ong, Walter J. *The Presence of the Word: Some Prolegomena for Cultural and Religious History*. New Haven: Yale University Press, 1967.

Ortega y Gasset, José. "On Point of View of the Arts." *Partisan Review* 16 (1949): 822–36.

Page, Norman, ed. *Tennyson: Interviews and Recollections*. London: Macmillan, 1983.

Parrish, Stephen M. *The Art of the Lyrical Ballads*. Cambridge: Harvard University Press, 1973.

Pater, Walter. "Wordsworth." *Appreciations*. New York: Macmillan, 1906.

Patterson, Rebecca. *Emily Dickinson's Imagery*. Amherst: University of Massachusetts Press, 1979.

Paul, Sherman. "The Wise Silence: Sound as the Agency of Correspondence in Thoreau." *New England Quarterly* 22 (1949): 511–27.

Peck, H. Daniel. *Thoreau's Morning Work: Memory and Perception in "A Week on the Concord and Merrimack Rivers," the Journal, and "Walden".* New Haven: Yale University Press, 1990.

Pitt, Valerie. *Tennyson Laureate.* London: Barrie, 1962.

Poe, Edgar Allan. *Essays and Reviews.* Ed. G.R. Thompson. New York: Library of America, 1984.

Porter, David. *Dickinson: The Modern Idiom.* Cambridge: Harvard University Press, 1981.

Priestley, F.E.L. *Language and Structure in Tennyson's Poetry.* London: André Deutsch, 1973.

Proust, Marcel. *Remembrance of Things Past.* Trans. C.K. Scott Moncrieff and Terence Kilmartin. 3 vols. London: Chatto & Windus, 1981.

Rajan, Tilottama. "Displacing Post-Structuralism: Romantic Studies after Paul de Man." *Studies in Romanticism* 24 (1985): 451–74.

– "Image and Reality in Coleridge's Lyric Poetry." *Dark Interpreter: The Discourse of Romanticism.* Ithaca: Cornell University Press, 1980.

Rea, John D. "Coleridge's Health." *Modern Language Notes* 45 (1930): 12–18.

Rosenthal, M.L. and Sally Gall. *The Modern Poetic Sequence: The Genius of Modern Poetry.* New York: Oxford University Press, 1983.

Rossetti, William Michael, ed. *Rossetti Papers 1862–1870.* New York: Scribner's, 1903.

Ruddick, Nicholas. "'Synaesthesia' in Emily Dickinson's Poetry." *Poetics Today* 5 (1984): 59–78.

Ruskin, John. *Modern Painters.* Vol. 3. *Works* (Library Edition). Vol. 5. Ed. E.T. Cook and Alexander Wedderburn. London: George Allen, 1904.

Sabin, Margery. "Symbolic Light." *English Romanticism and the French Tradition.* Cambridge: Harvard University Press, 1976.

Schiller, Friedrich von. *Naive and Sentimental Poetry and On the Sublime.* Trans. Julius A. Elias. New York: Ungar, 1980.

Schneider, Elisabeth. *Coleridge, Opium and "Kubla Khan".* New York: Octagon, 1970.

– *The Dragon at the Gate: Studies in the Poetry of Gerard Manley Hopkins.* Berkeley: University of California Press, 1968.

Scott, Sir Walter. *Journal.* 2 vols. Edinburgh: David Douglas, 1890.

Sewall, Richard B. *The Life of Emily Dickinson.* 2 vols. New York: Farrar Straus, 1974.

– *The Lyman Letters: New Light on Emily Dickinson and her Family.* Amherst: University of Massachusetts Press, 1965.

Shea, F.X. "Another Look at 'The Windhover'." *Victorian Poetry* 2 (1964): 219–39.

Shelley, Percy Bysshe. *Complete Poetical Works.* Ed. Thomas Hutchinson. London: Oxford University Press, 1960.

– *Shelley's Prose.* Ed. David Lee Clark. London: Fourth Estate, 1983.

Smith, J.C. *A Study of Wordsworth*. London: Oliver, 1944.

Snyder, Alice D. *Coleridge on Logic and Learning*. New Haven: Yale University Press, 1929.

Sprinker, Michael. *"A Counterpoint of Dissonance": The Aesthetics and Poetry of Gerard Manley Hopkins*. Baltimore: Johns Hopkins University Press, 1980.

Stein, Barry E. and M. Alex Meredith. *The Merging of the Senses*. Cambridge: MIT Press, 1993.

Stevens, Wallace. *Collected Poems*. New York: Knopf, 1961.

– *Letters*. Ed. Holly Stevens. New York: Knopf, 1966.

– *Opus Posthumous*. Rev. ed. Ed. Milton J. Bates. New York: Knopf, 1989.

Stoddard, Eve Walsh. "The Spots of Time: Wordsworth's Semiology of the Self." *Romanticism Past and Present* 9 (1985): 1–24.

Stonum, Gary Lee. *The Dickinson Sublime*. Madison: University of Wisconsin Press, 1990.

Tennyson, Alfred Lord. *Poems*. Ed. Christopher Ricks. 3 vols. Berkeley: University of California Press, 1987.

Tennyson, Hallam. *Alfred Lord Tennyson: A Memoir*. 2 vols. London: Macmillan, 1899.

Thomas, Dylan. *Collected Poems*. New York: New Directions, 1957.

Thomas, Heather Kirk. "Emily Dickinson's Renunciation and Anorexia Nervosa." *American Literature* 60 (1988): 205–25.

Thoreau, Henry D. *Journal*. 14 vols. Ed. Bradford Torrey and Francis H. Allen. New York: Houghton Mifflin, 1906.

– *Journal Volume 1: 1837–1844*. Ed. Elizabeth Hall Witherell, William L. Howarth, Robert Sattelmeyer, and Thomas Blanding. Princeton: Princeton University Press, 1981.

– *Journal Volume 2: 1842–1848*. Ed. Robert Sattelmeyer. Princeton: Princeton University Press, 1984.

– *Journal Volume 3: 1848–1851*. Ed. Robert Sattelmeyer, Mark R. Patterson, and William Rossi. Princeton: Princeton University Press, 1990.

– *Journal Volume 4: 1851–1852*. Ed. Leonard N. Neufeldt and Nancy Craig Simmons. Princeton: Princeton University Press, 1992.

– *Major Essays*. Ed. Jeffrey L. Duncan. New York: Dutton, 1977.

– *Walden*. Ed. J. Lyndon Shanley. Princeton: Princeton University Press, 1971.

– *A Week on the Concord and Merrimack Rivers*. Ed. Carl F. Hovde, William L. Howarth, and Elizabeth Hall Witherell. Princeton: Princeton University Press, 1980.

Tolstoy, Leo. *A Confession and Other Religious Writings*. Trans. Jane Kentish. Harmondsworth, England: Penguin, 1987.

Trevor-Roper, Patrick. *The World through Blunted Sight: An Inquiry into the Influence of Defective Vision on Art and Character*. Rev. ed. London: Allen Lane, 1988.

Trilling, Lionel. *The Opposing Self: Nine Essays in Criticism*. New York: Harcourt Brace, 1978.

Vargish, Thomas. *Newman: The Contemplation of Mind*. Oxford: Clarendon, 1970.

Vendler, Helen. "Reading Walt Whitman." *The Music of What Happens*. Cambridge: Harvard University Press, 1988.

— "Whitman's Placing of the Aesthetic in Two Early Poems: 'There Was a Child Went Forth' and 'The Sleepers'." *Delta* 16 (1983): 19–32.

Vinge, Louise. *The Five Senses: Studies in a Literary Tradition*. Lund: Publications of the Royal Society of Letters, 1975.

Wand, Martin and Richard B. Sewall. " 'Eyes be Blind, Heart be Still': A New Perspective on Emily Dickinson's Eye Problem." *New England Quarterly* 52 (1979): 400–06.

Weisbuch, Robert. *Emily Dickinson's Poetry*. Chicago: University of Chicago Press, 1975.

Whalley, George. *Coleridge and Sara Hutchinson and the Asra Poems*. Toronto: University of Toronto Press, 1955.

Wheeler, Kathleen. "Coleridge's Theory of Imagination: A Hegelian Solution to Kant." *The Interpretation of Belief*. Ed. David Jasper. New York: St Martin's, 1986.

— *The Creative Mind in Coleridge's Poetry*. Cambridge: Harvard University Press, 1981.

Whitman, Walt. *Complete Poetry and Collected Prose*. Ed. Justin Kaplan. New York: Library of America, 1982.

— *Leaves of Grass: Facsimile Edition of the 1860 Text*. Ed. Roy Harvey Pearce. Ithaca: Cornell University Press, 1961.

— *Leaves of Grass: Facsimile of 1856 Edition*. Norwood Editions, 1976.

— *Notebooks and Unpublished Prose Manuscripts*. Ed. Edward F. Grier. 6 vols. New York: New York University Press, 1984.

— *Whitman's Manuscripts: Leaves of Grass 1860*. Ed. Fredson Bowers. Chicago: University of Chicago Press, 1955.

Wolff, Cynthia Griffin. "The Wrestle for Dominion: God's Supernatural Redefined." *Emily Dickinson*. New York: Knopf, 1987.

Wolfson, Susan J. "The Illusion of Mastery: Wordsworth's Revisions of 'The Drowned Man of Esthwaite,' 1799, 1805, 1850." *PMLA* 99 (1984): 917–35.

Wordsworth, William. *Poetical Works*. Ed. E. de Selincourt and Helen Darbishire. 5 vols. Oxford: Clarendon, 1940–49.

— *The Prelude 1799, 1805, 1850*. Ed. Jonathan Wordsworth, M.H. Abrams, and Stephen Gill. New York: Norton, 1979.

Zaehner, R.C. *Drugs, Mysticism and Make-Believe*. London: Collins, 1972.

— *Mysticism Sacred and Profane*. New York: Oxford University Press, 1961.

Index